FOR LOVE
&
DECEITFUL
Intentions

Aaron McDougall

ISBN 978-1-959895-15-2 (paperback)
ISBN 978-1-959895-14-5 (eBook)

Printed in the United States of America

W E S T P O I N T
PRINT AND MEDIA

Part I

CHAPTER 1

Maude Derringer was regarded by many people living in the inner circle of Hollywood as a highly sophisticated socialite from the prosperous community of Beverly Hills but to those who really knew her that wasn't where the story of her life began. That event actually occurred in the beautiful state of Arizona however due to the extenuating circumstances surrounding her attempt to get a higher education, she eventually made her residence in California. Obviously, one of the driving forces behind her decision to reside there had to do with the fact, Maude loved being near the ocean. As to just exactly why that was, she didn't know however that particular aspect of her personality followed her all the way through life. At any rate, in the due course of wanting to get a higher education, Maude took up residence in California. Needless to say, like most people her age, she wanted to get some type of college degree so it made all the sense in the world to move to the area where she would be going to school. Initially, it looked like Maude was taking a step in the right direction for beginning a professional career, perhaps in the field of medicine but not long after relocating to the area, a couple of unforeseen circumstances created some problems for her. Of course, at the time, Maude had no way of knowing that or she might have never ventured away from her home state of Arizona. At any rate, as stated before, Maude wanted to get the best education possible. It was at this point in her life, she was giving a lot of very serious thought to becoming a nurse. At least, it sounded like the right thing to do and if for some reason that didn't work out for her, she would look into another profession. In fact, at one time or another she must have changed her mind a million times about what she wanted to study in college however that's pretty typical of what most young people do anyway, nevertheless, her goal and objective was to succeed in life, and with a good steadfast, never say die attitude, the odds were in Maude's favor for being able to do that in the days ahead.

Anyway, without rambling off too far in a philosophical direction, it goes without saying, she had a couple of minor flaws in her personality. To begin with, Maude was the kind of person that liked to have her own way. To make matters worse if push came to shove, Maude pushed. I mean seriously look out, get the hell out of my way, may god have mercy on your soul. You get the picture! Furthermore, not only was she a little on the selfish side but she also had a very bad temper as well. Obviously, no one's perfect and neither was she however Maude would've been the first one to admit her short comings if you were to confront her about it. Whether or not that made her an asshole was debatable. In fact, there was room for discussion there, however if you were to ask her to describe her personality, she would've probably said she preferred to think of her personality as selective reasoning. At any rate, regardless of how you look at it, Maude was definitely her own person. Of course, on the downside of it all, if you've ever given any serious thought to having a long-term relationship with someone, you're more than likely in for a big let-down. Needless to say, relationships take time and they're founded upon trust, in addition to the obvious, what's mine is yours and what's yours is mine so if you just happen to be a very selfish person, you will probably have problems dealing with your newly found love. In this particular case, that did not bode well for Maude in the years to come because she was that kind of person. Anyway, the groundwork for her personality took shape when she was a young child growing up in the state of Arizona. As you might suspect, her parents spoiled her rotten and the end result of that was Maude had become extremely accustomed to getting whatever she wanted, the way she wanted it. In fact, believe it or not, even as a student in high school, she expected to get her own way. That's just the kind of person she was. At any rate, her parents promised to put her through four years of college, however like so many other kids her age, she didn't know what she wanted to do for the darn longest time. Finally, after giving it a lot of careful thought, Maude concluded, she would get a higher education. Needless to say, her parents were delighted about that and just as soon as she graduated from high school, Maude began making plans to attend a college in the state of California, where she planned on getting a degree in nursing. In the days ahead, it would actually turn out to be a degree in education however her strong work ethic and a commitment to succeed would eventually pay off for her down the road. Perhaps, not the way, Maude originally thought her life would go however professionally speaking, she did well for herself. It did take a little time to accomplish that though. In the meantime, she thought it would be a good idea to get involved in as many social activities as possible to try and get over her shyness. Needless to say, that wasn't a bad plan. At the very least, it would give her a much better footing in life on things that were important to her. Actually, Maude's decision to attend college was obviously, a step in the right direction and what she eventually accomplished there also went onto shape her life in a very positive way. In fact, thanks to something she accidentally stumbled upon in more than one way, she never had to want for anything in the way of money ever again. Granted, that might not be the most important thing in life however it's certainly a basic necessity in the 21st century. As for Maude's other characteristics, like I said before, in addition to being a little selfish, she had a very bad temper, and that posed numerous problems for her as well. Anyway, no sooner did she graduate from high school, and she was off to college with the intention of becoming a nurse. As stated before, that's what the original plan was anyway. Then, not too long after starting college, she began putting a lot of serious thought into getting a degree in education with the emphasis on becoming an elementary grade schoolteacher. That was an obvious change of plan, but it wasn't a bad route to follow either. Ironically, at this point in her life, Maude accidently stumbled upon something that would inevitably change her life forever, and that was the creative art of telling a story through the gift of being able to write a manuscript. Needless to say, a very prolific career in the field of literature began for Maude during the second semester of her third year in college when the psychology class she was taking required her to do a term paper on the nature of man. Well, that was all good and fine, but it was also going to be a very challenging experience for her because that was something she hadn't ever done before. Anyway, for some unexplained reason, everything very quickly fell into place and soon she was writing for her own personal enjoyment. Actually, just to be able to write something was a major accomplishment but she did so well with it, that by the time her summer vacation was over, Maude had written a full-length novel about a young couple who fall in love and go onto prosper in the stock market. At any rate, at the advice of one of her friends, she found a publisher that was willing to take a chance on her book and the rest was history.

From that point on, writing novels became a way of life for her.

Anyway, due to the immediate success she achieved as a writer, money wasn't a problem anymore so just as soon as she graduated from college, Maude began looking around for a house. Well, as you might think, after a very in-depth search, a short time later, she made the decision to purchase a home in the upscale community of Beverly Hills. At any rate, Maude found what she was looking for in a relatively short period of time and over the course of four weeks, she moved into her new home. In fact, as you can well imagine, it was adorned with every possible amenity known to mankind, in addition to a luxurious spa with a full-service bar, an in-ground swimming pool, six bedrooms, five baths, a four-car garage, a one-of-a-kind meditation garden, and last but not least, a physical fitness room. At any rate, she quickly took a liking to her new home, and in the years ahead, it would turn out to be the place she always called home.

Anyway, as time went by, Maude continued to come out with a new book every year until she left her twenty something years behind. The degree she received in education soon became a passing memory because the success she attained in the field of writing literature left her without any need to be a teacher. In fact, as more time went by, Maude eventually took to a way of living that was synonymous with the lifestyles of the rich and famous. Actually, I am sure, most people would've looked at that as a blessing and as you might think, she did as well. In addition to that, it can also be said, Maude was more than satisfied with what she had accomplished but like most things in life, there was always room for improvement and that's the way she looked at it as well. At any rate, with that aspect of her life already decided, she would be able to move forward with her personal life now so with that said, her next goal and objective was to find a special person to raise a family with. Of course, that's not always an easy thing to do and for some people like her that was going to be a very difficult thing to do. The truth of the matter is she didn't really have the right personality for marriage and what it entails however her motherly instinct was trying to convince her having children and raising a family was the correct thing to do. Actually, in many instances, marriage isn't always the way to go anyway because not everyone is cut out for living with another person and it sure as hell isn't going to solve all your problems. In fact, think of all the problems you'll inherit the day you get married. Say, instead of having a couple of problems, you'll more than likely have two-fold after that. Think of your marriage partner as company that comes to visit you and decides never to leave. Then, you have children, and the size of your self-acquired family gets even bigger until you're literally living with a commune of people. Granted, the children you have will be flesh of your flesh, but if you don't like constantly having someone around, you aren't going to be too happy with the adventure you are embarking upon. Don't get me wrong, being in love is a great thing and if you're fortunate enough to find a special person to share your life with that is what life is all about however some people will have a hard time with that endeavor. Well, you guessed it, with regards to Maude, she just happened to be that kind of a person. For that reason, there were going to be some difficult days for her in the days to come although she didn't have any way of knowing that at the time. Needless to say, for some people, the hardest things to see in life are the most obvious even if it comes right down to the nose upon your face. That also includes understanding and seeing your own personality. Anyway, she was a bit short sighted in that area as well and of course that led to some additional problems for her. In fact, one of those so-called problems had to do with dealing with what she saw as an intrusion into her privacy and of course, I am referring to public appearances and what someone else may do that you have no control over. Perhaps, that isn't the best way to put it, but it had everything to do with the fact, Maude found it difficult to deal with things that didn't go her way and things you would normally associate with being a celebrity. Anyway, not too long after realizing these things, she wrote another novel and like before, she was successful in doing that. Unfortunately, for that reason, as time went by, she began having a very difficult time dealing with the notoriety of being a celebrity however in her case, what she took issue with actually went along with being a notable writer. In fact, in many instances, what she actually thought was a problem was in fact nothing to be concerned about. Unfortunately, Maude was a very deep person, so it was hard for her to see the simplest things in life and that did not always bode well for her. Actually, what did her well though was shortly after writing her third novel, she suddenly found herself getting a lot of good reviews and praise for the work she had done in the field of literature. Needless to say, it was the kind of praise Maude needed and it gradually helped boost her confidence in doing some things. Yes, Maude was a bit shy when it came to dealing with the public and celebrity stardom, but that was her nature and Maude tried to deal with it the best way she knew how by pulling her hair back into a ponytail and wearing sunglasses wherever she went. Obviously, it did not solve all her problems however it did help some. At any rate, as time went by, it became apparent she was going to have to make some adjustments in her personal life or something catastrophic was going to happen to her. Furthermore, due to the flaws in her personality, Maude managed to stay single all the way through the early years of her writing career. Actually, she wasn't trying to get that kind of an end result however every time Mr. Right came along, something would inevitably go wrong, and Maude would have to say, she wasn't ready to settle down yet. It was not that she didn't want to get married. She just simply hadn't found the right person, that's all. Anyway, in addition to her flawed personality, she was also a little to set in her ways for a good relationship to take root. Did she realize this? No, and believe it or not, Maude wasn't aware of this, so she had a lot of trouble with personal relationships. Perhaps, on the plus side of it all, she was a very attractive woman and that was something she was proud of as well.

Anyway, as it turns out, after living in the Los Angeles area for a little over ten years, she eventually concluded, it was time to get away from the lifestyle that shaped her life since having enrolled in college. Needless to say, it was a lifestyle, she had grown accustomed too however it was also making a wreck out of her life. For that reason, she had decided to make some changes in her life. Of course, that would mean finding another place to live but she had done that before and she could do that again. In fact, after many less than desirable dealings with the news media and some highly stressful public appearances, she thought it would be a good idea to take a new direction in life. Not necessarily changing what she did for a living but perhaps move to a place where she could have a little anonymity. In addition to that, she was getting very frustrated with a bad relationship she was in because the guy was using her to get whatever he wanted whenever he wanted it. It wasn't a very good situation and the stress of it all was dragging her down but if the truth were made known, it was actually a drug addiction to a couple of commonly prescribed tranquilizers that was ruining her life. Unfortunately, the very often fast paced living Maude had become accustomed too had caught up with her. At any rate, like so many people do at one time or another, she began taking tranquilizers and sleeping pills whenever the need arose and that did nothing but add to her drug addiction.

Anyway, as fate would have it, Maude's boyfriend dropped by her house one evening and found her sprawled out on the bathroom floor in a totally unconscious state. Needless to say, he immediately checked for a pulse but there wasn't any, so he began mouth to mouth resuscitation in an effort to bring her around. Unfortunately, she wasn't responding at all so rather than waste any more time on what appeared to be a lost cause, he called 911. At any rate, about ten minutes later an ambulance arrived at her house and it wasn't a moment too soon. Anyway, as you might think, the paramedics quickly assessed the situation and came to the conclusion, it was necessary to rush her to the nearest hospital, so they put her in the ambulance and took off down the street as her boyfriend looked on in silence. The truth of the matter is, she damn near died on the way to the hospital that evening but thanks to the medics and her boyfriend's quick action she pulled through the ordeal. In hindsight, it was also extremely apparent if Ken hadn't come along when he did, Maude would've been just another statistic in the state coroner's office. At any rate, the end result of what Ken did, gave her a second chance on life.

Anyway, as you might think, after struggling with the idea she was going to have to make some changes in her life, a short time later, she came to the undeniable conclusion, it was time to get her life in order. Not just simply moving on with her life, but after several months of living a very unhealthy lifestyle and nearly dropping dead, she had decided to leave the area. That wasn't an easy decision to make because she liked living in Beverly Hills however after getting through that horrible night, it was the only practical thing to do. Something had to change, or she didn't have a prayer's chance in hell of making it to her next birthday. Of course, by this time, she was aware of that undeniable fact. Furthermore, and also realistically speaking, Maude needed to get away from the fast-paced living she had become accustomed too over the past few years. As you might think, it didn't have anything to do with where Maude was living however it did have to do with a couple of other things though. First, her boyfriend was to blame for much of her problems and when you figured in her flawed personality, some changes were in order. Obviously, running away from her problems wouldn't solve anything however she thought a change of scenery was a step in the right direction. In this particular case, she was also in a very abusive relationship with someone and since that was something she had control over that issue was fixable. With regards to a couple of other things, she would have to move somewhere else to fix the problem. The fact of the matter is the past couple of months had been difficult for her to get through anyway so you might say, she was more anxious than ever to begin a new chapter in her life. Anyway, with that said, Maude began thinking about where she might want to live outside the Los Angeles area. In fact, right at the moment, any other adjustments she made in her personal life would have to wait a little while longer. At this point, Maude looked up the coast a ways. Believe it or not, her first thought was to move to the state of Alaska and the fact she was actually contemplating doing that really said it all. Next, she thought about moving to the Lake Tahoe area but that didn't appeal to her either because it was a tourist haven. Admittedly, one of the things she wanted to accomplish was to find a place that would give her some anonymity from the public as well as the very often unrelenting news media but in all probability, Lake Tahoe would not be able to help Maude with that. Obviously, the community of Beverly Hills and the surrounding area wasn't able to provide her with any kind of protection from that sort of thing anymore and that was part of the problem. Needless to say, ever since Maude broke into the entertainment industry, she was forever running into someone who wanted an autograph or something like that. In most instances, it didn't really amount to any more than an acknowledgment of who she was and that was the end of it, however there were times when she didn't feel like dealing with that. Actually, part of the issue was just a matter of human nature kicking in however with regards to Maude's boyfriend, as far as she was concerned, all Ken Stackford wanted was a piece of her ass. Perhaps, that's a very tacky way of putting it however that was the reality of the situation. In fact, quite frankly, the way she looked it was all he wanted to do was party. You know like yahoo look what I did! Let's go have some fun! Well, in Maude's defense, he more than likely had a lot of growing up to do because he had a very promiscuous, fun-loving personality and that didn't fall in line with her serious take charge personality. At any rate, between an immature boyfriend and an often less than kind news media, she turned to prescription medications to try and alleviate the undesirable circumstances, and of course, that didn't turn out well for her. As for the people she didn't personally know, well, more often than not, someone would inevitably end up asking a question like, "Don't I know you from somewhere? My god, you look familiar. Wait a minute! Aren't you the one who wrote …?" At this point and long before she had a chance to answer the persons question, they would reflect for a minute on who she was, trying to bring a name to the tip of their tongue that would identify her. Anyway, they would inevitably say, "I thought that was you, Maude. Well, if this isn't a pleasant surprise. Not in a hundred and ten million years did I ever expect to meet you here however now that I have, I want you to know, I'm a really big fan of yours. I mean that sincerely. In fact, your last book was fantastic. I loved it!" Then, the next unavoidable question would ensue, "Would it be too much to ask for an autograph?" Actually, most people didn't mean any harm by doing that however there were times when Maude found it to be a little annoying. Needless to say, time and time again, she ran into similar situations and time and time again she would try to be as polite as she possibly could. Unfortunately, that came with the territory and as much as she hated to admit it, that was just part of being a celebrity, that's all. On the other hand, she was only human and to be honest with you, there were times when she would have preferred a little less notoriety. In the eyes of the public, she was a celebrity first, and then she was an everyday person who had a life of her own. It also goes without saying, since her fans were the ones who bought the books, she always tried to be as cordial as possible but as stated before, that wasn't always an easy thing to do. In most instances, all of her fans were actually looking for was an autograph or a picture of them standing together so it didn't usually entail that much. Every now and then she would run into someone who wanted to get personal with her by taking her out to lunch or going to a movie but that didn't happen very often. As for the reason why, she wanted to move away from the city of Beverly Hills, she would've probably said, it had to do with the stress of everyday living even though in reality, a combination of things was actually responsible for her decision to move away from the area. Needless to say, in the broadest of terms Maude was burnt out really badly so she thought it would be a good idea to take a different direction in life. At any rate, with that in mind and also at this point in her life, she soon began thinking about moving to the state of Oregon. At the very least, it would get her away from the over-bearing playboy that was using her. Granted, that wasn't going to solve all of her problems but it was definitely a step in the right direction.

Now, with regards to the state of Oregon, the way Maude looked at that was, it wasn't as heavily populated as the state of California so Oregon should give her some relief from the news media. Secondly, and equally as important, she would be moving to a region of the country that had mild winters. In addition to that, if she chose to live on the coast there, it was an opportunity to maintain a residence near the ocean somewhere and she had every intention of doing that if at all possible. Needless to say, Maude wasn't used to getting snow and that's the way she wanted to keep it. In fact, it's one of the reasons why she originally came to the state of California. As for the state of Oregon, it looked like it would be an ideal place to live, and like everything else she touched ground upon at one time or another, she was probably right about that too. Anyway, as you can easily see, things didn't go the way she thought it would and now she wasn't entirely sure how everything would go in the days ahead. The truth of the matter is not only did Maude stop taking the prescription tranquilizers that had become a hindrance to her health, but she also thought it was best to get away from the hectic fast-paced living she had become accustomed to over the past few years. Needless to say, sometimes things have a way of catching up with us at some point along the way and in this case, it did with her as well. In fact, quite frankly, she had reached her breaking point! Now, as far as she was concerned, the only question remaining was whether or not she would make her next residence in the state of Oregon. All things considered and under the circumstances, the only logical thing to do was to start looking for a new home so with that in mind, Maude began searching through the classified ads of a local newspaper to see if she could locate some real estate listings that were of interest to her. At any rate, after a fairly extensive search, she spotted a listing that caught her eye. In fact, this one actually read so well, it took her all of two seconds to realize this might be what she was looking for. Anyway, it goes without saying, when you're looking to purchase a property out of state somewhere, it stands to reason, the property in question will be located a good distance away from where you currently live. Obviously, she didn't see that as a problem because Maude was looking to get away from the area she was residing in anyway. The truth of the matter is the property she was interested in on the northern coast of Oregon would more than likely achieve two things. First, it would be a much easier to move to the state of Oregon than it would be to relocate to the state of Alaska and secondly, the real estate listing that caught her eye was near the ocean. For that reason, there was a very good possibility this property might give her the peace of mind she was looking for so the only logical thing to do was go see it. Anyway, after giving it a lot of thought, she concluded, it would be a good idea to take a look at the property so with that in mind, she left instructions with one of her neighbors to keep an eye on things while she was gone. She didn't think it would take very long to look into the matter and with any luck at all, maybe that's the way everything would turn out in the end. If for some reason she was away longer than a day or two, her neighbor said she would continue watch over things for her until she returned home and that's really all Maude could really ask for. Of course, there was always possibility her plans might change in the days ahead but if it did, she would take everything in stride and deal with the situation when it arose.

Anyway, early next morning, shortly after breakfast, she threw a few pieces of clothing in to a suitcase and proceeded to take a shower. Everything was going well, and right on schedule I might add, so the prospect of it being a good day looked promising indeed. Actually, the sun was out shining brightly and there wasn't a cloud in the sky, so it was shaping up to be a nice day. Of course, it goes without saying, that's always a good thing. At any rate, with all of her housework taken care of and everything seemingly in order at home, she was ready to hit the road. The time had come to head up to the state of Oregon to look at the property she was interested in and with her appetite having been satisfied for a while, she made one last trip to the bathroom. Then, after a quick check to make sure her physical appearance looked okay, with a suitcase in one hand and a pair of sunglasses in the other, she headed out the door to her car. Once outside, she wasted no time getting into her Ferrari, then, after starting the engine, she threw the car in gear and quickly sped off down the road. She was now officially on her way to the state of Oregon. In fact, to be more precise, she was headed to tierra Del Mar. Needless to say, after countless days of dealing with a lot of unnecessary bullshit, she was finally taking the appropriate action to try and put an end to all the unwanted shit she had been dealing with. In the meantime, the prospect of getting some badly needed rest looked better than ever now. There was even a possibility, she might go on vacation somewhere. Granted, that was something she hadn't done in a while, but it sounded like a great idea, so she was thinking very strongly about doing that now. Of course, that wasn't carved in stone or anything like that, but if the circumstances were right in the days ahead, there was a very good possibility she might take a vacation after all.

CHAPTER 2

As anticipated, Maude had a fairly long distance to drive before she reached the town of Tierra Del Mar however that was something she had already taken into consideration so that was fine with her. The fact of the matter is she wasn't on any kind of schedule, nor did she have any desire to be on one, so it stands to reason, she wasn't in a hurry to get there. Besides, if she were to travel up the coast of California the way she wanted too, she would have an opportunity to see the entire state and like so many other things she hadn't done before, this was something she had been wanting to do for a long time. During her years in California, she didn't have the time to do a lot of things because of business matters associated with publishing so on most occasions, after that was taken care of, Maude didn't do too much of anything. Of course, from time to time, she did a little shopping or went to see a movie, but other than that, she led a fairly quiet life. At any rate, at this point in her life, she thought it would be a good idea to try something different for a change, like utilizing her leisure time in a more efficient way. You know, like getting some good old-fashioned r and r. In fact, it's one of the reasons why Maude wanted to find another place to live, and right at the moment, it looked like it was going to be the state of Oregon. Of course, at this point in time, that remained to be seen but she appeared to be headed in the right direction.

Actually, what she saw as important in all of this was if she moved to the state of Oregon and it looked like that was the direction everything was headed in, Maude thought it would be a good idea to be located near the city of Portland. Needless to say, on occasion, she had business matters to attend too so being within driving distance of the city of Portland would make things a lot easier for her. In fact, from a strategist's point of view, Portland was in an ideal location, so it would be beneficial to her if she found a property in the area. Anyway, with that in mind, Maude continued to weigh out all the pros and cons of living in a small community like Tierra Del Mar, and she concluded, it was definitely close enough to the city of Portland that made this a doable place for her to live. The truth of the matter is there was a lot to take into consideration however the more she thought about it, the more she was convinced, living in Tierra Del Mar might work out for her after all. Of course, the overall condition of the house she was going to see would be a factor in her decision to move there as would be a couple of other things. Needless to say, she was accustomed to living in a city and that had been the case for a fairly long time now so living in a small community where they more than likely rolled up their sidewalks at five o'clock in the afternoon would take some getting use too. On the other hand, there were obviously some good aspects to living in the country. One being, it was a much slower way of life. Perhaps, the other positive aspect to it all was country living would give her an opportunity to enjoy the quieter side of life and that would be a welcome change from things in recent days. Needless to say, between fighting drug addiction and being in a bad relationship with a guy who was stuck on himself, she was ready for a change. In fact, quite frankly, it was imperative she get her personal life back in order before something bad happened to her and moving to the state of Oregon might remedy the situation. The truth of the matter is there weren't too many options available to her, nevertheless, she would get Ken Stackford out of her life and everything would be fine from that point on.

Anyway, thanks to some very good planning on her part, she arrived at her destination in Tierra Del Mar the following day. Of course, because she had traveled the entire distance by car, she was a bit tired however that was to be expected and she didn't have any qualms about having done so either although the reason why she chose the state of Oregon for beginning a new life for herself was just sheer coincidence. In fact, it was the desire for a better life that motivated her in to doing this. Needless to say, without taking some corrective measures, she would've more than likely headed further down the road to self-destruction, which was exactly what she was doing in recent months. At any rate, she was there to look at a real estate property in Tierra Del Mar so on one day, late in the month of July, totally drained of all emotion, Maude found herself in the town of Tierra Del Mar.

The drive up the coast had been a good one for her and she was very thankful for that. In fact, the route she used for travel added a whole new dimension to the word scenic and she didn't have any regrets about having chosen to do things this way. Anyway, as you might think, Maude immediately began scouting around the community for a place to stay, and after a brief search, it came as a great relief to know, she had found what she was looking for. As it turns out, the Cozy Arms Motel was her first choice for a temporary place of refuge. It wasn't anything to lavish but it would serve the purpose of what she wanted it for and that's all that really mattered. Needless to say, until she bought a new home or went back to her estate in Beverly Hills, this would be her home away from home. At any rate, as stated before, feeling a little exhausted from the drive up to Tierra Del Mar, she had decided to try and unwind a little before getting in touch with the real estate agency so with that in mind, she checked into the Cozy Arms Motel. That didn't take very long. Perhaps, as little as ten to fifteen minutes. Anyway, feeling satisfied that everything was in order, Maude headed off to her room and begin unpacking her suitcase. Then, after methodically laying out a fresh change of clothes on top of the bed, she stepped into the shower to freshen up a bit. That didn't take very long either and soon destiny found her completely at rest in one of the chairs inside the room, where she proceeded to write down a few questions she wanted to ask the real estate agency representative when she saw him. Needless to say, her reason for doing this in advance was so she wouldn't stumble around in total ignorance over real estate matters she knew nothing about. In fact, in most instances, Maude wasn't a very prolific speaker anyway, so it was probably a wise thing to do. At the very least, she would be well organized with lots of ideas and thoughts regarding her desire to purchase a new home and since organizational skills were one of her better traits, it made all the sense in the world to do that.

In the meantime, because she was a very deep person in all matters having to do with the inner psyche, at this point, she began using her time to reflect on things. Actually, there wasn't a hell of a lot she could do in a motel room anyway, so it certainly didn't hurt to do that. The truth of the matter is most things usually have a way of working themselves out with time, and as you might think, the problems she was experiencing over the past few months would eventually work for her as well. Unfortunately, when it came right down to the simplest things in life, more often than not, she was as blind as a bat however that was fairly typical of her personality. At any rate, not only did she begin reflecting on the things that were hopefully behind her, but she also began reflecting on what may lay ahead of her as well. Actually, that took in a lot of territory, however with all kinds of time on her hands she opted for deep reflective thought and so she whiled away the rest of the day with a world of things on her mind. First, it was business matters, then, it was boyfriend problems, then, it was news media problems, and then it was health problems. In fact, if it wasn't one thing, it was another however Maude felt the need to do this, and considering the circumstances, it seemed like the only logical thing to do.

Anyway, like usual, the day went by quickly and after having a bite to eat and watching a little television for a while, she opted to call it a day and went to bed. The truth of the matter is a considerable amount of time was spent on the road over the past couple of days so Maude felt the need to get a little extra rest. At any rate, for that reason, along towards the hour of nine o'clock, she turned out the lights inside her room and tried to get some sleep but with business matters on her mind that wasn't any easy thing to do. Obviously, it made no sense to worry about the things that hadn't actually happened yet, however, she was the kind of person who fretted over the least little thing anyway, so it turned out to be a fairly typical evening for her. In this case, that meant it would be a sleepless night, however a little rest was eventually attained, but it wasn't until the early morning hours of the next day before she finally fell asleep.

Anyway, shortly after eight o'clock in the morning, Maude got up from her short night's sleep, had breakfast, took a shower, and then with everything seemingly in order, she proceeded to give the real estate agency in Tierra Del Mar a call. At any rate, it was her steadfast intention to get an appointment to see the property so rather than putting the matter off any longer, Maude took a moment to speak with one of the representatives in the front office. Anyway, upon doing so, she found out no one was living on the premises so there wasn't any reason why she couldn't look at the house whenever it was convenient for her to do so. Needless to say, that fit in really well with her desire to see the property so he suggested they meet at the old Kimball mansion at three o'clock in the afternoon. Anyway, as you might think, a few questions followed, as Maude tried to learn as much as she could about the place. Of course, that also led to a very meaningful conversation with a lot of information shared between them as the realtor told her everything he knew about the house. That's when she learned who the former owner of the property was and a bit of additional information that she found very unsettling. An unsolved murder was committed there a while ago. Obviously, that was the last thing Maude wanted to hear the man from the real estate agency say however such was the nature of the past history of the house. Actually, Maude was lucky he was being up front with her about what took place at the Kimball mansion because she wouldn't have known something terrible happened there at some point along the way during the ownership of the property. Anyway, according to the gentleman at the real estate agency, the previous owner of the property came home one day and much to his surprise, he caught someone trying to steal the priceless antiques he had stored in his attic. Well, one thing led to another and in a last-ditch effort to stop the thief from stealing the antiques, the hoodlum pulled out a gun and shot the owner dead. Of all the possible things that could have happened there and as it turns out a murder was committed at the old Kimball mansion. Actually, what complicated things to some degree was Tierra Del Mar was a very small community. That meant if anything went on in town there wasn't any way something like that could be kept a secret, so when the incident took place, rumors quickly began flying around the community that the owner was mixed up in some type of marketing scheme however that was never proven. In fact, by the time the law enforcement guys arrived at the house that day, there wasn't anything they could do. The owner of the old Kimball mansion was sprawled out on the living-room floor in a pool of blood and the person who pulled the trigger of the gun was nowhere to be found. In fact, very uncharacteristic of the community, the thief was never apprehended and the murder remained unsolved. Anyway, when she learned this, her initial reaction was to hell with the property. Needless to say, Maude could always find another one, but she liked the looks of this one really well so for the time being she was going to stay the course. She wanted to see it! Furthermore, at this point in their conversation, she was a little reluctant to hear any more about the place or its former occupants however it can be further noted, the past history of the house was not going to prevent her from taking a look at it. Maude was a very determined person and in most instances she didn't take no for an answer and on this occasion, such was the case as well. Anyway, the man from the real estate agency said he didn't know any more about the murder that was committed there. The realtor did say, it was probably the reason why the house wasn't selling. In fact, the property had been on the market for a while now however as stated before, with it being a small community, no one dared to buy it. Actually, it was more than likely the reason why most of the people living in the area were reluctant to go near the property. In addition to that, and also in hindsight, the realtor said if his memory served him correctly, there was another mystery surrounding the house as well, however he stated it was only a rumor. He had heard the old Kimball mansion was haunted, however in reality, there was no evidence to back the claim up so Mr. Brewster went onto say, he preferred not to elaborate on the subject any more than was necessary. At any rate, at this point in their conversation, he also took a moment to tell her the property she was interested in buying was in need of a few repairs, but with it being an older home that didn't come as any surprise. Unfortunately, by this time, she was also beginning to have second thoughts about purchasing the property and with good reason. Based on what Mr. Brewster said, there were too many things wrong with it. In addition to that, after finding out a murder had been committed there, you might say Maude was a little reluctant to purchase it, and that was understandable, nevertheless, she had a decision to make. She didn't know whether or not it was a good idea to buy the property as it was or if she should look around for something else. Needless to say, for more than one reason, it was a difficult decision to make because the property was very appealing to her. At this point, she thought it out a little more and concluded, she would take a look at it anyway. At any rate, while listening to what Mr. Brewster had to say about the property, she continued to give the situation a little more thought. Not only was the past history of the house in question but what if she was targeted by the same person that committed the murder there. If that turned out to be the case, she might end up losing her life as well. In addition to that, with the estate in need of a few repairs, perhaps, the property wasn't the right fit for her after all. In that case, it would probably turn out to be another great big headache for her. Obviously, if Mr. Brewster was being honest with her about disclosing everything to her about the property and she didn't have any reason to believe otherwise, then in all probability, all she had to do was put a little money into it and she would have a very nice home. Of course, it's actually quite possible he may have failed to mention something about the estate she should have been made aware of and if that turned out to be the case, then, not only was she wasting her time with Mr. Brewster, but she was also wasting her time giving consideration to buying the property as well. Needless to say, after a little more procrastination on her part, she eventually decided to keep the three o'clock appointment to see the property after all. Anyway, like you might think, at this point in their conversation, she thanked him for being so up front with her about the property and a moment or two later, she hung up the phone. The truth of the matter is there wasn't a heck of a lot more that could be said about the property anyway so even though Mr. Brewster was a bit winded by the length of their conversation, he still liked to talk however by now, Maude opted to end the conversation in favor of getting something to drink, so their conversation came to an end. At this point, she proceeded to get a cold beverage out of the apartment size refrigerator that was in her room and then, she sat back down to think the situation out a little more. By this time, she was at odds with herself over whether or not she would even bother taking a look at the property, however regardless of her indecisiveness, that's what she wanted to do. At any rate, by this time, she realized it would be just a question of what needed to be fixed and how much money she had to put into it. In most instances, houses are capable of being restored as long as they aren't in too much disrepair, and in all probability, this one fell into that category as well.

At any rate, as you might expect, Maude wasn't familiar with the town of Tierra Del Mar at all, so she left the Cozy Arms Motel a little earlier than normal to make sure she wasn't late for her appointment with Mr. Brewster. In this particular case, the property she was going to look at was located on the outskirts of town so she figured it wouldn't be hard to find and as it turns out, she was right. It was very easy to find so in literally no time at all Maude found herself standing in front of a large white house with black shutters. Needless to say, it was obviously the one she drove all the way up from California to see, however much to her disappointment, the house was in need of a few repairs just like Mr. Brewster said. Actually, the truth of the matter is, like most of the classified ads that list real estate properties for sale in a newspaper, this one didn't give her a good accurate picture of what the house really looked like so you might say, she was somewhat dismayed at the condition of the house. Anyway, within minutes of having arrived there, judging by the overall appearance of the exterior of the house, she could immediately see, it was going to need a few repairs to get everything back in good working order however if no major renovations had to be done to it, given a little time, most of those other things could be fixed rather easily and probably in a fairly short period of time. That was a very encouraging sign. Besides, the overall architecture of the house was actually quite impressive. Needless to say, someone must have put a lot of careful thought into the building of the house. At any rate, Maude took a few minutes to walk around the perimeter of the house to make sure she wasn't overlooking anything that might turn into an unwanted headache in the days ahead. Thankfully, there didn't appear to be anything she had to be concerned about. In fact, the house actually had some strong points. For starters, it was in an ideal location so for that reason alone it was worth giving a lot of consideration. As for the other strong points of the property, the panoramic view a person got from the west side of the house was truly magnificent. In addition to that, due to the highly remote nature of the property, the house afforded her plenty of privacy as well and that was obviously a big plus. At any rate, a very determined person in the name of Maude Derringer took a look at the foundation next and it appeared to be in order, so she proceeded to inspect the grounds of the estate. It was at this point that she gazed off in the distance and noticed, the only other house located on this stretch of road was the one over to the right of the lighthouse. Everything else tied to the community was found back in town however that's one of the things that sparked her interest in the property. The house was definitely in a very good location. Perhaps, it wasn't in the most idealistic of locations for a lot of people but it was what she was looking for. Anyway, by this time, Maude was thinking the property might serve her purpose well in the days ahead and that was the only thing that actually mattered. In truth, she liked being near the ocean anyway so that only reinforced her decision to find a house that afforded her the opportunity to do that. At any rate, this particular house sat on a bank of soil overlooking the Pacific Ocean, so she took an even greater liking to it. Needless to say, that was something she wasn't able to get any enjoyment out of when she was a kid growing up in the state of Arizona however after moving to the state of California, the ocean very quickly became a part of her life. In fact, quite frankly, she came to like it so much, from that point on, it was a requirement for wherever she lived. Actually, with regards to the beach, the only fly in the ointment there was that's where she met Ken. Of course, the beach in the state of Oregon was in an entirely different area than California however as much as she tried to deny it, the memory of where she met Ken continued to haunt the hell out of the back of her mind. Anyway, as you may recall, Ken was the one that saved her life from an accidental drug overdose a few weeks earlier. In fact, it should be noted, their relationship started out very good but that all abruptly came to an end the night she caught him in bed with another woman. From her perspective, he wasn't ready to settle down yet and perhaps that was true, however rather than sitting down and trying to work their differences out in a civilized manner, she told him where to go. Not only was it hard for her to do that but in the end, the horrific barrage of words she levied at him left Ken crushed as well. At any rate, when it became apparent things weren't going to work out between them, it came as no surprise to Ken that she was leaving the area and now destiny had her searching for a property in the state of Oregon. Actually, if she were to think about it, she still missed Ken a lot, however her decision to call an end to their relationship was the right thing to do. Unfortunately, his very selfish need to be with a woman was the stumbling point. In fact, wherever there was a brunette, blond or redhead, that's where Ken could be found and you might say, that's not what she had in mind. Anyway, as you might think, she informed Mr. Stackford he had one too many girl friends for her liking and of course that didn't settle well with Ken but Maude was just being honest with him. Regrettably, Ken wasn't the perfect match she thought he might be. At any rate, to make a long story short, most women can tell when a man is screwing around on them, and such was the case here as well. In fact, so much so, it didn't take Maude very long to figure out what Ken was doing. Anyway, as stated before, everything came to light one evening when she dropped by his apartment and found him in bed with another woman however it wasn't until sometime later that she learned who the woman was. Yes, Monica Albert, a seemingly, bright individual with a great body was the one he was having sexual relations with although for some reason, she could never remember her last name. At any rate, not only were they having an ongoing affair, but it was one they had been involved in for several months. Anyway, the evening Maude became aware of all this also just happened to be the evening she gave Ken a call to remind him how much she really cared for him. In fact, the way everything unfolded, it was on this occasion that they made plans to have dinner together the following evening. Normally, that would have been a good thing but in this particular instance, that couldn't have been further from the truth because she was about to make a very unpleasant discovery. Anyway, now, looking back on it all, Maude could still recall what Ken said to her that evening. "Hey baby, what's happening? I've been thinking about you a lot lately. In fact, every time I look at your picture sitting on my nightstand, I can literally hear a voice calling out to me, beckoning to me, reassuring me, like the voice of an angel, stating you're my only reason for living. Yes, it's that bad, Maude. Anyway, I love you dearly. By the way, I'm not doing anything tomorrow evening. Would you like to have lunch with me? Believe it or not, that's one of the things I've been meaning to get around to asking you, but I've been busy lately. Business matters, you know. That sort of thing. Anyway, we'll have a great time. I guarantee it. In fact, consider that a promise." Then, long before Maude had a chance to give him an answer, he was in the quick process of wrapping up the conversation by saying, "Well, what do you say? I haven't got all day. I'm a very busy person. You do realize that don't you?" At that point, she was a little startled by his very abrupt fast way of speaking, however, coming from Ken that was not anything to unusual. Anyway, she quickly agreed to have dinner with him the next day. The truth of the matter is Maude had been thinking about Ken a lot in recent days however they never seemed to connect. He always seemed to be in a hurry to go somewhere. Well, this time, unless Maude was overlooking something, she would have an opportunity to spend some time with him. Furthermore, due to a lack of being able to connect with him, Maude had decided to give him the royal treatment after they had dinner tomorrow evening. If everything went as planned, she was going to rape the hell out of him. Needless to say, the intimate side of their relationship was very rarely seen. Like I said before, Ken always seemed to be occupied with something else. Well, as you might think, this was her chance to nail him. Actually, she thought it was something he had been pursuing for some time now however for more than one reason, Maude had been extremely reluctant to give into his demands. Anyway, as it turns out, after speaking with Ken that evening, she went into the bathroom, put on some make up, slipped into a very seductive dress, and left to go over to his apartment. Needless to say, she would surprise him. At any rate, upon her arrival at his residence, she discovered the door wasn't locked so rather than ringing the doorbell, she let herself in. At this point, she made a very unfortunate discovery. Much to her regret, there was a trail of women's clothing scattered about the living-room floor and it led all the way up the stairs to his bedroom. Of all the low-down despicable things he could have done, she mused to herself. At any rate, as you may have already guessed, she felt as if Ken had sucker-punched her right in the gut because the woman's clothing that had taken up residence on the floor of his living-room apartment wasn't her own. That meant only one thing. Ken was cheating on her! Actually, that was something Maude had suspected for some time now but with indisputable evidence now laid before her, she wasn't sure of what would be the best way to proceed. Initially, she was in a state of shock. Then, there was the state of denial. In fact, Maude even went as far as thinking maybe her eyes were playing tricks on her as a way of making her more receptive to his sexual needs. It was all very unsettling to say the least. Then, Maude took a moment to look about the room one more time. No, as much as she would like to say this isn't happening to me, she couldn't. There was a trail of women's clothing scattered about his living-room floor and it was quite real. Who in the hell does he take me for she thought to herself? Surely, he has better things to do than this. Unfortunately, what was keeping him busy of late was now extremely obvious. In fact, her worst suspicions had been confirmed as a very humiliating experience was about to unfold right before her eyes. At that point, regardless of the circumstances, she did what any other all-American girl would've done upon learning their boyfriend was screwing around with another woman. Maude took a long, slow, deep breath of fresh air into her lungs and slowly proceeded up the stairs to his bedroom with the intentions of confronting him about who this other woman was. Anyway, with all the courage of a lioness, after having reached the top of the stairs, she peered directly into his bedroom. At first, she was overwhelmed with the desire to vomit all over the floor because Ken and Miss whoever she was were engaged in sexual activity on top of his bed, and then reality set in. Damn, this is actually happening to me she said to herself. So, this is what Ken was doing in his spare time. Needless to say, from what she could see, Ken wasn't being honest with her about too much of anything. Her initial reaction was to kill the son of a bitch but she quickly dismissed the thought in favor of finding a less desperate measure for making him aware of how much she disapproved of what he was doing. Seriously, there had to be a better way to resolve the matter. Obviously, murdering him was a sin in the eyes of God and certainly against the law as well. In fact, it would not be a very wise thing to do. Unfortunately, the person she thought the world of had broken her heart, and now she had to decide what she was going to do. At this point, Maude wanted to tell him where to go but she also quickly concluded, that might not be the best thing to do after all so she headed back downstairs to the living-room to try and cool off a little before she said or did something she might regret. Needless to say, she could always tell the no-good son of a bitch where to go another day. Right at the moment, she was just concerned about the situation in his apartment and what she might possibly be able to do to put the message across to Ken that he was a good-for-nothing asshole. At the very least, it would let Ken Stackford know she didn't care for, nor did she approve of his behavior. At any rate, that quickly led Maude into some deep thought for a moment or two as she proceeded to weigh out all the pros and cons of sequestrating some type of retaliatory action against Ken for screwing around with another woman. Then, like a bolt of lightning in the sky above, an idea was struck into Maude's mind so she slipped into the kitchen for a moment to find some type of bucket she could use for the purpose of filling up with water. Anyway, once that goal was achieved, Maude took the bucket, pail or whatever you want to call it and walked over to the kitchen sink where she filled it up with the coldest water known to mankind. Then, to make sure what she planned to do had the desirable effect she was seeking to attain, she got into the refrigerator and loaded the bucket with as many ice cubes as she could. Needless to say, it was quickly determined, there was enough ice to remedy the situation so with only one thought in mind, she made her way back up the stairs to where he was joyfully banging his brains out in the comfort of his girlfriend's arms and dumped the bucket of cold water on top of them. Not unexpectedly, what happened next would be etched into her mind forever. In fact, quite frankly, within seconds of having done this, two very loud blood curdling screams could be heard echoing throughout the house. Then, ever so slowly, as the peace and tranquility inside his apartment came to an end, she leveled a few, good, choice words at Mr. Stackford to tell him just exactly what she thought of his promiscuous behavior, but first, Ken broke the silence by saying, "I know what this probably looks like, however as you know, appearances can be very deceiving so please don't jump to any conclusions, Maude. This woman is just a friend, that's all. Perhaps, I should formally introduce the two of you. Maude, this is Monica. Monica, this is Maude, and well, it goes without saying, you both know who I am. There, now that formal introduction's out of the way, I suppose there isn't any reason why we all can't be friends. Believe it or not, Maude, all Monica was actually trying to do is give me a hand with something and things got a bit out of hand, that's all. Obviously, in my eyes, this was something you didn't really need to know about, however, since you dropped in totally unannounced, there isn't any need to pretend we love each other anymore. As a matter of fact, if you really want to know, Maude, I was hoping in the worst possible way you wouldn't have to know about Monica but I can clearly see that isn't going to be possible now. Furthermore, judging by the look in your eyes, I'd say this relationship is over and that may very well be the case but before you do anything irrational, take a minute to think about what you may or may not do. Please keep in mind I'm only human, so I ask your forgiveness for what you probably see as an inexcusable act of foolhardiness." At this point, silence filled the air inside the room as they continued to stare at one another for a few more seconds. Actually, until now, it had been a one-sided conversation between the two of them, because the moment Maude doused them in ice cold water, Monica left the room. Needless to say, for that reason, they were alone to battle things out in the privacy of Ken's bedroom. At any rate, after what seemed like an eternity and a half, when in reality, not much more than a few seconds of time had gone by, Ken went onto say, "Why did you ever come over here, Maude? Did I not say, we'd go out to dinner tomorrow evening? Well, unless my heads stuck so far up my ass I can't see the light of day, I'd say you've got your days mixed up. Didn't I make myself clear, you were not to come over here under any circumstances unless you called first. Well, apparently, you don't understand English. In fact, I don't know how you could be so inconsiderate. Look at what you've done! A perfectly good relationship is about to go down the drain because of your stupidity! Well, what have you got to say for yourself?" At this point, Maude was seething with anger at his awfully ridiculous statement, yet she remained silent for another second or two. Then, all of a sudden, the hell and fury of a woman's wrath proceeded to bounce off every wall inside his bedroom as she yelled at him at the top of her lungs, "You god damn miserable piece of shit," she screamed! "How dare you imply we're the best of friends! In fact, quite frankly, if you can be so blatantly ignorant as to do this behind my back, you can go to hell, Ken. Needless to say, what you've been doing to me is very disgusting, not to mention very unbecoming of a gentleman. You should be ashamed of yourself, Ken. Do you realize what you said to me a moment ago is an absolute total disgrace and fooling around with this woman is a poor excuse for pretending to be a man? You're nothing but a little boy, Ken! You're no man! A man is a grown and that's something you're not. In fact, who in the hell do you take me for anyway? I don't want to be a puppet on a string. Neither was I born yesterday. Do you really think I am that numb? Furthermore, it's extremely obvious, you have been using me. I realize I don't own you, Ken, but what you've been doing behind my back is despicable!" At this point, she paused just long enough to catch her breath, and then she went onto say, "May you rot and burn in hell for this injustice, Ken! In fact, as of right now, you don't exist anymore! Do you hear me? I've got better things to do than to put up with your bullshit. If and when you try to take me out again, you can drop dead! I refuse to waste my time on you, or this cursed relationship anymore. This friendship is officially over, and furthermore, just in case there's any question about it, you are the biggest asshole I ever met in my life." Then, in a very disheveled manner, Maude quickly stormed out of his bedroom, ran down the stairs, and left his apartment with a world of tears flowing down the side of her face. Well, so much for that cursed relationship, she thought to herself. Enough is enough! Unfortunately, there are times in our life when things don't work out the way we would like them too and such was the case for

Maude as well. At any rate, by this time, she had decided to bring an end to her relationship with Ken. She would move onto other things and Ken could shove Monica what's-her-name right up his ass. In the meantime, she was going to try and put that unfortunate matter behind her.

Anyway, the way everything proceeded to unfold, a couple of days after having that bad falling out with Ken, he coincidentally stopped by her house in Beverly Hills to apologize to her for his inexcusable behavior the other night. Well, it appears, after ringing the doorbell a couple of times and not getting an answer, he had a feeling something was wrong. In fact, quite frankly, he sensed something was terribly wrong because at the very least, she would've come to the door and told him to get lost. Needless to say, that didn't happen so after finding out the door was not locked, he let himself in and made his way through the house until he found Maude lying on the bathroom floor in a totally unconscious state of mind. At any rate, within seconds of having run into the situation as it stood and not being able to bring her around, Ken very quickly concluded, it was going to be necessary to call for help so he rushed into her bedroom and dialed 911 from a phone that was sitting on her nightstand. After that, there wasn't really anything else he could do except wait for the ambulance to get there with a trained medic. Needless to say, Ken could only hope it was in time to save her life. The truth of the matter is little known to him, due to the fight they had the other day, she had taken an overdose of prescription medication and time was of the essence. Anyway, as it turns out, a short time later, after the paramedics arrived on the scene, she eventually regained consciousness at the hospital and was fine however it was Ken's quick action that saved her life.

At any rate, now, as she looked back on it all, it was becoming more and more apparent it was a miracle she was still alive and even though Ken was the one who saved her life, with every passing day that went by, Maude realized bringing an end to their relationship was the right thing to do. Anyway, that whole unfortunate incident was behind her now and Maude was using all of newly found time to concentrate on some other things. First of all, a little common sense told her there was a very good chance better days were coming however in the reality of everyday living, that could also mean, there might be some more difficult days ahead as well. Needless to say, at this point in her life, still being young and all, there wasn't any way to be certain how everything would turn out for her in the years to come however she felt very strongly that getting away from the area she had been living in was a step in the right direction. In this case, Maude had a chance to start a new life for herself in the state of Oregon, and perhaps, if she got lucky, she might even find someone to share her life with too. Obviously, her last boyfriend wasn't the right person for her however there are all kinds of fish in the ocean and with any luck at all, she would be able to find a new love interest somewhere down the road as well. Of course, right at the moment, with everything in her life having gone south, that wasn't her first priority. She had already decided to take things slowly, but if Mr. Right came along, there was always a possibility she might have an opportunity to raise a family after all. Needless to say, that was still quite possible, however the chances of that happening anytime soon was very unlikely. As a matter of fact, at this point, she was trudging through a fairly good amount of self-pity because of her break-up with Ken but she wasn't the kind of person to let something like that get her down for any length of time and such was the case with her as well. Perhaps, the biggest thing to come out of what happened to her in in Beverly Hills was she became a much more cautious person with regards to relationships and in the days ahead that way of thinking would follow her wherever she went.

Anyway, putting all that aside, it's not unfair to say, she had a lot on her mind and I really don't know of better way of saying that. At any rate, at this point in her reverie, Maude realized, she had fallen into a very deep thought pattern again, however her attention was soon directed to the sound of a late model pick-up truck pulling up into the driveway of the property she came to see. Surely, that must be Mr. Brewster, she thought to herself as she glanced at her watch to see what time it was. It was indeed 3:00 o'clock and since that was her scheduled appointment time, she immediately assumed it was the man from the real estate agency. Thankfully, that turned out to be the case because Maude wasn't sure how much longer she could wait around in anticipation of seeing the inside of the house. In truth, she had been waiting for Mr. Brewster to arrive for the past fifteen to twenty minutes although in all due honesty, it felt more like a few hours to her. At any rate, now that he had arrived, she was going to see the interior of the house after all, and that was obviously all that really mattered. In the meantime, like a person on a mission to buy a new home, Maude quickly got her emotions in order and within seconds of having done so, she arose from the front steps of the Kimball mansion where she had been sitting and slowly walked down the driveway to meet Mr. Brewster. It was time to take care of business and in this case, she was very anxious to get started on things. Actually, even though business matters were normally very important to her, on this occasion, it was an entirely different circumstance, so with everything to gain and nothing to lose, she proceeded to get herself in the right mind-set, and got ready to look at the property with Mr. Brewster. In fact, with any kind of luck at all, she wouldn't have to look any further for a new home.

CHAPTER 3

The person from the real estate agency was a slightly balding man with gray hair. He had a very pleasant smile and walked with sort of a gait, however the most impressive trait she found this man to have, was he appeared to be a happy, go lucky guy, who enjoyed his job. Needless to say, Maude knew from past experience, they were the best kind of people to deal with. The fact of the matter is she didn't like aggressive salesmen. Generally speaking, individuals like that are a little too pushy in their sales technique for her liking. On the other hand, it was a real, pleasure to do business with someone who really liked the profession they were in. So many times, in the past, she had been turned off by someone trying to oversell a product or service they didn't know anything about. In this particular case, Mr. Brewster fit the description of a real estate broker in every sense of the word and you might say, she was extremely pleased about that. As a matter of fact, it can be further stated, she could see, he was going to be up front with her in their business dealings and from her perspective, that was the most important thing of all. Needless to say, she had only the highest amount of respect for a person with that kind of character and since, he just happened to remind her of a friend she use to know in school, she felt good about doing business with him. Anyway, at no surprise to her, just as he was about to show her the inside of the house, Mr. Brewster began to ramble on about the real estate market and why he had made the decision to get into that profession so late in life. Well, as you can easily surmise, that wasn't what Maude traveled up to Oregon to hear however he was very persistent about sharing that information with her so she knew from the onset, she would have to listen to what he had to say, regardless of how anxious she was to see the inside of the house. In this particular instance, due to the fact, he was a really nice man, she didn't mind listening to him and it goes without saying, she was lucky that was the case, because he was very long winded. Anyway, as you might think, Mr. Brewster told her a little about himself and then, he elaborated on how strong the real estate market was, which by the way, wasn't originally what she thought he was going to say at all. Actually, she was more interested in seeing the house however Mr. Brewster was extremely flamboyant with words so it stands to reason, Maude was going to have to wait a little while longer before she would be able to do that. Apparently, the gentleman from the real estate was a little lonely because he wouldn't stop talking. Needless to say, that happens sometimes. In fact, from time to time, she got lonely herself, however unlike Mr. Brewster, she very seldom ran off at the mouth. Anyway, as it turns out, according to what he stated to her, it was necessary for him to supplement his pension with a little extra income until social security kicked in but that didn't come as any big surprise because money is hard to come by sometimes or at least, that would be the case for some people anyway. Unfortunately, money is one of those things people cannot live without because it pays the bills. In fact, in some instances, we become victims of the environment we live in, and it goes without saying, when that happens, it can be hard for some of us to step into a better situation. Actually, Maude realized, a lot of people have a hard time making ends meet from time to time. She was just grateful that was something she didn't have to worry about. Anyway, the man from the real estate agency went onto say, the profession he was now, working in was turning out to be a very interesting and rewarding job. Not only did it give him a very flexible work schedule, but it was also something he liked doing as well, and she could immediately see that was important to him. Anyway, it didn't take her very long to realize this and in that understanding, she could honestly say, she was happy for him, because so many people get stuck in a profession they don't actually care about. Like I've said many times before, life is very short so to be able to do something you really enjoy doing is obviously a blessing. In fact, under those circumstances, consider yourself lucky, because if the shoe were on the other foot and you were miserable in your job, you would not have the pleasure of doing something that's agreeable to your personality.

Anyway, another moment or two went by, before Mr. Brewster got around to introducing himself. Initially, she thought it may have been an oversight on his part, however due to the fact there wasn't any urgent need to get things done, she didn't mind listening to him ramble on about this, that, and everything else as well. Besides, it didn't make any difference to Maude if it was a little while longer before she got to see the inside of the house. Realistically speaking, she wasn't in all that big of a hurry to see the house anyway, so she had decided to be patient. Admittedly, it was something she was anxiously awaiting to do, however a few more minutes obviously wasn't going to change anything, in particularly, her highly instinctive plans for totally restructuring her personal life. Anyway, after a little more time went by, Mr. Brewster came to realize, it was time to move on with their conversation so without any further ado he said, "First of all, I'd like to say, I apologize for rambling on the way I have for the past few minutes however I tend to get carried away with most things in life and this just happens to be a good example of that. The fact of the matter is, I have a short attention span. I don't mean anything by it, ma'am. It's just the kind of person I am. At any rate, please accept my apology for being so inconsiderate and let's get down to business. My name is Jedediah Brewster however you may call me Jed if you prefer. In fact, most of my friends call me Jed. Anyway, here's my business card. Hopefully, I'll be able to help you find a property here. I presume, you are the lady I spoke with earlier in the day," he finished saying. "Yes sir, I am," she replied. "I'm Maude Derringer. It's a real pleasure to meet you, Mr. Brewster." At this point, they formally shook hands, and a moment later, they continued on with their conversation. "You know, Mr. Brewster, I drove all the way from southern California to see this house so if it's not too much to ask, I would really like to a look at it," she stated. "Sure, that won't be a problem at all," he replied. "In fact, it will be a pleasure to show it to you. I hope you have your walking shoes on though because it's a fairly good size home and it's going to take me a few minutes to show it to you." Anyway, as it turns out, immediately following that statement, Mr. Brewster smiled ever so graciously at Maude and motioned for her to follow him up the front steps of the house. At this juncture, he very casually pulled a key out of his pocket and unlocked the door. "Come in, Ms. Derringer," he said. "I really don't think you'll be disappointed with the property however like I said earlier in the day, the house needs a few minor repairs to spiff it up a little though. All in all, it's a very nice home, ma'am." Anyway, with that said, they went inside the house and much to her surprise, Maude took an immediate liking to it. The fact of the matter is, it had beautiful oak floors, ornate kitchen cabinets, a huge cathedral ceiling in the living room, a couple of built-in dish cabinets, two brick fireplaces, and a lot of very exquisite woodwork laid out in many different patterns throughout the house. Needless to say, the building certainly had a lot of character for an older home, and it did not take her very long to realize this either. Initially, the only thing she really wasn't all that pleased with was the strong, musty odor that had come to inhabit every square inch of the house however that was something that could always be fixed by opening up a few windows when she moved in. Admittedly, that really wasn't a big deal at all so Maude brushed the matter aside and continued on with the tour of the house. Other than that, she was actually quite pleased with the interior of the house. In fact, quite frankly, it was in excellent condition. On the other hand, it was also quite apparent, the exterior of the house needed repairs. Actually, for what it's worth, Maude's first impression regarding that was nothing major had to be done to it, however due to the undeniable fact, the house was built back in the 1800's, there were a few things that had to be replaced. The most important thing of all was the house only needed a little tender loving care so it stands to reason, if she put a little extra time and money into it, all that should be taken care of. Anyway, as she walked around the property, she continued to put a lot of very serious thought into purchasing the house. At this point, Maude could honestly say, it was just a question of whether or not the property was worth what the current owner was asking for it, that's all. As for the overall character of the house, you might say, this one had a lot of old fashioned, country charm. Anyway, with that in mind, Maude continued to mull the whole thing over until she came to the conclusion, the house would do just fine. That meant she was going to take a chance on purchasing it, after all. Initially, she wasn't certain that was going to be the case however at this juncture, the pros outweighed the cons so she was inclined to believe, she would buy it. Actually, Maude was also very pleased with the way Mr. Brewster was handling the sale of the property so that was a positive point as well. In fact, not once did he try to pressure her in to buying it and you might say, that was greatly appreciated. As for what the previous owner of the property was asking for the house, that was actually quite reasonable so rather than giving it anymore thought, Maude made him an offer. Furthermore, since money wasn't an issue, it really wasn't all that imperative that she think about it anyway. It was just a question of whether or not, she liked the property, and it turns out, she liked it really well. Besides, if she were to wait much longer about making a decision on buying the property, in all probability, absolute, sheer anxiety would more than likely get the best of her. Not a very pleasant thought but that was the nature of her personality. For that reason, it would be a good idea to get this business matter taken care of as soon as possible. Needless to say, it was the only way, she was going to be able to start a new life for herself in the state of Oregon. Anyway, to make a long story short, the offer she made for buying the house, just happened to be in the ballpark of what the owner wanted for it, so it wasn't necessary to haggle out an agreed upon price. Furthermore, in this particular instance, due to the nature of a couple of things, there really wasn't any reason why the sale of the house wouldn't go through quickly, so Mr. Brewster pulled out a contract of sale from his briefcase. Actually, it was a mere formality that had to be taken care of before they could proceed with Maude's acquisition of the property. Needless to say, it is what had to be done to get things moving along in the right direction. Now, it would be just a matter of waiting out the process of transferring the ownership of the property to her. Mr. Brewster said, not only was it a formality, he had to follow but it was also a standard procedure that had to be adhered too in the due course of taking care of real estate business. Actually, that was something Maude hadn't paid any attention too for quite some time now. Anyway, regardless of what he had to do, he wanted her to know this so there wouldn't any room for disappointment somewhere down the road. Realistically speaking, it would take a little time to process all of the paperwork that went into the sale of the house anyway so based on that premise, she was going to have a little more time for him to get things in order before she would be able to move into her new home. Mr. Brewster did go onto say, he would start working on the sale of the property just as soon as he got back to the office. As for Maude, she was content with what he told so for the time being, she was satisfied with the way things were.

In the meantime, after having explained her situation to him, he advised Maude to go on vacation somewhere for a while or at the very least, find something to occupy her time until everything was taken care of. Actually, she had a feeling that is what the man from the real estate agency was going to tell her and as it turns out, she was right about that. Unfortunately, that's the way the ownership of a real estate property is transferred, so for the time being, she had a little extra spare time on her hands. In reality, that wasn't actually a bad thing however it definitely meant, it would be a while longer before she would be able to move into her new home. At this point, Mr. Brewster went onto say, there wasn't any way to know for certain how long the process would take however he promised to let her know the status of everything just as soon as the necessary paperwork that went into the sale of the property was taken care of. Anyway, while keeping this in perspective, before leaving that day, she made sure Mr. Brewster had her telephone number so he would be able to reach her when it was necessary to do so.

Now, as to what she was going to do with herself over the course of the next two or three weeks, she wasn't sure however for the time being, she would be in Tierra Del Mar. Whether or not everything remained that way, she wasn't certain. As a matter of fact, there was a very good chance that would change in the future. Realistically, most of what she wanted to do would have to wait a while anyway because it would entail fixing up her new home so for the time being, she would have to be patient. At this point, it should also be noted, with regards to how things would go over the course of the next month, right at the moment, everything was definitely up in the air. In the meantime, nothing was going to change until she moved into her new home. Perhaps, she was not aware of that because of the depth and complexity of her personality however regardless of that undeniable fact, she had already set things in motion for beginning a brand-new chapter in her life. In reality, there would be a lot of changes for her in the days ahead even though some of those changes would infringe upon her past way of life. Normally, that isn't a bad thing however in her case, it was bound to cause some problems for her in the days ahead. Of course, like most things in life, Maude wasn't aware of that however it would eventually become more apparent to her as time went by. In the meantime, she had decided to concentrate on some other things but at the time, had she known what was ahead of her, chances are Maude would have done things a lot differently. Needless to say, for whatever reason, shit happens sometimes and when it does, all a person can do is try to remedy the situation or they don't have a prayer's chance in hell of getting things headed in the right direction. The truth of the matter is, everyone makes mistakes at some point in their life and you wouldn't be human if that weren't the case however because she was a very headstrong person some of the things that happened to her in the days ahead was more than likely her own doing while some of what happened was undoubtedly the fault of another person.

Anyway, just as soon as her conversation with Mr. Brewster was finished, Maude headed off down the road to the Cozy Arms Motel in anticipation of a nice, warm shower and something good to eat. The fact of the matter is she wanted to relax for a while and like most things Maude contemplated doing, that is what she did. Actually, to be more precise, she had a lot on her mind and that had been the case for quite some time now, so she was slightly fatigued regardless of the fact, that was something she had become accustomed to in recent months. In truth, it didn't make any difference to her when the sale of the house went through. She just simply had a lot of stress to deal with, that's all. In this particular instance, after giving it some thought, Maude also came to the conclusion, she didn't want to just sit around and do nothing during her stay in Tierra Del Mar. If she did that there was a very good possibility, not only would she be bored to death with the way things were, but she would get restless as well, right to the point of literally climbing the walls of the Cozy arms Motel to maintain her sanity. As you know, she was accustomed to living life in the fast lane so if she were to do something as sedentary as just sitting around a hotel room and watching television for the better part of two or three weeks, it wouldn't be a very easy thing for her to do. Besides, just the thought of not having someone around these days was enough to make her feel lonely. Actually, the news media was responsible for causing a lot of her problems however not having someone around to do things with was also giving her reason to reassess her life in general. As far as her literary fans went, they usually meant well, however every now and then someone would do something that made things difficult for her, and when that happened, it was not unusual for her to get a little depressed or regret having gone into the profession she did. Needless to say, those were the days she would go onto ask herself if it was worth the occasional aggravation that came along with being a celebrity and like a true realist, Maude would shrug the whole thing off as being part of the job. Of course, there's a lot of pros and cons, that go hand in hand with being a very recognizable person in the entertainment industry and not unexpectedly, I believe that was something she had to deal with every day of her life now. The fact of the matter is, everyone reacts differently to celebrity stardom and the stress that goes along with it, although most people find a way to cope with that sort of thing somewhere along the way. For those of us that don't, it can be a hard road to walk down. In particularly, for those people that travel around the world to do music concerts. Needless to say, living your life inside a hotel room isn't my idea of paradise, and I'm sure had that been something Maude Derringer had to deal with she wouldn't have cared too much about doing that either. In fact, in my opinion, the life of someone working in the music industry isn't an easy job regardless of how easy they make it look. I would say, it's a tough way to make a living. Granted, there is a lot of money to be made in that profession, but that kind of lifestyle wouldn't be something I'd want to do. As for Maude, thankfully, she didn't have to deal with that way of life because had that been the case, she would've probably walked out the door of the nearest auditorium, stadium or arena and never went back. Anyway, so much for the professions some of us get into. Now, with regards to Maude, over the course of time she became more at ease with the celebrity stardom she had attained although that didn't necessarily mean she was fond of it. In truth, she didn't mind being acknowledged for her accomplishments. Needless to say, that was fine but all those cursed questions that pried into her personal life were not favorably looked upon. In fact, quite frankly, she very often found that irritating because on occasion someone from the news media wouldn't respect her privacy, however when something like that happened, they more than likely weren't fans of hers anyway. At any rate, under those circumstances, their behavior was very hard to tolerate, so she would inevitably try to refocus on something more pleasant and go from there. That's really all she could do, and it was something she came to realize shortly after she began her career in writing.

Anyway, putting all that aside, she was now giving a lot of additional thought to a couple of other things. For instance, what if she were to take the initiative and do something that was a little out of the ordinary for a change, like take a vacation. You know, the kind where you pack a suitcase with a few of those necessities you can't do without and then leave everything behind for a while. The idea certainly had a lot of merit. Not only would it solve the immediate problem of what she was going to do in her spare time over the course of the next two or three weeks but she would also get a badly needed vacation as well. Actually, an inner voice inside her head told her she would probably do herself a favor by doing so. What the hell, she mused to herself. In truth, she didn't really have anything to lose by doing so and probably everything to gain by taking the initiative to do something like that. Believe it or not, until now, the idea of taking a vacation had not occurred to her, however now that it had, she was convinced the best thing to do would be to go somewhere for a few days. That meant the next thing that had to be done was commit herself into making a decision on where to take a vacation. After that, it would be just a matter of taking the initiative to make reservations with a travel agency to wherever it was she wanted to go, then with any luck at all, she would be off on a new adventure. More importantly, Maude would have something to look forward too for a change. In recent days, most of her time had been spent on a past friendship that now fell into the category of a great, big mistake although Maude tried not to think about it anymore than she had too. In fact, as far as she was concerned, her overall thought process was headed in the right direction now. Not only would that help Maude get her life back in order but the odds of it pacifying her mind were in her favor as well. As for taking a vacation, somewhere, that was something she had wanted to do for a long time so it had all the makings of a win, win situation for her and you might say, if she followed through with her plan to do that, it stands to reason, she would be better off for having done so.

CHAPTER 4

Maude's decision to stay at the Cozy Arms Motel had more to do with the actual location of the facility than anything else. In addition to that, she was extremely pleased that a restaurant occupied the space directly across the street from where she was staying because Maude was the kind of person who liked having the convenience of a restaurant nearby. At any rate, since there wasn't anything else she could do until the paperwork for her new house was all taken care of, it came with the greatest of pleasure to be able to begin focusing on a few other things, which right at the moment just happened to be what she planned on doing over the course of the next month. In fact, quite frankly, the idea of taking a vacation somewhere kept sounding better and better all the time. Of course, if she really put her mind to it, there were probably a lot of other things she could do as well however the way everything was unfolding, the most likely thing to happen was a vacation. Actually, for most people being idle isn't necessarily a bad thing however she wasn't the kind of person to sit around and do nothing if she didn't have too. In the years ahead, Maude would eventually get over the "I've got to have something do syndrome" and she would take on new interests, however at this point in her life, she liked to keep busy. At any rate, it was for that reason, she wanted to find something to do for a few days and taking a vacation was at the top of her list. The truth of the matter was she didn't have any new and exciting plans on the horizon so that prompted her to do some more thinking. As stated before, Maude was tired of dwelling on a couple of things that were making an absolute total wreck out of her life, however the thought of finding a special person to share her life with kept her going. Granted, she wasn't really ready to do that, however as long as she were alive, there was always a possibility that might happen. At any rate, after having reached her breaking point, and without being able to take anymore shit of any kind, she was more determined than ever to make some changes in her life. In fact, that's the reason why she was moving to the state of Oregon. Needless to say, it more than likely wouldn't solve all of her problems, but it was definitely worth giving it a try. In fact, quite frankly, Maude didn't have anything to lose by doing so.

Anyway, with this and a hell of a lot more racing through her mind, she walked over to a small refrigerator located against the wall inside her motel room and got out a can of iced tea to drink. Fortunately for her, with a little foresight, she remembered to stop by a convenience store on the way back to the motel, so the refrigerator was filled with a few things to eat and drink. At this point, just as she was about to sit back and watch television for a while, the restaurant across the street caught her eye. In this particular case, that just happened to be the Frenchman's Friend. In fact, what better place could there be to get a good meal, she thought to herself. Obviously, it was a restaurant that served French cuisine and probably everything else under the sun and being hungry, that was the only logical thing to do. Anyway, with that ever so pleasant thought lodged inside her in head, she headed across the street to get something to eat. At any rate, one thing led to another and long before Maude realized it, she was walking through the door of the restaurant. Then, with nothing but hunger on her mind, upon entering the establishment, a young personable waitress escorted her to a table, took her order and promised to return with her meal shortly.

Anyway, not unexpectedly, she kept tossing the name of the restaurant around inside her head until it finally dawned on her. What better place could there be to take a vacation than to go to France. Not only would it give her something to do for a few days, but it would also be a very cultural experience for her as well. In fact, quite frankly, the more she thought about it, the more she was convinced, taking a vacation to France would be a good thing to do. At any rate, at this point, her mind very gradually began to wander off in other directions like it was so accustomed to doing however this time her train of thought was focused on what she would be able to do on a vacation to France. It was as simple as that. Then, with that ever so challenging thought planted firmly in the back of her mind, the complacency of the past few days literally went flying out the door, and it couldn't have come at a better time. She was ready to experience life again. First, it was with great desire that she see the city of Paris. Even as a young child growing up in the state of Arizona, that was something she had always wanted to do. So many times, Maude had dreamt about going there. Whether it was an opportunity to enjoy one of their fine art galleries or one of their gift shops or sampling some of their fine cuisine at one of their many restaurants, she was at a loss for words for describing how she felt about going there. In fact, she had every intention of taking in a theater show as well, and perhaps, she would even take a boat tour on the Seine River. Then, if everything went well, she planned on visiting all of their museums too. Needless to say, there were a lot of other things she could do as well, including a walk down the Champs-Elysée's and a stop at the historic Arc of Triumph. Last but not least, she wanted to take an awe-inspiring excursion up the Eiffel Tower, and that would conclude her visit to the city of Paris. From there, it was her intentions to travel to the west coast of France where one of the most important battles of World War II was fought. Of course, I'm referring to the beaches of Normandy, where the tide of the war took a favorable turn for the Allied Forces in their effort to defeat Germany. Needless to say, had it not been for their heroic efforts that day, hard telling how the war would have gone. Anyway, that area was not to be left out of her vacation itinerary and certainly a place never to be forgotten through the annals of world history. From there, if everything continued to go well, she would take a train down to the southern coast of France so she would be able to see the beauty of the French Riviera. Needless to say, she had heard many wonderful things said about it and with a little time on her hands, what better place would there be for a little rest and relation. In fact, it was of interest to Maude for one other reason and that was the possibility of living there at some point in her life. At any rate, with the better part of these thoughts ravishing her mind, she could hardly contain her excitement now as the thought of taking a vacation to France was beginning to overwhelm her. At this point, she glanced at her watch. It was around 4:30 in the afternoon and the better part of the day had already slipped by. She had been daydreaming again however that wasn't anything unusual. In fact, quite frankly, it was something she did fairly often even though she probably wouldn't have ever admitted that. Needless to say, it was a bad habit of hers and if push came to shove, that wasn't going to change anytime soon. As a matter of fact, probably not in her lifetime. It's just simply the kind of person she was. Anyway, just as Maude was about to head off to the lady's room to powder her nose, the waitress returned to the table with her dinner so instead of doing that she chose to eat first. Actually, Maude was hungry anyway and with the quality of the food being very good, the lady's room could wait a little longer. In the meantime, she took the initiative to order a daiquiri to go along with her meal. Normally, she didn't do that at this time of the day, however with circumstances as they were, she thought a drink might help her unwind a little and as anticipated, it did. Anyway, as you might think, she continued to savor the fine cuisine that was laid out on top of her table until it was gone. At this point, she realized, it was time to be on her way anyway so rather than ordering some type of dessert or perhaps, one more drink, she chose to go back to the Cozy Arms Motel. The fact of the matter is Maude spent the better part of an hour inside the restaurant getting her appetite satisfied so she had to be going or nothing was ever going to get done. In this case, it was a reference to making reservations for a vacation to France, however if she didn't get busy that more than likely wasn't going to happen that day. Of course, you could always make the argument, there's always tomorrow however due to the fact she wanted to go on vacation, the matter couldn't wait any longer. At any rate, it turns out, what began as a day of taking care of business was about to turn into a brand-new adventure for her and you might say, she was excited as a person could be about that.

Anyway, with her mind made up about what she wanted to do, Maude proceeded to pull her back behind her ears, slipped on her sunglasses, and headed out the door of the restaurant. It was time to do the inevitable. She was going to make reservations for a vacation to France. As a matter of fact, the moment she got back to her room at the Cozy Arms Motel, that's what she did, and a few minutes later everything was all taken care of. Granted, it was all done on a very short notice, however she was more than satisfied with the way she took care of things. As for the rest of the evening, not too much of anything was done. She watched television for a while and gave some more thought to the vacation she was going to take. Needless to say, if everything went the way she thought it would, she would be in the city of Paris sometime the following day and at no surprise to her, that was the last thing on her mind before she fell asleep that night.

CHAPTER 5

Every possible runway at the airport was alive with activity the day Maude was supposed to fly to Paris for a vacation to France however that was a fairly common occurrence there. As a matter of fact, in many instances, it was even a lot busier than that. Actually, many of the flights that originated there were international flights so it stands to reason, there would more than likely be a good amount of traffic on the runways. Anyway, now seemingly readier than ever for a trip to France, destiny found her waiting patiently inside the airport terminal for her plane to take off. In this case and also as anticipated, she had to be there a little earlier than usual, but that was due to the tighter airline security measures that were being implemented. In fact, it's the reason why she had a couple of hours to wait before her flight took off however that certainly didn't dampen her spirits any. Being the headstrong person she was, you know like, come hell or high water, or in this particular case, perhaps, better stated, come hell or high altitude, Maude intended to enjoy her flight to France. Chances are, everything would be fine and the overall prospect of having a good flight was actually in her favor. As for her plane's itinerary, the first leg of her journey was relatively simple. It was a direct flight to Boston. From there, she would have to change planes and then, it was onto the magnificent city of Paris.

Anyway, due to the amount of time Maude had to wait before her plane actually took off, she began getting a little restless however that wasn't really anything unusual. In fact, if the truth were made known, because she had a tendency to be a little hyperactive anyway, even if she had been accustomed to flying, her nerves would have probably gotten the best of her. Actually, that was something she had to deal with from time to time and chances are that wouldn't ever change. In this particular case, perhaps, the most important thing of all was in less than twenty-four hours she had secured a first-class seat on a 757-jet bound for Boston. Anyway, regardless of how she came about making reservations for a vacation to France on such a short notice, she would soon be on her way. In fact, if things continued to go well, after a change of planes in Boston, Maude would be in Paris a few hours later. At any rate, while she waited ever so patiently for her plane to depart that day, she began focusing on a few other things to try and take her mind off her fear of flying. Obviously, the combination of a passenger train and a cruise ship were an option, but had she done that, it would've taken forever to get there. For that reason, Maude chose to fly to France even if she was afraid of confined spaces and high altitudes.

Anyway, after a little while, she glanced over at the clock on the wall inside of the airport terminal and noticed it was nearly time for her plane to take off. Thank god for that, she thought to herself because the wait was making her more nervous than ever now. In fact, you might even say, she was as tense as a wild goose in heat. Well, if you can picture that, then you'll understand what happened next. Anyway, shortly before she was to board her plane, all of a sudden, without a warning of any kind, her heart began to race out of control. In a matter of seconds, Maude was literally out of breath. Then, panic and fear began to overwhelm her as she tried to get control of the situation. What could be wrong, she thought to herself? Her chest was a little tight and there was numbness in the lower part of her jaw. Obviously, something was wrong, but she had yet to figure out what was going on. Her first thought was she was having a heart attack however she was also an optimist so she quickly ruled that out in favor of taking a couple of aspirin and a few deep breaths to try and slow her heart rate down. Thankfully, it worked because if it hadn't, she could have dropped dead on the floor of the airport terminal and you might say that wasn't at all what she had in mind. Anyway, be so as it may, shortly thereafter, she was fine. Chances are her doctor would've said, "In all probability, it's just a little anxiety. It will pass. Give it a little time and you'll be all right." Of course, a statement like that would not change the seriousness of the situation because the symptoms were real, nevertheless, it was comforting to know she would be all right. Hopefully, it wouldn't happen again, Maude mused to herself because if it did, perhaps, she wouldn't be as lucky next time. Needless to say, shit can happen on a moment's notice, so it was probably a good idea not to dwell on it too much.

At any rate, a few minutes later, her plane was ready for boarding, so Maude grabbed her carry on and headed for the gate her plane was taking off from. In fact, in literally no time at all she was all buckled into her seat and ready to go. At this point, it was just a matter of waiting for the rest of the passengers to be seated and they would be on their way to France. Anyway, after a good deal of anticipation and a lot of very tedious waiting, around twenty minutes later, the plane she was on taxied down the runway and took off. Needless to say, it was a smooth transition into the air and the plane reached its flying altitude in literally no time at all, nevertheless, Maude still had a long ways to go before she landed in Paris. Of course, that prompted her to begin thinking about all the things that could go wrong on a flight so after Maude changed planes in Boston, she had a couple of drinks to calm her nerves into believing she was sitting at home in her easy chair. In the meantime, she was having second thoughts about flying. Between all the things that could go wrong and her uncontrollable fear of being in a confined space, you might say, she didn't feel comfortable flying. At any rate, while trying to keep all this perspective, her flight continued on its way and without any problems, I might add. In fact, quite frankly, thanks to the consumption of a little alcohol, she had a hard time remembering too much of anything after changing planes in Boston. Anyway, like everything else a person does in life at one time or another, time passed by very quickly and in the matter of a few hours, the flight she was on landed in the city of Paris. Needless to say, after being confined to the inside of a jet plane for a few hours, Maude was now more anxious than ever to see the country of France so she unfastened her seat belt, disembarked from the plane, and headed for baggage area of the airport terminal. There, Maude picked up her luggage, then, after a bit of indecision on her part with regards to where she would stay while she was in the city of Paris, she walked down the main corridor of the airport terminal and exited the building. At this point, feeling satisfied with how everything had gone since she left Oregon, she flagged down a taxi and went in search of a place to stay. It was time to do some sight-seeing in the country of France. Needless to say, it was a place she had always wanted to see and now that she was actually there, that was finally going to happen. Yes, excited as ever at the very thought of what she would be doing while she was on vacation in France, she quickly began formulating ideas inside her head on how to get the most out of her vacation.

CHAPTER 6

Well, it didn't take Maude very long to realize the country of France was everything she thought it would be and a whole lot more, however she did forget to take a couple of things into consideration. First of all, the French culture was a lot different from what she was accustomed to in the United States, and even though it fascinated her greatly, it posed some problems for her as well. Secondly, there was a language barrier she had to find a way around because she didn't know how to speak French however like so many other things in her life that she had to deal with from time to time, she would find a way to deal with that too. Not that there was anything wrong with the French language however other than a few words, she couldn't speak it. At any rate, she refused to let those things get her down. Come hell or high water, she was going to have a really great vacation. Anyway, it was now extremely apparent, she was going to have to make a couple of adjustments in the way she did things if she was going to get all she could out of her vacation in France so with that in mind she bought a small handbook that converted French to English. It obviously wasn't going to solve the language barrier between her and the French people however it would make things a lot easier for her. As for getting familiar with the French culture, that was something that wouldn't happen overnight however she would find a way to manage that as well.

At any rate, as stated before, after arriving in the magnificent city of Paris, Maude took a taxi from the airport and went in search of a place to stay. Well, as luck would have it, she found a nice room at the Piedmont Hotel and a short time later, she began the tedious task of unpacking her suitcase. Anyway, once that was taken care of she had a bite to eat at a nearby restaurant and then, after a long day of travel, she headed back to her room, where she proceeded to get herself settled in for the night. At this point, the beauty of the city of Paris was beginning to overwhelm her as she took a few minutes to gaze out upon the city from a balcony in her room. In fact, quite frankly, it was actually breath-taking to do so. Needless to say, she had been there for only a few hours and she was already beginning to fall in live with the city. Anyway, as lights of every kind, glowed ever so brightly throughout the night sky, typical of her personality, Maude found herself engaged in deep thought again. First, thoughts of an old boyfriend emerged, then, ever so slowly she began thinking about fond memories of her childhood and after ten to fifteen minutes of time had gone by, Maude was feeling melancholy. Not lonely or rejected but satisfied with herself for having taken the initiative to be where she was now. At any rate, after a few minutes of thinking about past and present matters, she went back into her room and began jotting down a few things a person might want to do and see while they were in France. That didn't take her very long. In fact, after making a couple of inquiry's and studying some tourism literature on France, she was able to do that in a fairly short period of time. Anyway, it was at this point she learned the city of Paris was renowned for preserving some of the greatest cultural exhibits in the world. Of course, that took in a lot of territory, however it was also proof positive that some very notable works of art, sculpture and literature had been left behind there. Perhaps, only rival to what the country of Italy has to offer a person. At any rate, regardless of which country had more museums, the city of Paris certainly had its share and they housed some of the finest cultural work ever created. As a matter of fact, all things considered, Paris would be right up there on top of the list of cities in Europe that went out of its way to preserve those cultural works. In addition to that, Paris is also known for creating a very relaxing atmosphere, where feelings of love and romance usually take hold in a very short period of time. I guess for that reason alone whenever Maude turned around or opened a door, she inevitably found a young couple in love. Yes, believe it or not, that is just the way the city of Paris is. If you have an open heart, and give it some time, chances are you'll feel the love that's in the air. Furthermore, a person wouldn't have to be in love with someone to enjoy this feeling either. It's just simply the wonderful feeling you get the moment you're in the city. Perhaps, not everyone would see it that way however she most certainly did. Anyway, after putting a lot of thought into planning out her time in Paris and the country of France that day, she headed off to bed. The truth of the matter was, after a long day of travel, Maude was ready to get some rest.

At any rate, the next day, she made her way around the city of Paris, taking in all the sites she wanted to see. Yes, this here and that there and god only knows what else kept her busy for a week or more. No stones were left unturned in that very short period of time however with other things to do and see, she was ready to move onto some other things. At this point, you might say, she also had a very strong desire to see the countryside of France so after taking a few minutes to secure a seat on one of those new modern passenger trains, she traveled around some of the rural areas of that country for a couple of days. Then, after her curiosity had been satisfied, she set out for the beaches of Normandy. In fact, a trip to France would not be complete without going there at some point along the way. Needless to say, that is where the Allied Forces made their invasion of Europe in June of 1944. Yes, D-Day. How could anyone forget a military operation like that? It was a terrible point in world history and someone had to rise to the occasion to bring an end to the Third

Reich or even more people were going to lose their lives to the mentally unstable man that was leading Germany down a road to death and destruction. At any rate, with patience and a lot of perseverance, the Allied Forces eventually succeeded in defeating Adolf Hitler and the rest of the world was much better off for their having done so. In hindsight, had that not happened, it would have been a Nazi driven, socialist world lead by a dictator who wasn't fit to hold power of any kind. Needless to say, that's a very sad thought but it would have been the reality of things if Hitler had been victorious in World War II.

Anyway, after she spent a little time walking upon the beaches of Normandy, she went to visit three museums that were in the area. The Overlord Museum, the Big Red One Museum and the Coleville Museum with her last stop being at the Normandy American Cemetery. In fact, the whole thing was an extremely heart-warming experience for Maude and when she left there, she was harboring a very grateful feeling inside, knowing darn well, she was free thanks to the heroic efforts of all the men who died in that war. Anyway, like it so often does, time passed by quickly and in not wanting to miss seeing a couple other things while on vacation, Maude chose to travel off in the country again, only this time, she took a train down to the French Riviera. Actually, the reason why she wanted to go there had to do with the fact, that part of the country was known for having a warm climate and number one, second to none, gracious hospitality.

In fact, the second she arrived at her destination, she could see why it was regarded by many people as a great place to live. Needless to say, between the palm trees, fine cuisine, panoramic views and a lot of very iconic architecture, the area certainly had a lot going for it. Admittedly, many people made their home there for those reasons, in addition to the warm climate that was favorable to the area. At any rate, she took an immediate liking to the French Riviera or perhaps, better said, she fell head over heels in love with the city of Nice. Whether it was the warm ocean breezes blowing in from the Mediterranean Sea or just simply the city life that encumbered the area, it didn't matter at all to her. She took an immediate liking to the French Riviera, in particularly, the city of Nice. As a matter of fact, after spending a few days there, Maude was certain she would be able to live there in the days ahead if the right opportunity came along. Needless to say, it was reassuring to know that and like anyone who knew what they wanted to get out of life, she made a note of that in the back of her mind for future reference. In the meantime, Maude immediately took to enjoying the final week of her vacation and with everything turning out really well, she was extremely pleased with the way things had gone since she arrived in France.

At any rate, like all good things in life, they don't last forever, and such was the case with Maude and the vacation she took to France as well. Anyway, with a bit of sadness in her heart, a short time later, she traveled back to the city of Paris, where she intended to fly back to the state of Oregon the following day. It had undoubtably been a great vacation however it was also time to go home so with that in mind, late one evening, shortly after returning to the city of Paris, she packed up her suitcase and got ready for a return flight to the United States. Needless to say, her time in France turned out to be as good of a vacation anyone could have ever wished for but now she had business to attend too in Tierra Del Mar so she booked a flight on the next plane headed to New York City, where a connecting flight would take her back to the city of Portland, Oregon. Granted, like before, it was all done on a very short notice but do to her fear of flying, perhaps, it was best she did it that way anyway. Actually, the most important thing of all was she had gotten some badly needed rest during her vacation and with the prospect of moving into her now home when she returned to the state of Oregon, she felt really good about things. In fact, quite frankly, it was the best Maude had felt in as long as she could remember. Now, if only things stayed that way, perhaps, she would be able to redirect her attention to some other things.

Anyway, later that evening, a couple hours before midnight, Maude turned out the lights inside her hotel room and called it a day. You might say, she was slightly exhausted from all the traveling she did over the course of the past three weeks but she was more than satisfied with her current state of affairs because it had turned out to be a very memorable vacation however it was time to give Mr. Brewster a call because she wanted to see how the acquisition of the property in Tierra Del Mar was coming along. At any rate, for varying reasons, she fell asleep rather quickly that evening. I guess between the thought of returning home and moving into her new house, she was able to get a good night's sleep and it was probably a good thing she did because Maude had a long flight ahead of her the following day.

Anyway, after a quick breakfast the next morning, she soon found herself redirecting her attention to some of the things she would have to do when she returned to the state of Oregon. It wasn't anything unusual for her to be in deep thought and once again, she took to thinking about what was ahead of her in the days ahead. Actually, in addition to wondering how the paperwork for the sale of her new home was coming along, she was extremely worried about her health and well-being, which in this particular case was something she was now taking very seriously. That meant no smoking tobacco and no alcohol of any kind, in addition to implementing exercise into her daily routine. Realistically, she was doing really well getting her physical and mental health back in order with the exception of one thing and that was the consumption of alcohol. Needless to say, in that area, she wasn't doing as well however once she got settled into her new home, she thought that problem would take care of itself. In the meantime, she was side-stepping that issue every chance she got in favor of imbibing a little more alcohol. Perhaps, part of the problem was her steadfast stubbornness to change something she got pleasure in doing. At any rate, such was her state of affairs as she continued to contemplate the situation and the flight that was ahead of her. Anyway, after a quick bite to eat, she got things in order, grabbed her suitcase, and called for a taxi. It was time to leave the magnificent city of Paris. Regrettably, after spending some of the most memorable days of her life in a country she had always wanted to see, she had the taxi take her to the airport, where upon arrival, she checked in at the airline reservations counter and about an hour later, she was on her way back to the United States. Anyway, since, everything was now headed in the right direction, she took a moment to get comfortable by slipping off her shoes and then, she closed her eyes and tried to sleep off as much of the flight as possible. Obviously, with circumstances as they were, it was undoubtably the best to do. In fact, if there had been a way to be more relaxed on her flight back to the United States, she would have pursued that route sooner but in this case, her only option was to have a couple drinks. At any rate, once that option was so necessarily achieved, she slept through the better part of her flight home, and after one brief stop in New York City, her plane continued on its way until it landed in Portland, Oregon. Now, there was business to attend too. Mr. Brewster, you're next, she mused to herself. At this point, it was just a question of how many times she had to sign on the dotted line, that's all. Anyway, by now, she was more anxious than ever to begin a brand-new chapter in her life, so Maude pushed all of those thoughts out of her mind and began thinking about what was ahead of her. Yes, everything will all be taken care of shortly, she mused to herself. Perhaps, a day or two, she wasn't sure. In the meantime, without having any qualms about having taken a vacation to the country of France even though it was on the spare of the moment, Maude returned to the place she was staying at in Tierra Del Mar, and before the evening was through, destiny found her savoring the memory of a really great vacation.

Part II

CHAPTER 7

A couple of days later, Maude was sitting patiently in the waiting room of Mr. Brewster's office listening to the sound of thunder echoing off in the distance. Needless to say, the town of Tierra Del Mar was experiencing a severe electrical storm however that wasn't anything unusual. In fact, she found out that was a fairly common occurrence in that part of the state, but that didn't dampen her spirits any. The truth of the matter is, she had become used to a lot of sunshine over the past few years so if it rained all of the time in Tierra Del Mar that might turn out to be a little disappointing for her. At any rate, from what she heard, that really wasn't the case at all, but if it did rain often, it was going to be a problem. Actually, in all due fairness, without having lived in the state of Oregon before, she couldn't in good faith make a statement on the matter but the door was open to that possibility in the days ahead. Right at the moment though it didn't really matter because she was safely inside Mr. Brewster's office so the wind and rain that was pelting the hell out of the area wasn't of any concern to her. She would deal with the seemingly persistent rain if it became necessary to do so. Hopefully, that wouldn't be the case because she liked sunny days and warm weather, so an abundance of sunshine would be seen as a blessing to her.

Anyway, as you might think, her entire train of thought had been thrown off course by the sound of the pouring rain beating down upon the windows inside Mr. Brewster's office and being a little on the nervous side, you might say, she was anxious to get her business with Mr. Brewster over with. Actually, her doctor called it anxiety, compounded by fear of the unknown but Maude preferred to think of it as nothing more than having a few butterflies in the stomach. At any rate, regardless of what you want to call it or how you actually look at it, it was a health problem she had to deal with from time to time. Usually, it wasn't anything to get all worked up about and in this case, that was true as well. The truth of the matter is, there's a very fine line between stress and anxiety and what most doctors would probably say is, the stress that a person is dealing with is more than likely what's causing the anxiety. In fact, it goes without saying, some people are a lot better at handling stress than other individuals however she preferred to think she did all right with that particular health problem and perhaps, she was right about that. One way or another, it is just an aspect of being human. Obviously, if everyone had an identical personality, it would be a very boring world however the bottom line of it all is, everyone does what they can to survive.

Anyway, putting all that aside, Maude continued to wait for Mr. Brewster to finish up his business with a client that was already in his office. The fact of the matter is, he was a very busy man and she understood that however like you might think, she was also very anxious to put this business matter behind her. Anyway, for that reason, regardless of the amount of paperwork that went into the overall transfer of the property that conveyed the deed over to her, she was anxious to move into her new home, so she continued to wait ever so patiently inside his office. Finally, after a few more tedious minutes went by, Mr. Brewster came out of his office and offered her a cup of coffee, saying he would be with her shortly. At that point, Maude knew it would be only a matter of time now before they sat down and went over the paperwork that would officially sign the Kimball mansion over to her. Anyway, as it turns out, about five minutes later, Mr. Brewster emerged from his office with the client he had been conversing with and showed him to the door. That meant she was next. Thank God, she thought to herself. Obviously, there are times when a lot of patience is in order however with regards to this business matter, she had definitely waited long enough. At any rate, after a couple more minutes went by, Mr. Brewster finally got around to beckoning her into his office. Needless to say, it was time to get down to business and with all the paperwork already having been done ahead of time, that simplified things enormously. Now, in all probability, it would be just a matter of tying up a few loose ends and the Kimball mansion would be hers to do whatever she wanted with it.

At this point, the depth of Maude's personality began to surface again as her mind began to wander off onto some other things. Like I've more than likely said before, she had a tendency to reflect on things and that isn't necessarily a bad thing but to someone who didn't know her, it probably looked like she had her head stuck up her ass. Of course, there was no truth whatsoever to that assumption, nevertheless, it was a perception that many people may have had of her over the years. Anyway, right at the moment, Maude was engaged in more depth thought. Actually, it was a very short relapse of mind however in a matter of a few seconds, she managed to run a lot of things through her head. Perhaps, the most troublesome issue that continued to badger Maude was the bad relationship she had with her previous boyfriend. Needless to say, she thought a lot of him however Ken Stackford was definitely using her so she called an end to their relationship. Anyway, to make matters worse, because of that incident, she didn't want any men in her life for a while. In fact, quite frankly, at this point in her life, she was scared to death to get involved in another relationship. Obviously, the fear of being hurt again was still present. Actually, it wasn't until she left the Los Angeles area behind before things began to go in the right direction for her. Anyway, she was about to make her residence in the state of Oregon. Furthermore, Maude was hoping in the best possible way it turned out to be a good move on her part, but time would tell whether or not that was the case. Needless to say, she thought the move would allow her to get her life back in order, and if everything went as planned, perhaps it would, however, if the right opportunity came along to go back to her home in Beverly Hills, Maude would more than likely do so. Unfortunately, right at the moment, due to extenuating circumstances, she didn't see that happening, but as long as she was alive, there was always the possibility that might happen. For the time being, she wanted to live elsewhere and that was going to be in the state of Oregon.

As for the business at hand, that had to be taken care of next. In fact, quite frankly, from what she could see, every indication seemed to indicate everything was progressing along rather well. Mr. Brewster appeared to be content with the way things were and was now in the process of making sure everything was in order. Actually, he was going through a pile of paperwork one last time to ensure he hadn't overlooked anything. Then, if she didn't miss her guess, she would be able to sign her name a few times and another prospective sale of property would be finished. Needless to say, Maude was fine with that although as more time passed by, it also became quite apparent, the electrical storm that was dumping a large amount of rain on the community had yet to move out of the area.

In fact, much to her disappointment, it was actually still raging away in the early morning sky over of Tierra Del Mar. At this point, Maude was convinced the storm was directly overhead because the sound of thunder was so loud it was deafening to her ears. At any rate, not unexpectedly by any means, in the short attention span of another moment, like so many times in the past, Maude's highly sophisticated mind began to wander off on some other matters of importance. Philosophically speaking, she was a very deep person, and it goes without saying that probably wouldn't ever change. For that reason, her attention span tended to be on the short side at times and when it wasn't, she was usually busy doing something. Anyway, as it turns out, at first, she began thinking about her home in California. Then, her train of thought centered on her old boyfriend for a few minutes and eventually on her days of youth in Arizona. Needless to say, many memorable days were spent in both Arizona and California so it didn't come as any big surprise that's what she was thinking about. Anyway, soon, her mind wandered off even further as the innermost caverns of her mind got philosophical for a moment. Actually, Maude was just trying to stay focused on why she was sitting in Mr. Brewster's office however in her down time, between answering questions and signing her name a few times, she couldn't help thinking about some of the things most people never think of. Anyway, like usual, Maude was in the process of running all of these thoughts through her head at the most inopportune time. It's just the kind of person she was. Maude's character was deep, complex, and she was always trying to understand things in the best possible light. Needless to say, that took in a lot of territory but that is how she looked at everything in life. In fact, quite frankly, it was her natural instinct to do that. She was a seeker of knowledge, in particularly, anything and everything that had to do with the nature of things, both spiritual and physical. Perhaps, Maude missed her calling in life by not becoming a scientist or a minister of theology but as you can readily see, that's not the path she chose in life. Anyway, at this point, a loud clash of thunder could be heard echoing throughout Mr. Brewster's office again as more strikes of lightning could be seen through the window Maude was sitting at. Needless to say, that's what broke her concentration, however in this particular instance that was probably the best possible thing that could've happened because there was business to attend too. Actually, without being too rude and obviously unintentionally meant, she was hoping in the best possible way, Mr. Brewster hadn't noticed her inattentiveness, so she very quickly glanced across his desk to see how he was coming along with the paperwork. Needless to say, she could see, he was still working on it, so no harm had been done by the absent-minded thoughts that were going through her mind. In reality, it would be a little while longer before she would be able to sign all the proper documents that transferred ownership of the property over to her. In fact, a good deal of those so-called required signatures had already been signed however there was a little more to go. Unfortunately, there are laws governing the sale of a house and there wasn't anything Maude could do to change that, regardless of how really frustrating it was sitting around his office doing absolutely nothing. Obviously, there are procedures to follow, and she did not want to be the one to screw up that process. Generally speaking, she wasn't the kind of person to make waves about something anyway and a situation like this certainly wasn't going to change anything. She would have to wait until Mr. Brewster got everything in order. In the meantime, the gentleman from the real estate agency continued to work on getting all the paperwork organized so everything would be easier for her to understand. All most there, Maude thought to herself. Perhaps, another five or ten minutes might do it. At this point, bored to death with the way things were going, Maude began to daydream a little more. Actually, she had already covered a lot of ground in the way of in depth thinking that morning however Maude's heart was also centered on her days of living in Beverly Hills. Needless to say, she spent a considerable amount of time there and she was going to miss the area a lot however like I said before, she was also a very determined woman and with that in mind, she had every intention of getting her life back in order, regardless of what she had to do to accomplish that even if it meant staying away from the Beverly Hills area forever. As a matter of fact, it was the best possible thing she could've done. Anyway, as much as she hated to admit it, she found herself dwelling on that matter again however because it was her nature to do that, it was just a natural reaction for her. Besides, right at the moment, there wasn't really much she could do anyway other than wait around for Mr. Brewster to convey the warranty deed of the property over to her. At any rate, time continued to go by quickly and even though it seemed like she had waited in his office forever, in reality, it was only for a short period of time. Perhaps, not more than an hour or so. The truth of the matter is, Maude hadn't been watching the time closely so she wasn't sure. At the very least, she was expecting a thirty-minute wait, perhaps, longer but that would inevitably all boil down to the specifics of what she had to sign. Anyway, the ever so persistent sound of hard pouring rain continued to beat down upon the real estate office's roof as she pondered things a little more. Hopefully, it wasn't a sign of things to come, Maude mused to herself because if it was, she was going to be greatly disappointed with her decision to make her residence in Tierra Del Mar. It was more than likely just coincidence. In fact, according to what she was told, the weather was usually quite nice along the immediate coast of Oregon, so Maude wasn't overly concerned about that particular matter at this time. At this point, she took notice of what Mr. Brewster was doing, and it appeared he was in the process of finishing up what he was doing. Well, thank god for that she mused to herself because her patience was beginning to wear thin. Anyway, as it turns out, after a couple more signatures and perhaps, a yawn or two, the flat, outright ownership of the old Kimball mansion was finally hers. Now, it would be just simply a matter of getting a few renovations done on it and everything should be alright. Actually, as you might think, she was fairly certain that could be taken care of rather easily, even if it meant hiring someone who was an expert in the field of home improvements. Obviously, the little things she would be able to do herself. The fact of the matter is, Maude liked keeping busy anyway so that wasn't going to be a problem. Perhaps, at some point, even a new love interest will make its way into her heart. Who knows what was in store for her because life's so darn unpredictable? In the meantime, she was giving some very serious thought to starting a new hobby, like oil painting on canvas and maybe even becoming an established artist. Actually, on second thought, perhaps she could find something that was a little easier to do and a little less conspicuous than being an artist however at this point, that was only speculation on her part. The truth of the matter was, she was beginning to get a desire to find an interest that would give her something to do in her spare time. Obviously, to some degree, the property Maude was in the process of purchasing would keep her busy anyway. In fact, the more she thought about it, the more she concluded, perhaps, she would take up a hobby like stamp or coin collecting. Not only would that give her an opportunity to do something constructive, but it would also give her an investment over time. On the other hand, if she were to pursue the idea of becoming an artist, she had a great place to do that, right in Tierra Del Mar. Needless to say, it was a very picturesque area, so it would make the perfect back drop for oil and watercolor paintings, not only of the ocean, but for anything else as well. At any rate, by the time she had finished running all these thoughts through her head, Mr. Brewster was ready to give her the keys to her new home. At this point, she shook hands with him and that's all there was to it. She was now the owner of the old Kimball mansion. Furthermore, since, there weren't any additional snags or other problems associated with the transfer of the deed to the property, it was a finished business matter, and she was as happy as a person could about that. Anyway, with the thought of moving into her new home bouncing around inside her head, she quickly gathered up her copies of the paperwork concerning the sale of the house and left Mr. Brewster's office in good spirits that afternoon, knowing darn well, she had more than likely taken another step in the right direction for getting her personal life back in order. At any rate, with that in mind, she was soon on her way out to the parking lot, where she got into her car, put the key in the ignition and sped off down the road in the direction of the Kimball mansion. Because it was still raining, she had to make two stops along the way. The first one was at the Cozy Arms Motel. There, she got a fresh change of clothes and then, she headed off to a convenience store to pick up something to eat.

Anyway, once those matters were taken care of, Maude continued on her way. Needless to say, it was time to look the Kimball mansion over really well in order to determine what needed to be fixed and what could be left the way it was. After that, it would more than likely be just a matter of determining what should be done first and what could be left for another time however regardless of how that went, she was going to be busy for a while. It was just a question of how long it took her to get the Kimball mansion fixed up, that's all. In the meantime, patience was in order however with her never say die attitude and a strong desire to succeed, the odds were in her favor for accomplishing everything she wanted to do.

CHAPTER 8

As anticipated, Maude immediately began the long slow process of inspecting the house from every possible angle to make sure nothing that was in need of repair got overlooked, and it was probably a good thing she did because after taking a closer look at the property, she realized the mansion needed a new heating system, a new roof, some new windows, a couple pairs of new steps, up to date wiring and a fresh coat of paint. Needless to say, that didn't surprise her any but she did learn the house was in need of a few repairs she didn't know needed fixing. Anyway, her goal and objective, if you want to call it that, was to try and restore the Kimball mansion back to its original condition. Granted, that would take some time, but she would see the project through until it was finished. Between the age of the house and the fact, no one had been living there for a while, it was going to require some extensive renovations after all. Perhaps, on the bright side of it all, she was fairly certain everything could be fixed however it was going to take some time to do that. In the meantime, Maude definitely had a project to work on, which in this case meant she had a lot of cleaning to do. Actually, most of the renovations on the house would have to be done by someone who was in the business to do home improvements however some of the things that didn't require any skill or dexterity, she would do herself.

At any rate, with that in mind, Maude didn't waste any time taking the initiative to begin working on things around the house or nothing was ever going to get done. As you know, there's only so many hours in a day a person can utilize to get things done so she had to get busy. First, she thought it would be a good idea to go into town and buy some furniture because there wasn't any way she would be able to live there until she did. Then, if everything went well, Maude had every intention of going in search of some new curtains, after which she planned on shopping for some new appliances. Finally, last but not least, she would purchase a few gallons of paint from a local hardware store and then, she would be able to spruce the house up a little. Anyway, once those things were all taken care of, Maude headed off to the grocery store to purchase some food. Actually, as silly as it may sound, she wanted to stock up on as much food as possible. Needless to say, by doing so, she wouldn't have to run to the store every time she wanted something good to eat. At any rate, in a matter of forty minutes to an hour, she managed to amass enough food in her shopping cart to last for several days. Then, after getting her affairs in order, she dropped the better part of what she purchased off at the Kimball mansion and headed back to the Cozy Arms Motel. Needless to say, by this time, Maude realized she would be all moved into her new home in about twenty-four hours. In the meantime, she planned on spending another night at the Cozy Arms Motel. The truth of the matter is, waiting one more day to move into her new home wasn't going to make any difference. Needless to say, she had waited this long to get things moving in the right direction so what the hell was another day. Besides, it would give her a little more time to think things out as well. At this point, she began to reflect on what she had accomplished over the past few months. Actually, having lived in California and traveled to France, you might say, that took in a lot of territory. In fact, she could honestly say, been there, done that. Not only did it leave her with a good feeling inside but what she had seen were definitely places worth seeing as well. Anyway, the end result of it all left her with memories that would last a lifetime and she didn't have any regrets about having done so either. Obviously, most people wouldn't have been able to afford to do what she did, however putting that aspect of her life aside, her time in France did her a world of good. In fact, in hindsight, Maude wished she had done that sooner however it unquestionably opened the door to a lot of new possibilities for her and if she were to think about it, that was the most important thing of all.

Anyway, with regards to this particular day, Maude had already decided to try and get as much rest as possible, which by the way was something she hadn't gotten a lot of in recent days. As for the circumstances that led to the problem of her sleep deprivation, well, that was another matter entirely and Maude didn't want to think about it anymore than she had too. In fact, quite frankly, it was one of the things that led to Maude to her drug addiction some time ago. Anyway, regardless of the adjusts she had made in her personal life, her immediate remedy to the situation was to watch a little television. Actually, between finding a way to relax and by making a really good commitment to stay away from the things that were ruining her life, Maude was confident she was on the road to recovery. As I said before, she thought the first step in the right direction was moving to the state of Oregon. The second step was obviously a vacation to France. Since Maude had already done both, she felt good about her attempt to get her life back in order. Now, with any kind of luck at all, the healing process would begin. In the meantime, it was in her own best interest to not only take care of herself but to also get an ample amount of sleep. Anyway, at no surprise to her, the moment she went to bed, like so many times in the past, her mind began to think about Ken Stackford again. Needless to say, once upon a time, they were good friends and had he not been trying to lay everyone woman in Beverly Hills and the surrounding area, they'd more than likely still be together. In fact, she still missed him from time to time, but for obvious reasons, it was best she brought an end to their relationship. At any rate, as she began to run this troublesome thought through her head, she also began giving a lot of serious thought to finding a special person to share her life with again even though that probably wasn't a very wise thing for her to do at this point in her life. In fact, quite frankly, she had everything to lose and nothing to gain by doing so, however no one could tell her otherwise. Unfortunately, once she set her mind to doing something, woe unto anyone who tried to tell her otherwise. Needless to say, that's just the kind of person she was. Anyway, as for how she would proceed with finding another person to share her life with, for more than one reason, that was not going to be an easy thing for her to do. Admittedly, there was always the possibility someone might use her for her money much the same way Ken Stackford did. Of course, the other way to look at that is, perhaps, something like that may never happen again. Obviously, that was the optimistic way of looking at it. Perhaps, it was still possible to find someone to raise a family with after all however the next person she let into her life would have to be a little more considerate to her wants and needs than Ken was. He seemingly had only one thing on his mind, and that was where he could stick his dick. Actually, she could sympathize with him to some degree because in being human, there would always be a desire to put it somewhere however he could've asked her first but instead he went elsewhere for his piece of ass. In fact, quite frankly, he was the most irresponsible, ungrateful person she ever met in her life however there was a physical attraction between them that kept her wanting to see him. He had a very nice personality, it's just Ken seemed to have an uncontrollable desire to get a piece of ass anywhere and everywhere he could, regardless of the consequences of what he did. Yes, in common sense terms, a person could easily make the argument Mr. Ken Stackford was a playboy first and then, perhaps, in the broadest of terms, a really nice guy. Of course, depending on how you want to look at it, most women probably wouldn't want to deal with a man like that, and neither did she for that matter. Actually, in Maude's case, there was a lot more to it than that because a lot of money was involved. She was a very wealthy person, not necessarily filthy rich, however she had more monetary assets than most people do. At any rate, for that reason, Maude was very cautious when it came to dealing with men. In fact, as stated before, that was probably the reason why Ken Stackford pursued her because he didn't seem to be too interested in sticking his dick into her. The truth of the matter is, at the time they met, he was working as a lifeguard at a beach on the outskirts of Los Angeles so if she were to give it some thought, a job like that sure wouldn't pay much money so it gave credence to the idea, he was after her money. Actually, that wasn't determined for certain however she still firmly believed that was the case. Additionally, it can also be noted, she wasn't an easy lay anyway and that may have been a factor in Ken's desire to look around for someone to have intercourse with. At any rate, whatever the reason was, Ken was usually in another woman's bed and that didn't go over well with Maude. In fact, she found it extremely frustrating to be in love with someone who was inevitably interested in nothing but sex. Granted, that's a wonderfully pleasurable thing to do, however there's a lot of things in life beside that. Actually, the straw that broke the camel's back was the night she caught him in bed with Monica Jean _ _ _ _ something or other! In truth, she could never remember her last name. All she knew was Ken Stackford had broken the bond of trust they had between them and at that point, their relationship was officially over. No, as much as she hated to say it, Ken had a lot of growing up to do, and in the end, that's what motivated her into making the decision to move on with her life. At any rate, that's the reason why she dumped Ken and you might say that came as no surprise to anyone who knew her. Perhaps, the saddest part to the whole thing, she was fairly certain he didn't know Monica's last name either and that gave great credibility to the fact, in all probability, Ken had numerous one-night stands during the time they were going together.

Anyway, putting all that aside, in realizing her mind had wandered off far enough for one day, she concluded, it was time to get a little rest because the next day would more than likely be another busy day for her. At this point, it wasn't clear what Maude would do next but it was safe to say, she intended to start working on some of the things around the house that were in need of tending too. After that, she would hire a contractor or at the very least someone who was skilled at putting on a new roof and installing new windows. In truth, there were a few other things that needed repair as well and that would inevitably require an expertly licensed plumber, in addition to a skilled carpenter, however she would deal with those things when it became necessary to do so. For the time being, she was content with the way things were, so she took a moment to push those thoughts out of her mind, and went to bed, where she drifted off to sleep a little while later.

CHAPTER 9

The next day everything started out pretty much the way she wanted it too. Shortly after getting out of bed, Maude had breakfast, took a shower, and headed back over to the old Kimball mansion to begin the long, tedious job of cleaning it up. Anyway, with that in mind, the moment she arrived at her new home, she proceeded to put up new curtains in every room of the house so it would be adorned in the finest drapery anyone could have wished for. Next, she washed down all of the walls inside the house and then, for good measures, she washed and waxed the floors as well. Once all those things were taken care of, she moved onto stocking the kitchen shelves with the food she purchased the day before. From there, Maude unpacked a few of the necessities she would using from one day to the next so no unpleasantness would be experienced. Then, later in the morning, her appliances arrived so things were shaping up rather quickly. In fact, at this rate, she would be all settled into her new home in literally no time at all. As for the furniture that was to be delivered to the house, thanks to a little monetary persuasion on her part, that showed up at 1:00 o'clock that afternoon so everything was going as planned. At this point, it's also not unfair to say, she was working harder than ever to make living in her new home a better experience. In fact, not only did Maude have a tendency to be somewhat of a perfectionist at times, but she also took a lot of pride in doing things right as well. At any rate, by now, Maude concluded, she was going to give everything inside the house a new fresh coat of paint, in addition to having given it a thorough cleaning. Needless to say, not only would that make the house look more presentable in the event she had company, or the news media showed up but she would also be satisfied with the way everything looked as well. Anyway, with that thought in mind she proceeded to work on this particular aspect of her new home for the better part of the afternoon. Finally, at the hour of four o'clock, she took a break. In this case, all that really amounted to was going into the kitchen and having a cup of coffee. Normally, Maude didn't do that at this time of the day however with circumstances as they were, she had decided to do things a little differently for a change. At the very least, she would've managed to gain a little extra energy by doing so and she didn't see that as a bad thing.

Anyway, after a refreshing cup of coffee, a few minutes later, she went back to work with a scrub brush in one hand and a bucket of water in the other. First, she began cleaning the living-room, in particularly in and around the fireplace because it looked like the previous owner hadn't cleaned it in years. Needless to say, the inside of the firebox was full of soot, in addition to being in a state of disrepair so if she had any intention of using it in the days ahead, it obviously had to be cleaned. In fact, after giving it a little more thought, she wisely concluded, it would be a good idea to have someone inspect the chimney as well. In this case, it was undoubtedly the only way she would be able to make sure it was in good working order. In the meantime, Maude had a lot more cleaning to do. At this point, she went to retrieve a vacuum cleaner from one of the closets and then, she proceeded to vacuum out the fireplace. Actually, what's really interesting to note is the house was built with two identical fireplaces. There was one in the living-room and the other one was upstairs in the master bedroom. Whoever built the house, added some very nice features to it and this was obviously one of them. At any rate, she continued to clean around the fireplace in the living-room until she came across a small knob located to the right of it. Obviously, it was very perplexing to her because there wasn't any logical reason for it being there so Maude gave it a turn. All of a sudden, the built-in bookcase adjacent to the fireplace gave way and moved off to one side leaving a great big gaping hole in the wall directly in front of her. At this point, she was speechless! Anyway, astonished beyond disbelief, she thought about it for a minute and then, she made the decision to investigate things further. The truth of the matter is there was some type of passageway located directly behind the fireplace and it was up to her to find out where it led. In fact, quite frankly, it was mind boggling to say the least. By now, Maude had also concluded, the passageway led somewhere down beneath the house but as to where it went, was anyone's guess. Then, Maude paused for a moment to assess the situation. What if the passageway wasn't safe to walk through or worse yet, what if it was infested with rats? Since the old Kimball mansion was built back in the late 1800's, it undoubtedly left a lot of uncertainty running through her head. At any rate, by now, she had regained her composure enough to peer down the flight of stairs to see what, if anything could be seen. Unfortunately, it was too dark for Maude to see down the stairs, so she went into the kitchen to get a flashlight and some matches. Needless to say, the flashlight would give her the light she needed to make her way down the passageway and the matches may come in handy at some point along the way as well. At this point, Maude thought she was ready to investigate where the passageway behind the bookcase led so she headed back into the living-room to check things out. Anyway, with that in mind, she turned the flashlight on and gradually began to inch her way down the flight of stairs into the darkness below. Then, carefully, ever so carefully, Maude proceeded down the stairway to see if she could find out where the passageway led. Needless to say, she had always been a little nervous about exploring the unknown however in this case, it was also the only way she was going to unravel the mystery of what may be lying down beneath the house. At any rate, she continued her descent down into the unknown until the stairway gave way to a dirt floor. By now, Maude had come to the bottom of the stairs and it was extremely apparent she had entered some type of room. Of course, at this point, that didn't really explain much so she quickly pointed the flashlight to the interior of the room and began the long, slow methodical process of looking around the perimeter of the chamber. At first, the only thing she could discern in the dimly lit room was black empty space but after taking a closer look, she became aware of something sitting on the floor on the far side of the room. Needless to say, that immediately piqued her curiosity, so she took a deep breath and slowly made her way over to the object she spied sitting on the floor. When she reached her directive, her jaw must have dropped at least ten feet because sitting directly in front of where she stood were hundreds of old coins in a seaman's chest. Her initial guess was the coins must have been someone's life savings because there were so many of them it would have taken someone years to amass. Anyway, as you might expect, she was totally dumbfounded! In fact, right at the moment, there really wasn't a word in the English language that could accurately describe her feelings. At this point, Maude shook her head in absolute total disbelief. Of all the possibilities of what she could have found, and it turns out, she discovered someone's life saving beneath her house. Needless to say, in real life, things like this just don't happen, Maude mused to herself, yet at the same time what she saw sitting on the floor in front of her was very real. It wasn't a dream, mirage, or anything else for that matter. She was alive, awake and totally aware of her surroundings, yet, at the same time, she was taken aback by what she saw. Maude even took a moment to try and humor herself into believing she had been watching too much television as a way of explaining what she saw however that didn't appease her mind either so she immediately began to hypothesize, she might be suffering from a delusion of the mind. Needless to say, that wasn't a very pleasant thought, but if it explained the situation before her, she would be satisfied. At this point, she dismissed the thought after having reached out and touched some of the coins that were sitting in the trunk. Not only were they real but she could also see, the coins were worth a lot of money as well. Anyway, as you might think, seconds later, she looked around the room to see if there was anything else sitting in the room but nothing immediately materialized. Then, she saw a wick lantern mounted on the side of the wall. At this point, Maude took the matchbox she brought with her out of her pocket and withdrew one of the matches in inside the box and used it to light the lantern so she could see around the room. It was then determined, there were three more wick lanterns inside the room, one on each wall so she lit all of them as well. Then, after having regained her composure, she began to look around the room. That's when she discovered the room had two exits. One appeared to go up a flight of stairs, most likely to the master bedroom on the top floor of the house, and the other one went in opposite direction, perhaps, towards the shore of the ocean. Actually, with regards to the one that more than likely led up to the bedroom upstairs, that made all the sense in the world to her, since there was an identical fireplace upstairs. Needless to say, a bookcase was attached to that one as well however she quickly made the decision to look into that at a later time. Right now, she was more intent on seeing where the other passageway led so with that thought tucked firmly away in the back of her mind, Maude turned her flashlight back on and headed down the narrow corridor that led to another point beneath the house. She was inclined to believe, it led down to the ocean somewhere because the passageway appeared to be headed in that direction. Whether or not she was right about that remained to be seen however she would have an answer shortly. At any rate, regardless of where the corridor actually went, she wanted to find out what it led too so with that in mind, Maude proceeded forward very slowly, not knowing what to expect. After two or three minutes went by, she had her answer. The narrow passageway she had been following opened up to another room. Anyway, upon seeing this, she took the flashlight she had with her and shined it about the room to see if this one had more of those wick lanterns attached to the walls and it did. Obviously, that was to her advantage, so she lit the lanterns so she would be able to see the inside this room as well. At this point, it was becoming extremely obvious, someone went through a lot of trouble to construct these rooms and corridors beneath the house. At any rate, the moment she looked about the room, she saw six more seaman's chests. Actually, four of them were precisely identical to the one in the other room however two of them were a bit different. Surely, there had to be a reason for that and of course, that made her more curious than ever why those chests were set apart from the one in the other room. Needless to say, it was very perplexing to say the least however without knowing what took place on this property years ago, Maude assumed whoever built this place knew what they were doing because everything appeared to be well planned out. Anyway, at this point, she walked over to where the chests were and after seeing four of the six chests were filled with more silver and gold coins, she headed over to the far side of the room to take a closer look at the other two trunks. In fact, after taking a closer look at them, she thought the other two chests looked more like a coffin. Holy horrors, she mused to herself. If that were the case, it would mean there were bones of a dead body inside and she immediately shuddered at the very thought. At any rate, these chests were not displaying any coins in them, and both of their lids were shut tight. That wasn't a good sign, she thought to herself. Obviously, it was for a reason and like most people in a situation like this, Maude was scared shitless at the thought of what she may find in them if she were to open up those two chests. Needless to say, by now, her curiosity had gotten the best of her and a moment later, she flipped open the lid of the chest. At this point, if there had been anyone around, you would have heard a loud blood curdling scream coming from one very terrified Maude Derringer because like she suspected, the bones of a body were inside that chest. At any rate, she quickly tried to regain her composure by taking a couple of long, slow breaths, all the while she kept telling herself, this can't be happening to me. Of all the possible things, she could've discovered inside the chest, and it had to be the skeletal remains of a person. Admittedly, she was quite shaken by the series of events but there wasn't any sense of dwelling on it because whoever the person inside of the trunk was, that person was obviously deceased. In fact, there was a very good chance, the person who was laid to rest there had been dead for many long years ago. What an awful thing to find down beneath the house, she thought to herself. In fact, as much as she hated to say it, something in the back of her mind told her this might happen, and it did. Not only was it a very disturbing thing to see but it was also one of the most repulsive things she ever had to deal with. At this point, she took another deep breath to try and regain her composure a little however it was extremely questionable as to how well she was actually doing. Anyway, as you can well imagine, Maude wanted to know what was in the other chest, so she popped open the lid of that one as well. Needless to say, if it contained the remains of another human skeleton, there was a very good chance, she would sell the house. In fact, as it turns out, all the other chest had in it was a few personal belongings and a diary. Thank god, she thought to herself because by this time, she wasn't in the mood for another unpleasant surprise of any kind. Anyway, moments later, after having collected her thoughts, once again, Maude set off down the passageway again. Needless to say, she still hadn't come to the end of it, nevertheless, she wanted to know where it led. Well, once again, a few minutes later, she had her answer. Up ahead of the passageway she spied a small ray of light, which common sense told her, the end of the secret corridor was in sight. Anyway, as she made it to the end of the passageway, she could discern a few rays of light emanating from outside somewhere. At this point, Maude inched her way up to the aperture on the side of the tunnel and from where she stood, not only could she see the ocean, but she could also see the lighthouse in the distance as well. That meant she was right next to the shoreline and only a few yards away from the ocean. Needless to say, due to the fact the entrance to the passageway she was following was almost completely blocked by rocks, trees and other debris that had accumulated over the outside of the entrance through the years, Maude wasn't able to go any further. In fact, anyone who was walking along the shoreline wouldn't be able to see there was actually a tunnel that ran from the shore, all the way up to the underside of her house. Perhaps, as much as ninety-five percent of the original opening was obscurely hidden from sight. No wonder, no one knew there was a hidden passageway there. It also goes without saying, it would more than likely take a lot of work to reopen the entrance, so Maude just headed back towards the house. The fact of the matter is if it came right down to it, she could always do that another time however it would definitely require some assistance. In the meantime, she was quick to turn around and head in the other direction, which entailed going back up the tunnel and passing by the room with the chest that had the remains of a human skeleton in it, and then it was onto the first room she came too. At this point, she wanted to see where the other stairway led so she took another deep breath and headed up that one as well. A few minutes later, her suspicions were confirmed. As she thought, the other passageway, led up to the bedroom on the top floor of the house. In fact, the hidden stairway stopped behind the fireplace of the master bedroom up on the second floor of the Kimball mansion. Needless to say, it was a very interesting setup and one that left a lot of questions in her mind. Apparently, someone designed it that way for a reason. It was just a question of what the person had in mind when they constructed it, that's all. Anyway, right at the moment, Maude was more intent on finding out how to get into the bedroom from the passageway she was presently standing on without going back down the stairway and up through the other stairway that led into the living-room. At any rate, after careful observation, she could see there was a way to do that as well. In fact, quite frankly, she figured out how to get into the bedroom upstairs without retracing a step of her way back to the living-room. Actually, the way all that unfolded was she tried pushing on the back of the fireplace to see if that would give way first however that didn't work. The fireplace wouldn't budge an inch. At this point, Maude took her flashlight and inspected the perimeter around the back of the fireplace. Upon doing so, like in her living-room, there was a small knob to the right of the fireplace and like she suspected, the platform she was standing on swung around to the other side of where she wanted to get too and a second or two later, she was standing inside her bedroom. Holy shit, it was just as she thought! In addition to that, after looking at the bedroom side of the fireplace, Maude soon discovered she could go right back to the other side of the room where the secret passageway was by turning one of the scones located above the mantle in front of the fireplace. Believe it or not, when a person did that, whoever was standing in front of the fireplace would be swung around to the other side of the structure. Actually, as far as she was concerned, the person who designed this house must have been very smart. Of course, that didn't explain the reason why the person did what they did however regardless of what the designer of the house had in mind; she was impressed by the way everything was set up. In fact, quite frankly, after thinking about it for a moment or two, Maude chuckled at the thought of what she would've used it for had her old boyfriend been around. She would have gotten him to stand in front of the fireplace, then, she would have turned the scone to the right and gotten the no-good son of a bitch right out of her bedroom. Perhaps, that's what the person who designed this amazing setup had in mind. Who knows? Furthermore, at this point in her investigation, there wasn't any way of knowing whether or not it was the builder of the house or one of the previous owners of the estate that made all that possible. Anyway, regardless of the circumstances behind the construction of this very unique setup, she could honestly say, she liked it really well. By now, it was also apparent, that was all the excitement Maude could take for one day, so she headed downstairs to the living-room. From there, she quickly closed up the entrance to the other passageway by hitting the button on the side of the fireplace. At this point, she made the decision to look into the matter further another day. Obviously, what was hidden beneath the house was not going anywhere so for the time being, she was going to let things be as they were. Actually, by doing things this way, it would give Maude time to absorb what she had discovered beneath the house. Anyway, with that in mind, she concluded, it was time to take another break, so she went back into the kitchen and made herself another cup of coffee. After about forty-five minutes, as stated before, she also concluded, she would look into this monumental discovery in her spare time on another day, so she locked up the house and headed out to her car. The truth of the matter is, it had been a long day and she was getting hungry, so Maude got into her car, threw it in gear, and sped off down the road in a frame of mind that was highly reminiscent of a person who had their head stuck up their ass. Of course, that wasn't the case at all, nevertheless, Maude was still slightly bewildered by the discovery she made a little while earlier. Anyway, due to the fact she hadn't eaten in a few hours, she was intent on getting something to eat at one of the fine restaurants in Tierra Del Mar, which in this case, just happened to be the Frenchman's Friend. It also goes without saying, their food was very good so she thought it would be a good place to get a bite to eat. Perhaps, she would even have a nightcap when she got back to the house. In fact, it sounded like a great way to end the day. In the meantime, she intended to enjoy her meal, which in this case was clams on the half-shell, a fresh garden salad, breadsticks, and a glass of iced tea. In fact, not only did the meal sound good, but it hit the spot really well too. Anyway, she was in and out of the restaurant in not much more than an hour and then she was on her way home.

As for the earth-shattering discovery Maude made earlier in the day, you might say, there were a few troublesome questions in her mind. First of all, why would anyone want to be buried down beneath their own house? Secondly, where did all those silver and gold coins come from? Thirdly, could the whole unbelievable discovery have something to do with the murder that was committed there some time ago? Needless to say, that was a very scary thought however without having a little more information about what was buried beneath the house, there wasn't any way to be certain of anything. Perhaps, given a little time, she would be able to figure things out. In the meantime, Maude wanted to get some rest so shortly after returning to the Kimball mansion, along towards the hour of eleven o'clock, she called it a day and went to bed. Unfortunately, rest didn't some easy though as a world of things continued to saturate her mind. Actually, there was a possibility the old Kimball mansion was haunted. Admittedly, Maude didn't believe in ghosts or the supernatural however there appeared to be a spiritual presence beneath the house. She was certain of that however for the time being, she had decided not to let it bother her. I guess on the bright side of it all, she was more than likely sitting on a gold mine. Needless to say, Maude was quick to realize, the silver and gold coins she found down beneath her house were worth a lot of money. How much money, she didn't know however something in the back of her mind told her probably several thousand dollars. In fact, that wasn't everything she had on her mind. Because there had been a murder committed at her house a few years earlier, she was also very concerned about that as well. At first, Maude didn't give that a second thought but after finding the skeletal remains of a body down beneath her house, it was definitely a concern. At any rate, she was now having second thoughts about having purchased the property. In fact, one of the last thoughts on her mind that night was whether or not Mr. Brewster had disclosed everything about the property to her. Actually, common sense told her, he wouldn't have known anything about either one of those things. Obviously, had he known about the coins, he would've taken care of the matter at some point along the way because they were worth a lot of money. Surely, anyone in their right mind wouldn't have been numb enough to look in the other direction on something like that. As for the mystery surrounding the house, that would more than likely depend on whether or not she was able to come up with an answer that would explain her unexpected discovery however if the circumstances dictated it, she would move to the Hawaiian Islands somewhere. Perhaps, Kauai or Maui, she wasn't sure. Needless to say, she had heard a lot of good things said about Hawaii, and if push came to shove in the days ahead, there was a very good chance she might head off in that direction. In fact, either she would do that or she would go back to California. Anyway, as you might think, a lot of things were bouncing around inside her head that evening however that was also fairly typical of her personality. As I've said many times before, her character had a lot of depth to it so she had a tendency to worry about things that other people wouldn't have given any thought too. Of course, that's not to say what she discovered down beneath her house wasn't something to be concerned about however that was Maude Derringer to the letter T. Anyway, for obvious reasons, she didn't get much sleep that night. In fact, quite frankly, she wasn't even sure if she was going to stay in Tierra Del Mar now. Obviously, due to recent developments, that may change in the days ahead however for the time being she had decided to keep her residence at the Kimball mansion. Needless to say, Maude didn't want to jump to any conclusions over what she found down beneath her house however she would move again if the circumstances warranted it, even if it meant finding another place to live.

CHAPTER 10

The following day, after a very restless night of sleep, Maude woke up a little earlier than usual however as stated before, she had a lot on her mind. The truth of the matter is, she thought there might be a connection between the unsolved murder that took place at the Kimball mansion some years ago and all the old the coins that were sitting down beneath her house. Maybe, that's what the murderer was after when the homicide happened. Furthermore, it may also explain why the remains of a human skeleton was found down beneath her house as well. In fact, at this point she wasn't even a hundred percent sure there weren't more bodies down there. Granted, she took in everything in sight, but perhaps, she overlooked something. Even as much as she hated to say it, that was quite possible. Hopefully, that was not the case however it was undoubtedly the most bizarre thing she ever encountered in her life. Anyway, now, more than ever, she wanted to solve the mystery of how everything came to be at her house, but until she had more information, there wasn't any way to be certain of anything, and that wasn't going to give her the peace of mind she was looking for. Needless to say, she could only speculate on what took place at the old Kimball mansion and really nothing more so for the time being, she didn't have any answers however she was still optimistic everything would eventually explain itself in the days ahead.

Anyway, immediately following a nice warm shower, Maude headed into the kitchen that morning to find something to eat. Obviously, after spending a restless night in bed, she woke up hungrier than ever that day and it was certainly all the motivation she needed to fix something up for breakfast. In this particular case, Maude had already decided to have a couple of eggs, a few strips of bacon and a glass of orange juice. Needless to say, this was one of her favorite things to have for breakfast and more often than not, it helped get the day started off right. Actually, from time to time, she liked to have pancakes and syrup and when it came right down to having a good breakfast, she made out really well with that too. As for a cup of coffee, that was something she had on occasion, however in most instances, it was only when Maude was hot under the collar or when she needed a little extra energy. Other than that, she usually had orange juice for breakfast and iced tea during the day. It was a daily routine Maude followed and she rarely did anything to the contrary. Anyway, as it turns out, after having finished breakfast, at no surprise to her, she set her mind to thinking about the bizarre discovery she made the day before. Actually, the thought of having the body of a murdered man laid to rest beneath her house was a little scary if that was in fact, the case. Needless to say, for that reason, until she had an answer, her mind wasn't going to be able to lay the matter to rest. Anyway, rather than letting it bother her some more and while keeping this in perspective, before leaving the kitchen that morning, she picked up her flashlight, grabbed some matches from a drawer in the kitchen, and then feeling satisfied that she had done everything necessary to investigate the matter down beneath the house further, she headed for the living-room. At this point, she was startled by the sound of the doorbell ringing. Who would be calling at such an early hour of the day, she thought to herself? She didn't know anyone in Tierra Del Mar so you might say, she was a little perplexed by who was at her front door. It wouldn't be the man from the real estate agency because the sale of the estate was finished. Furthermore, she was absolutely certain he would have called first. Perhaps, it was some type of salesman, selling something. That was always a possibility. Worse yet, maybe someone from one of the local area churches wanted her to become a member of their congregation however Maude didn't have any interest in doing that. Actually, there was one other possibility, perhaps, someone from the news media found out she was living in Tierra Del Mar and had showed up to try and get an interview out of her over a recent book she had published. Who knows? All she actually knew for certain was someone was paying her a visit.

At any rate, upon hearing the doorbell ring, she immediately set her flashlight aside and ran into the bathroom for a moment to look into the mirror. Like usual, she wanted to make sure everything was in order in case someone from the news media was at her front door. Actually, as things stood right now, she didn't think that was very likely but through the years, stranger things had happened, so she wasn't about to rule anything out. Anyway, like you might think, she was a very modest woman in most respects, in addition to the fact, she was also a very pretty woman so taking a lot of pride in how she looked was always a concern. In fact, most people her age would have probably been married a couple times over, however for more than one reason, that was not the case with Maude. She held her ground. Actually, what most people would've said is she just hadn't been lucky enough to find the right person. Needless to say, there always seemed to be an unwanted fly in the ointment, figuratively speaking and when that happened, things did not work out for her. Anyway, not in a hundred and ten million years did she ever expect to see the young man standing at her front door this morning however as fate would have it, that man was about to become her best friend for some years to come. At any rate, what Maude originally thought was going to turn out to be another business matter that had to be dealt with, things didn't go that way at all. In fact, little did she know the relationship she was about to get herself into would change her life forever, and it wouldn't be until some years later before she realized the mistake she was about to make would also end up causing her a lot of unwanted misery as well. Obviously, if she had known that at the time, where everything was headed and what would eventually come to be, I'm absolutely certain she would've done things a lot differently. Anyway, with at least a million and a half things bouncing around inside her head, she took one more look in the mirror to make sure everything was in order, and then like a woman who has business matters to attend too or an important date she didn't want to miss out on, she went to see who was at the door.

At any rate, the moment she opened the door, she was immediately taken aback to realize it wasn't the news media at all. No, rather than having to deal with that or a traveling salesperson who would inevitably try to sell her something, Maude found a handsome young man standing at her door. Anyway, long before she was able to make an inquiry into what the man wanted; it was a profound pleasure to find out he wasn't at all who she thought was at the door. "Good morning, ma'am," he stated. "I hope this absolutely splendid day finds you well. Furthermore, rather than beating around the bush to make acquaintances with you, I would like to take a moment to make this a formal introduction, as well as welcome you to the neighborhood. First of all, my name is Enrique Vestellini. You may call me Ricky if you wish. That's what most people who know me do. I live over there a ways, where that lighthouse is," he stated as he casually pointed off in the distance. "Well, if I'm not mistaken that makes us neighbors. Granted, it's a few hundred yards away from here however the distance isn't so great that we can't pay each other a visit. Actually, once upon a time, the property you see over there was my parent's home, but they passed away a short time ago. Needless to say, being the only child in the family, I inherited the property from them. The truth of the matter is they were getting up there in age, so there passing did not come as any surprise. In fact, I did my best to take care of them while they were here. Anyway, that's a quick overview of my life. There's actually a lot more that can be said about me however right at the moment, I would like to hear from you, ma'am." At this point, she was overwhelmed with emotion by what the young man just finished telling her, so you might say, she was at a total loss for words. Believe it or not, she had a tendency to be a little shy at times, and such was the case this time as well. Actually, Maude was so infatuated by the young man's appearance she literally forgot how to speak. Of all the possible things that could have happened however that was most certainly the nature of things at that moment. Anyway, for that reason, she immediately began to fumble around with the collar on her blouse, not knowing what to do or what to say. I know that probably sounds like the trait of a young child however whether she realized it or not, Maude had been smitten by cupids arrow. Anyway, a moment later after having regained her composure, she finally managed to say, "It's very nice to meet you, Mr. Vestellini. I mean that sincerely however other than welcoming me to the neighborhood, which really isn't a bad to do, may I inquire what your reason is for dropping by today? Actually, I would also like to say, it's obviously very kind of you to do that however in my profession that doesn't usually happen. In fact, due to the nature of my profession, usually when someone does that, they want something. Now, just exactly how may I help you, Mr. Vestellini?" At this point, Ricky paused for a moment before saying, "There isn't any particular reason for my visit, ma'am. Like I said, all I really wanted to do is welcome you to the neighborhood. In case you weren't aware of it no one has been living in this house for quite some time so my curiosity got the best of me. Anyway, when I noticed the house was lit up the other day, it piqued my curiosity so here I am. I hope this is not too much of an intrusion into your life because I didn't mean anything bad by taking the initiative to see who my new neighbor was. I would also like to say, if that's a little too personal for you, I most sincerely apologize for that inconvenience, ma'am. I assure you, there weren't any bad intentions on my part. Actually, there's one other thing I have to confess too and that's, I've been admiring that very eye-catching car of yours that's sitting out in your driveway, ma'am. Boy, she's a real beauty. I can't say I've always wanted to own a Ferrari, but it is definitely one of the finest cars I've ever seen. Anyway, that's more or less what I wanted to say to you so on behalf of everyone in the town of Tierra Del Mar, I welcome you to our community. I think you'll like it. Just give it a little time and keep in mind, we're a small town. In this neck of the woods, we probably do things a lot differently than what you're used too however we're very proud of our community and I think you'll feel right at home here. Now, if it's not too much to ask, you would take a moment and introduce yourself. I would really like to know who I'm having a conversation with. In fact, perhaps, we could have a cup of coffee together sometime. It would give us a good opportunity to get to know one another a little. Of course, don't feel so you have to do that, but the door is open to that possibility if you would like too," he finished saying. Needless to say, it suffices to say, Maude did like the young man really well however she was also at a loss for words. The fact of the matter is, it wasn't too often that she had an opportunity to meet someone as handsome as Ricky Vestellini was and right at the moment, her infatuation with him probably showed more than ever. I'm sure it looked like she was a very conceited person however that really wasn't the case at all. Maude was actually a very pleasant person once you got to know her however between being a bit shy and taken aback by Ricky's handsome appearance, it probably looked like she was indifferent to the occasion. At any rate, after another moment went by, without getting a response from her, Ricky gave up and started upon his way. Then, just as he was about to get into his truck and drive off, Maude yelled over to him at the top of her lungs saying, "Please excuse my hesitancy in responding to you, Mr. Vestellini but I was thinking about a couple other things and my mind went blank. That happens sometimes. I don't know the reason for that, but I sincerely apologize for my lack of response to you." Anyway, as you might think, the moment he heard Maude call his name, he came back to her doorstep and said, "I didn't think I was ever going to get a response from you ma'am. May I be so bold as to inquire who am I speaking too? What is your name, dear? I have been carrying on a conversation with you for the past fifteen or twenty minutes and I have yet to find out who I have the pleasure of speaking with." Believe it or not, she was still speechless. Needless to say, it wasn't her best moment ever and she continued to struggle to find the words she wanted to say. Finally, after another second or two of indecisiveness, Maude said, "First of all, Mr. Vestellini, I would like to apologize for not answering you sooner, but you're a very handsome man and right at the moment, I'm so darn flustered, it probably looks like my heads stuck up my ass. Believe it or not, that's not like me at all and this is a very embarrassing moment for me. In fact, it's so bad and I'm so nervous that I nearly forgot my name," she stated further. "In fact, quite frankly, I am glad you dropped by. I mean that sincerely. Anyway, please accept my apology for being such a thoughtless person for not having answered you sooner and let me introduce myself. My name's Maude Derringer. I'm actually a writer from the state of Arizona however in recent years, I have been living in southern California." At this point, Maude reached over and shook his hand. "It's a pleasure to meet you, Mr. Vestellini," she stated. "I do sincerely mean that." Then, long before she had a chance to say another word, he responded back to her, saying, "It's Ricky, ma'am. You don't have to formally address me as Mr. Vestellini. Ricky will do just fine. Besides, in case you haven't guessed it by now, that's how I would prefer to be addressed. Now, with regards to what you do for a living, I've heard of you Ms. Derringer. In fact, just so you know, I've read most of your books and I can even go as far as saying, I have also thoroughly enjoyed every one of them. You're very good author, ma'am. My compliments to you for having written such great works of literature." At this point, she was at a loss for words again. The truth of the matter is, she didn't think he would pick up on her name so quickly, but he had and you might say, she was extremely flattered by his compliment. At any rate, a moment later, after the better side of excitement flew through wildly her veins alerting her to the possibility she may have found someone after all, she replied back to Ricky. "Well, don't just stand there," she said, "come on in. I will put on a fresh pot of coffee and we can chat for a while. Actually, I was just about to start on a project that was in need of my attention however it can wait until later. Rome wasn't built in a day, and I am sure nothing around here was either so I don't see any reason why we can't spend a little time getting to know each other. In fact, come this way. No, on second thought, instead of making a trip into the kitchen, why don't we go out on the back terrace and have our coffee. It's really pleasant out there at this time of day and I'm sure you'll enjoy the view. After that, I'll give you a quick tour of the house. Please keep in mind, I still have a ways to go before it's completely done." At this point, she took a moment to explain what her plans for the house were and how she was going to proceed in getting some of the necessary renovations on it done. In the meantime, she told him a little about herself, in addition to delving into some small talk aimed at getting to no one another better. At any rate, after a couple cups of coffee and a lot of very productive talk, she gave him a tour of the house. Once that was taken care of, they went back out onto the terrace and talked for a little while longer. She did get a very nice compliment from him about how great the view was from her back terrace however that just happened to be the reason why Maude suggested having coffee out there. Anyway, after a couple hours of discussing this, that, and everything else under the sun, Ricky left to go home but more importantly, it appears, the seeds of a great relationship together had been sown in concrete. In fact, she was all but certain she would see him again. If that didn't turn out to be the case, she would be greatly surprised. At any rate, things went very well that day and before leaving, he invited her over to supper sometime however the invitation was very open ended because he didn't give a precise day and time on when that would happen, nevertheless, it left her with a wonderful feeling inside. Anyway, as you might think, right at the moment, Maude was literally walking around on cloud nine with her mind being off somewhere in a la-la-land of infatuation over Ricky Vestellini. In fact, so much so, she had a very hard time getting out of her own way of anything and it was very unlikely that would change anytime soon. Now, with regards to the open-ended invitation to have supper with him, obviously without a day and time attached to the invitation, everything was sort of left up in the air for the time being. He did say, he was working on a couple projects of his own so she immediately attributed his lack of giving her a definite answer to one of those so-called projects he was working on. At any rate, it wasn't any reason for concern. She was certain whenever he got around to it, he would have her over for supper and that's all that really mattered.

In the meantime, with Ricky no longer there, she went into the kitchen to find something to eat before heading back down the secret passageway in the living-room. Needless to say, she wanted to find out how everything beneath the house got there. For that reason, she was going to have to play private investigator until the mystery of that bizarre occurrence was solved. In fact, that's what she had set out to do when Ricky showed up at her door a little while earlier. At any rate, he had gone home so there wasn't anything standing in her way from doing that now. With that in mind, she sat down and had a bite. It was the modest of lunches but she wasn't looking to do anything more than satisfy her appetite anyway, so a tossed salad and a ham sandwich did the trick for her. After finishing her meal, she took the time to rinse off a few dishes that were sitting in the sink, then she got ready to go back down beneath the house. At this point, Maude began to put a little more thought into what it would be like to be married to Ricky Vestellini. Needless to say, due to her intense infatuation with him, she hadn't been able to get him out of her mind since they met and that limited her concentration on anything except Mr. Vestellini. As stated before, Maude wanted a family of her own, so it was just a question of whether or not he was interested in getting married and raising a family. Actually, there was a couple of things that concerned her about Mr. Vestellini and that was compatibility and trustworthiness. Of course, there wasn't any way she would be able to determine that at this point. That would take time. Needless to say, it could be such, Maude would get used again and if that happened hard telling what she would do. There certainly was a lot to consider and like a person with a personality that was as deep as the universe, the inner workings of her mind continued to devour one thought after another until she finally concluded, Ricky Vestellini was an ideal candidate for marriage.

At any rate, as stated a moment ago, Maude had something else she wanted to do or not a blessed thing was going to get done so she grabbed her flashlight and headed for the living-room. It was time to do the inevitable! Needless to say, she wanted to know how all those old coins got down beneath the house and the only realistic chance that had of happening was to go back down there. Since the previous owner was no longer alive, and Mr. Brewster didn't know anything but what he told her, that left her only one recourse, Maude would have to look into the matter on her own. If by some chance she got lucky and that's what she was counting on, she would be able to unravel the mystery behind the old Kimball mansion and of course, that's what she wanted to do. At any rate, with that in mind, that's what she headed off to do.

CHAPTER 11

Anyway, within a few minutes of having made the decision to look into the highly bizarre circumstances of what was down beneath her house, upon entering the living-room, Maude went to the fireplace and proceeded to turn the small knob that swung the bookcase around to the other side of the wall. Needless to say, it only took a second or two for that to happen and then, with a slightly bewildered look on her face, she turned her flashlight on and slowly inched her way back down the secret stairway to the chambers beneath the house. Actually, it was her desire to take a closer look at the seaman's chests that didn't have any coins in the. Perhaps, they would hold the answer to how everything got where it was. At any rate, upon reaching the bottom of the hidden staircase, Maude got out her matches and proceeded to light all of the lanterns that were attached to walls of the first chamber. This time, after taking a closer look, she came to realize there were actually four chests with coins in them, not just the one she saw the day before. Since, the other three chests were located on the far side the room, she didn't immediately see them. Needless to say, that meant there were even more silver and gold coins than she originally thought. Anyway, after taking a short respite, she started down the narrow tunnel that went directly to the shoreline of the ocean. She didn't have far to go. In fact, after a moment or two, she had reached the other chamber beneath the house. At this point, she proceeded to light all the lanterns on the walls of the second chamber until she could clearly see the two chests in question were made somewhat differently than the other ones. Obviously, that didn't mean anything to her but she figured there was a reason for that and in all likelihood, there probably was. Anyway, it appeared that one of the chests had some type of insignia written on the top of it and that only added more mystery to an already puzzling matter. At first, she thought the writing may have been written in some type of foreign language, possibly Latin however after studying writing for a moment, she concluded, that wasn't the case at all. What's really interesting to note is, all the chests with the tops flipped open were filled with silver and gold coins. In fact, it looked like someone left them that way for a reason however that was just speculation on her part. Perhaps, there was more than one person who set this whole thing up, she thought to herself. That might explain the overall differences in the design of the chests as well as the reason why there were two chambers, not just one. It was mind boggling to say the least! Actually, another possibility was maybe it was just bad planning on the part of the person who constructed the labyrinth of the tunnels beneath the house however in reality, there wasn't any way to know what the maker of the house had in mind. Anyway, as I said before, two of the six seaman's chests inside the second room were closed tight. In fact, she already knew one of them contained the remains of a man that was buried down here many years ago. The other one, she hadn't tried to open yet however that was the next thing she was going to do. Obviously, with any kind of luck at all, perhaps, this trunk would provide her with an answer as to how everything got where it was. Needless to say, if it didn't have some kind of identifiable thing inside of it, like a newspaper or a book, she was out of ideas. That meant she would not be able to figure things out after all. Until now, her attempt to get to the bottom of this very unusual matter had failed. Anyway, fortunately for her, the cover to this seaman's chest was attached by a couple of light weight metal clasps so with a little dexterity, she flipped open the lid. Maude's initial impression was the trunk contained nothing more than some old clothes, a bible, and a few other personal belongings that someone left behind. Then, all of a sudden, she spotted something she thought might be of interest. There, tucked off to one side, near the bottom of the chest was an old book. Naturally, Maude picked it up and went to the first page of it to see if it had a title. At this point, she could see it was a man's diary. Not only that; the handwriting was very neatly written and in English even though the print was slightly faded away from sitting down beneath the house for many years. Apparently, the writing was still legible, so it was obviously readable. Needless to say, without the diary, Maude didn't have a prayer's chance in hell of learning what happened here god only knows how many years before. Anyway, by now, it was quite apparent, this diary was going to shed some light onto the matter and that the diary was probably the story of the man who was laid to rest here. Anyway, within a moment or two of having made this very unique discovery, she pulled a pair of reading glasses out of one of the pockets on her blouse and proceeded to put them on her face. Then, she walked over to the far wall where one of the wick lanterns shined brightly and stood beneath it. Now, she was able to see things in a much clearer light. At this point, Maude looked closely at the writing on the first page of the man's diary and then, ever so slowly, she began reading the very first line of the diary. "In the summer of 1848, I, Charles Winston Kimball I, son of Elijah John Kimball, set sail upon the ocean as an indentured servant for a man by the name of Richard Deacon Smith." Well, it suffices to say, she didn't have to read any further to realize the diary was going to turn out to be the story of someone's life. In fact, more than likely, the life story of the person who built the house. Anyway, with that said, a moment later, she stopped reading the diary and stared off into space. Unfortunately, she wasn't able to concentrate. Too much had gone on for one day for her to be able to do that so she gently closed the cover of the diary and got ready to go back upstairs. She would get back to it another day. Maude was certain of that. Right at the moment, she had decided to head back upstairs and call it a day, so Maude quickly turned around and went through the secret passageway and up the hidden stairway until she was standing inside the living-room again. From there, she pressed the turned the small knob on the side of the fireplace and that in turn spun the bookcase back into its original position. Actually, the only drawback to the whole thing was when the bookcase swung around to the other side of the wall, a few of the books would inevitably fall out onto the floor in disarray however that was a very minor inconvenience.

At any rate, by this time, Maude planned on getting something to eat, then, she would sit down for a few minutes before going to bed. In fact, between the work she did the previous day and what she had to deal with today, she quickly concluded, she would go to bed early. Besides, with regards to reading the diary, she wanted to read it in its entirety and right at the moment, she was too fatigued to do that, so she opted to put that off for the time being. Perhaps, she would be able to get to the reading of it sometime the following day or possibly shortly thereafter. Right at the moment, she headed into the kitchen, and once again, she fixed herself up a quick lunch, then after making a stop in the bathroom to freshen up a bit, she slipped into her nightgown and went back into the living-room to have a night cap before going to bed. Actually, that wasn't anything too unusual for her to do. Anyway, at this point, she began reflecting on what she had done over the past forty-eight hours and then, like she planned on doing, a short time later, she went to bed. It was only a little after the hour of ten o'clock however quite uncharacteristic of most nights, all of a sudden, the peaceful tranquility Maude usually enjoyed at this time of the day was broken by the sound of the telephone ringing. Obviously, still wide awake, Maude glanced at the clock that was sitting on the nightstand beside her bed and took notice of the time. It wasn't even half past the hour of 10:00 o'clock yet. Who in the name of Christ would be so inconsiderate to call her at this time of the day? Surely, it must be a wrong number, she said to herself. Then, a little uneasy and somewhat reluctant about answering it, she slowly reached over to the nightstand and picked up the handset of the telephone. "Hello," she stated in a very inquisitive voice, "Who is calling," however there wasn't any response from the person on the other end of the phone. All she could hear was the persistent sound of someone breathing heavily into the telephone with obviously no intention of saying anything. At this point, perhaps, another second or two went by, and then the phone went dead.

CHAPTER 12

As unbelievable as it may be, after receiving that mysterious telephone call the previous evening, Maude still managed to fall asleep and that really said a lot about her character because she had a lot on her mind however with regards to was calling her at such a late hour, at least for the time being that would remain a mystery. In fact, by now, she had concluded, it was probably nothing more than a wrong number or a prank caller who didn't have anything better to do than to harass someone. Actually, there was one other possibility. The call may have been related to the murder that took place at her house some time ago but if that was the case, it meant someone was trying to find out who was living there now. Unfortunately, without knowing more than she did, you might say, it was very puzzling to her. At any rate, as she continued to speculate on who may have been behind that very disturbing telephone call, more uncertainty began to take root in the back of her mind. Granted, Maude had an old boyfriend living back in the state of

California who wasn't happy about her breaking off their relationship however he wouldn't do anything like that to her. He was a womanizer however he wasn't disrespectful to the law or to anyone else for that matter. No, to the best of her knowledge, she didn't have any enemies. Of course, once in a while someone from the news media would be looking for a story but they wouldn't do anything like that either. At any rate, for a couple of very apparent reasons, she had decided not to contact the police department this time however if the calls persisted, she would have to take appropriate measures. In the meantime, she was a little bewildered by everything because she had not given her telephone number out to anyone. At this point, Maude talked herself into brushing the matter aside for a while however she would monitor the situation closely and if necessary, she would go to the police. For the time being, she had decided not to worry about it.

Anyway, as it turns out, shortly after awakening that day, she proceeded to push all those unwanted thoughts right out of her mind in favor of getting out of bed and taking a shower. Like always, personal hygiene was one of her top priority's when she got out of bed in the morning, so she headed off to the bathroom. In fact, after a nice warm shower, the make-up went on, and just as soon as that aspect of being a woman was taken care of, she got dressed and went down-stairs to have breakfast. At this point, Maude took a look out of one of the windows in the house to see what kind of day it was going to be and with the sun shining brightly against a perfectly blue sky, she quickly surmised, it was going to be a nice day. In fact, quite frankly, there wasn't a cloud in the sky and that immediately appeased her mind. At any rate, to this point, satisfied with the way everything was going, she sat down at the kitchen table and had something to eat. Then, after her usual early morning hunger was taken care of, Maude proceeded to grab her purse and was about to head out the door to do some grocery shopping when the telephone rang. Needless to say, she froze! What if it was the same person who called the previous night? Anger, fear, and frustration immediately raced to the forefront of her mind. Then, in a tizzy, and near the point of panicking, Maude got a hold of herself and answered the telephone. "Hello," she stated, "who may I ask is calling?" At this point, the person on the other end of the telephone identified himself. "It's your next-door neighbor, Ricky Vestellini," he replied. "After having spoken with you yesterday, I'm surprised you didn't recognize my voice. I hope this isn't an inopportune time to call, but I need to speak with you for a moment. Actually, to make a long story short, I wasn't able to sleep at all last night. I couldn't get you out of my mind, Maude. I don't usually own up to a statement like that however you may rest assured, that's the god's honest truth. At any rate, the reason why I'm calling is, I would like to formally ask you over to supper this evening. Not only will it give us a good opportunity to get better acquainted but I make a great chicken linguine as well and I would love to have you sample some of it for me. What do you say? Would you be interested in having supper with me?" At this point, it was noticeably apparent, Ricky had caught her off guard again because like the previous day, she was flustered right to the point of being speechless. Actually, the truth of the matter was between the highly disturbing phone call she received the day before and trying to figure out how all those old coins from the 19th century ended up down beneath her house, she hadn't had time to assess the situation. Admittedly, Maude was aware of the fact, she had made a big impression on Ricky however she didn't expect to be asked to dinner so soon. In fact, quite frankly, it was very overwhelming to her. Anyway, at this point, she took a moment to think about his invitation to have dinner with him. The truth of the matter was, there as a couple of things she had to take into consideration. First, if she consented to have dinner with him, she was taking a chance on being screwed over again. That in itself was a reason for concern. Then, secondly although perhaps not as importantly, she would have to put off looking into the mystery behind the old Kimball mansion for a little while longer however it was unquestionably the right thing to do. At any rate, after a few more seconds went by, she finally gave him an answer and it probably wasn't a moment too soon because he had reached the point where he was beginning to get impatient with her. Anyway, at this juncture, she replied, "Ricky, I would love to have dinner with you. I'm terribly sorry about the delay in giving you an answer but I had a couple things on my mind, none of which you need to be concerned about. In fact, to put your mind at ease, both matters had nothing to do with you, Ricky. I was momentarily lost in thought, that's all. I'm sure in the due course of time everything will be fine." "Is there anything I can help you with," Ricky asked? "No, not really, but I will definitely keep what you said in mind," she answered. "By the way, would you like me to cook something up for you? I can bring it over with me when I come over this evening." "No, that won't be necessary," he replied. "Perhaps, another time, I'll take it to heart and let you do the cooking. Tonight, I'll do the cooking for the both of us. It will be my treat." "Okay, let me know if you change your mind," she said. "It would be a pleasure to cook you up something. Now, what time should I come over this evening?" At this point, Ricky took a moment to think about what she asked him. The truth of the matter is, he was so excited about having the opportunity to spend the evening with her that he forgot to specify a time. "Well, why don't you plan on coming over around six o'clock. If everything goes well, I should have supper ready by then." "Okay, I'll be there," she replied. "Then, I guess it's a date," he stated. "I'll see you later this evening," and with that said their conversation came to an end.

CHAPTER 13

Anyway, shortly after getting off the telephone with Ricky, Maude thought it would be a good idea to go into town and get her hair done. At the same time, she would be able to pick up a few necessities at one of the stores in the area so it was the only logical thing to do. As always, when it came right down to doing something, she wanted to look her best and a dinner date with Ricky Vestellini certainly fell into that category. Actually, most people would have said she was a very pretty woman and in reality, that was true. In fact, for that reason, she always tried to look her best. Obviously, with a pleasant personality, and a great philosophy on life, Maude had a lot going for her however like most people, she had problems too. As for her personality, like I said before, she always kept a good positive attitude and she never set her goals too high. In addition to that, she believed very strongly in living one day at a time. Needless to say, she thought if that could be done, then in all probability a good life would follow, and of course, like so many other things she believed in, that probably stacked up in her favor as well. Yes, she was an optimist in every sense of the word regardless of whether or not that was the best way to live one's life, and in most instances, that philosophy usually benefited her. When it didn't, Maude did the best she could with the situation and then, she would move on from there.

Anyway, on this particular day and as things stood now, she was only thinking about one thing and that was Ricky Vestellini. Actually, like most people who had been living alone for an extended period of time, she concluded, it was time to take a chance on life again. Obviously, in her case, all that really meant was she was going to try and find a husband over the course of the next few weeks. As you well know, most women have a way of knowing when a man has taken an interest in them, and she could easily see Ricky was so infatuated with her right that she could literally hear wedding bells peel away inside of her head. It would be just a question of whether or not he was ready to settle down yet. Needless to say, someone of Mr. Vestellini's stature sure as hell didn't need money or anything else for that matter so it was going to be a challenge to talk him into getting married. At this point, she began to reflect on her current situation. Perhaps, he wouldn't even be interested in having children anyway, and if that turned out to be the case, then she was going to have to look for another man. The truth of the matter was, she wanted to raise a family while she was still young and if that was going to happen, she couldn't wait around much longer because age was beginning to catch up with her. What concerned her most was men were usually only interested in one thing and that was the good old one-night stand. In this case, there was a lot of money involved so that was something Maude had to take into consideration as well. Actually, what pained her the most was the thought of being used again. Anyway, she eventually concluded, Ricky was worth taking a chance on. Yes, come hell or high water, she was going to pursue her interest in him and with any luck at all, perhaps, things would work out well for her in the days ahead. Of course, Maude couldn't honestly say, she didn't have anything to lose but she wanted to take a chance on winning him over with the hope it would lead to marriage somewhere down the road. Obviously, if things didn't work out that way, she would have to look around for another man however right at the moment, everything looked very promising.

At any rate, Maude was going to have dinner with Ricky that evening, and that appointed time arrived a lot sooner than she thought. In fact, as usual, time passed by quickly that day and destiny now found her standing in front of his house. Needless to say, in her mind, it was time to take a chance on life again and with that said, she walked slowly up to the door of his house and rang the bell. Seconds later, Ricky came to the door and let her in. Actually, it turns out, he just happened to be watching for her anyway, so she didn't have long to wait. Anyway, after a bit of small talk about how the day was going, they proceeded into the living-room where they wound up discussing all kinds of different things. As for the overall atmosphere of the occasion, Maude could immediately see the chemistry between them was good. In fact, it's more or less, what she concluded the day before. Needless to say, that meant they would be compatible with each other if they were to get married. Obviously, that was good news because she was really only thinking one thing and that was marriage. Anyway, after a little while, Ricky took a few minutes to show her around the house. As expected, she liked his home really well. She wasn't sure how old the house was, but it was definitely a lot newer than the one she purchased. Of course, Maude didn't have any complaints about purchasing the old Kimball mansion however it did need some fixing. In fact, like you might think, Maude had already made arrangements with someone earlier in the day to have new windows and a new roof put on the house. As for Ricky's property, it was in the best possible condition anyone could ever imagine and you might say, Maude took an immediate liking to it. Actually, her own property, would eventually be in good condition also however the Kimball mansion was a little older than his house. At this point in their conversation, it came to her attention, the lighthouse Ricky owned was built back in the late 1800's to help accommodate a growing number of sailing vessels in the United States. From there, he told her how his family came to own it. Needless to say, it was a very interesting story and at no surprise to her, she was actually quite impressed with how everything came to be. As a matter of fact, Ricky also took a few minutes to explain how important it was for a mariner to have a good working lighthouse in those days. In fact, quite frankly, Maude had no idea so much technology went into building one of those lighthouses. Admittedly, most of the lighthouses that were in operation these days were very easily maintained however she learned that many of them were nothing more than a symbol of the past now. Anyway, in the end, not only did Maude have a lot better understanding of what a lighthouse actually did but she also had a much better understanding of the historic significance the held in American history as well. At this point, Ricky went onto explain what had been done to preserve the heritage of the lighthouse even though it wasn't actually used anymore. Then, he further stated, the house he was living in was built after the lighthouse was constructed and more than likely by the owner of the property at that point in time. Needless to say, that was too many years ago for Ricky to even comprehend what it would've been like to have lived back then so he didn't want to speculate on it any further. Actually, Maude thought her house was around twenty years older than his however she wouldn't know that for sure until she had an opportunity to read the diary of Charles Winston Kimball I. In the meantime, there were a couple of things that were bothering her and both things were directly tied to the house.

Anyway, as it turns out, he promised to show her the inside of the lighthouse sometime if she was interested in seeing it, which of course sparked a lot of enthusiasm in her because Maude found the historical significance of the lighthouse to be very interesting. He did go onto say, not only were his parents responsible for purchasing the lighthouse but they were also the individuals who restored it back to its original condition. At any rate, since their passing, Ricky hadn't done anything to the lighthouse, except keep up the yearly maintenance on it so if he ever went to sell it, the property would bring in a lot of money for him. In the meantime, the lighthouse was his to enjoy even if it meant just sitting there admiring the beauty of it. Anyway, thanks to his parents, he was financially secure and that's all that really mattered. In fact, it was the inheritance he got from his parents that made everything he did these days possible so you might say, that was first and foremost on his mind whenever he gave any thought to it. One way or another, regardless of what he did with the property in the days ahead, he was extremely grateful to them for what they left behind to him.

At any rate, the evening was progressing along rather nicely however shortly after giving Maude his promise to show her the inner workings of the lighthouse, they could hear the distinct sound of rain beating down upon the roof of the house. Needless to say, that was not the kind of evening she was looking for however like everything else in life, one takes what they can get. In any event and in spite of that, rather than just sitting around watching it rain, they headed into the dining-room where they were about to sit down and have dinner together. Anyway, at this point, Ricky ran off into the kitchen for a moment to check on the meal he was preparing for them, and when he did, Maude used the opportunity to make a trip to the bathroom to make sure everything was in order. At any rate, like usual, Maude was satisfied with what she saw in the mirror, so she headed back to the dining-room where she found Ricky laying the food out upon the table, which meant it was time to eat. Needless to say, the moment of truth had finally arrived so without any further ado, Ricky made sure she was seated down at the table, and then he sat down in the chair next to hers. Now, if I haven't mentioned this before, it should also be noted, Ricky was a really handsome man with black hair, soft brown eyes, high cheekbones and being of Italian descent he had a distinct accent that stood out whenever he was engaged in conversation with someone. In addition to that, from what she could see, he had a very charismatic personality and that literally made her melt like an ice cube whenever she was in his presence. Anyway, right at the moment, that is what she was thinking. Obviously, Maude was only human and due to the close proximity of where Ricky sat in relation to where she was, their eyes very quickly interlocked for a moment as the unrelenting passion of what she had in mind took refuge in the heart. In fact, quite frankly, she felt rather warm for an environment that was naturally cool and was perhaps, blushing a little at the thought of getting him into bed, however that was the nature of things. At any rate, shortly after they finished eating their meal, Ricky quickly assed the situation and asked her if she would like to go upstairs to see the balcony. Of course, that easily fell in line with what she had in mind anyway, so she agreed to go upstairs with him. Actually, she doubted very much that the balcony was what he wanted to show her, however the bedroom would be, and right at the moment, that's where she wanted to be. Anyway, with absolutely nothing but sex on their minds, you might say, by now, neither one of them was in a very talkative mood as they made their way up the stairs to his bedroom. It was a quiet atmosphere. One so quiet that only the sound of the rain beating on the roof of the house could be heard. She felt at ease. In fact, she actually felt right at home and like she had known Ricky her whole life at the point she walked into his bedroom that evening. I believe it was then, that her eyes began to dart around the room to see what kind of a man Ricky was, when she noticed the beautifully designed French doors that led out onto the balcony. Yes, it was this he was referring to, she thought to herself and how beautiful it was even with the rain coming down a lot harder than she would have preferred it to be. Obviously, they couldn't walk out onto the balcony because the overhang above their heads did not extend out far enough from where they stood, nevertheless, she still grasped the moment, and such a peaceful serene moment it was as the rain continued to beat upon the roof. Yet, the rain didn't matter to Ricky as he held Maude's hand ever so tightly, not wanting to let go. Then, unhesitatingly he gazed into her eyes and kissed her passionately upon the lips and of course, she began to melt in his arms like an ice cube trying to find a cool place to chill amidst a long hot summer. Yes, passion, lust, desire, and everything else anyone could ever imagine soon began to overwhelm them. At this point, Ricky started to fondle her breasts and she moaned in delight. Then, like a man on a mission who knew what he wanted, he let his hand slip down between her thighs. His moves were very methodical, in fact so splendidly wonderful that Maude was hoping this moment in time would never end. It was undoubtably the most passion she had ever felt in her life. It was as if time itself had come to a standstill. Then, with no other desire than to be with the woman he was so fondly caressing, Ricky gently picked Maude up and carried her over to his bed, where seconds later, they were all wrapped up in the passionate thralls of love making. Not once, not twice but three times. It was all so quick, yet it was all so very pleasant. In fact, it was so wonderfully exhilarating that there wasn't any way she could describe her feelings or how she felt at that moment in time. It was as if she had ascended into heaven and been redeemed of all of her sins. Yes, it was really and truly the best sexual gratification she had ever experienced in her life. Then, after a while of enjoying the intimate side of their love making and having spent the better part of an hour in bed together, their love making gradually came to an end, and a short time later, Maude fell asleep in his arms. Then, ever so slowly, with the evening giving way to the night, soon they were both sound asleep amidst the magic one feels when they're in love. Oh, what a magnificent night it was. Yes, for a few minutes in time, there were no cares, worries or concerns or anything else for that matter, as the night slowly descended upon them. Needless to say, Maude felt as if she had finally found a man who really cared for her, and perhaps that was true, however at this point, there was no way to be certain of that. She would have to feel things out as she went along. At any rate, they both slept soundly through the remainder of the night until the first rays of sunlight found its way into Ricky's bedroom, alerting her to the fact, morning had arrived. Actually, she was the first one to awaken from a very restful night of sleep. Then, in realizing the night had come and gone, she slipped quietly out of bed, and took a moment to get dressed while Ricky slept. Needless to say, it was an evening she would always remember however to make sure he continued to pursue her, she wanted to plant the seed of desire into his heart, so rather than wait around until he woke up, she had decided to go home. Surely, if she left now, he would wake up and want her even more. If he didn't, Ricky would not be human. After that, if she didn't miss her guess, his every desire would more than likely lead him directly to her door. At any rate, with that said, she scampered quickly over to his bureau and picked up one of the pens that was lying on top of it. Then, in no more than the blink of an eye, she took a moment to write a short message on the back of an old letter that was sitting on his nightstand. It read as follows:

"My dearest, I am at a loss for words. Not only did you make it a night to remember, but you made it a joy to be with a man again. I really don't know how to thank you for that so I will try to do it this way by putting my feelings into words. You are heaven to me, Ricky. I want you to know that. Never have I enjoyed myself so much in all my life. In fact, you're the first person to ever care for me, and that is greatly appreciated. I mean that sincerely. Perhaps, we'll have an opportunity to do it again sometime. In the meantime, I've got some things I need to take care of at home so don't be misled by the fact I won't be here when you wake up. I love you dearly with all my heart and soul. Please feel free to call me when you get up. I will probably be busy doing something, perhaps, taking care of business however regardless of what I'm doing, don't hesitate to call me if you need something. You know where I live. In fact, you're welcome to come over anytime. Anyway, I have to go now, so for the time being, this is good-bye. Sleep pleasantly my dear. I leave you with many hugs and kisses and certainly all my love. Until we see one another again, take care, Ricky. You're in my thoughts every second of my life now. Love, Maude."

At any rate, with that said, Maude left his bedroom with a world of happiness rampaging through her heart that morning as she ran downstairs and out the front door of his house, leaving behind a night she would remember for as long as she were alive. In fact, she was so darn happy with the way everything went that night that she could have literally done cartwheels all the way across his property and into her own yard that morning. Needless to say, their ever so passionate love making the night before left her with an ever-lasting impression in her heart. Maude was in love, and she felt like she was walking around on cloud nine. In fact, it was a feeling she hadn't ever experienced before, however now that she had there was a very good chance her life would be turned upside down at some point along the way in the days ahead.

Anyway, feeling absolutely wonderful about things, when Maude got home that morning, she headed directly up to her bedroom and stretched out on top of her bed. Upon doing so, after taking a few minutes to reflect on things, she fell back to sleep. Actually, it was still early in the morning anyway so that was what one would expect to happen under circumstances such as this. At any rate, she unintentionally got a little more rest. To be more precise, another two and a half hours of sleep. Anyway, sometime around eight-thirty that morning, the telephone began ringing off the hook again. At this point, being half asleep from having fallen back to sleep, it took her a second or two to realize the situation, then, once that was determined, Maude reached over to the night-stand next to her bed and picked up the telephone because she was anticipating a call from Ricky. Well, sure enough, that's who was calling. In fact, Ricky just wanted her to know that he enjoyed the previous evening as much as she did and that they would do it again sometime. Yes, she thought to herself. That meant a relationship between them was going to go somewhere and perhaps, with any luck at all, it would lead to marriage. At any rate, she thanked him for calling and a moment or two later, their conversation came to an end.

Anyway, after having gotten a couple additional hours of sleep that morning, just as soon as she got off the phone with Ricky, Maude headed into the bathroom to take a shower. Needless to say, she wanted to freshen up a bit before doing anything else. Then, if things continued to go well, she would sit down and read the diary she found beneath the house. At least that's what the plan was anyway. Anyway, once her morning bathroom routine was all taken care of, she headed downstairs to have breakfast. In fact, by now, she was a very hungry woman because she hadn't had anything to eat since yesterday evening, so the only logical thing to do was to fix up a good meal and have something to eat before doing anything else. In this case, a serving of bacon and eggs with a glass of orange juice hit the spot. Anyway, once her hunger had been fully satisfied, she grabbed a pair of reading glasses that were sitting on top of the kitchen countertop and went into the living-room. Needless to say, it was time to read the diary of Charles Winston Kimball I. Obviously, this was something she could do another time, however she was looking for answers to a couple of things that were eating away at the back of her mind, so rather than opting to do it another day, Maude sat down in her easy chair, picked up the diary of Charles Winston Kimball I and began reading the story of a man, who, in all probability knew how everything came to be at her new residence in Tierra Del Mar.

Part III

CHAPTER 14

The diary read as follows: "In the summer of 1848, I, Charles Winston Kimball I, son of Elijah James Kimball, set sail upon the ocean as an indentured servant for a man by the name of Richard Deacon Smith. For the record, the long and arduous journey I was about to head out on began the day I heard that gold had been discovered out in the territory of California. I must say, that was a very big change from the usual run of the mill news that had a tendency to find its way into the port of New Orleans. Most of the time the news was about what President Polk intended to do or about a legislative bill that was kicking around in Congress back east, however this time, that wasn't the case at all. As a matter of fact, everyone living in the city of New Orleans as well as myself at that point in time, immediately welcomed the news as a blessing because that meant there was a good possibility something like that might bring more money into the area. Anyway, as you might think, I began thinking about what that would mean to me if I were to travel out to the California Territory to try and make good for myself by striking it rich. Actually, if I did that I saw it as an opportunity to see the world, and that in itself wouldn't be a bad thing at all. I will say, it sounded like a very favorable thing to do. In fact, just the thought of becoming well to do over the prospect of panning for gold weighed was very agreeable to me. Perhaps, I should also say, I'm the kind of person that likes adventure so when the news of gold being discovered out in the California Territory reached the city of New Orleans, it tickled my fancy so greatly that I was inclined to travel out there and give it a try. At the time I found out about this very extraordinary opportunity I was unmarried and living at home with my family so there wasn't anything holding me back from taking on an adventure like that. Anyway, like you might think, and also what did in fact happen, a friend of mine turned out to be the one who brought the matter to my attention. All I know is within a few days of learning about this great opportunity, the idea of traveling out to the California Territory was all I could think about. Admittedly, I was looking for a profession anyway so with that in mind, at the age of seventeen, I made the decision to join a merchant ship with a crew of seven men. It also goes without saying, at this point in time, everyone aboard the ship had the same objective in mind. We were going to brave the high seas for as long as it took, with the sole intention of making it to the California Territory to strike it rich. It was as simple as that. Actually, what made our upcoming adventure look so promising was after the better part of a year went by, the highly intriguing news of gold being found on the south fork of the American River was still making its way back to the state of Louisiana. As to the validity of that rumor, no one knew for sure, but most of the people living in the area thought it was true because everyone kept saying the same thing. Surely, if all of the seamen passing through the port of New Orleans said that, then it must be true. At any rate, being the kind of person I was, I didn't waste any time setting my mind to thinking about traveling out to the California Territory, and a short time later, as stated before, I made up my mind, this was what I wanted to do. In fact, I had every intention of trying to make good for myself out in the California Territory, so I joined the crew of Richard Deacon Smith, even though I realized there was a very good chance I would never see my home in Louisiana again. Needless to say, the endeavor I was about to embark upon was obviously the chance of a lifetime so rather than debating whether or not I was doing the right thing any longer, I bid my family farewell and we set sail from the port of New Orleans. As you might expect, the voyage our crew set out upon was a very long one indeed. We encountered several storms along the way and each one presented new challenges for us. In fact, for that reason alone, it wasn't an understatement to say, there was a tremendous amount of peril associated with the journey, but in my opinion, the risk was worth taking. At any rate, we managed to weather the storms and about three months later, our crew had the good fortune to make landfall out in the California Territory. It was definitely a very difficult journey for all of us, however someway, somehow, we managed to defy the odds and we eventually made it there. Actually, there were many times along the way when I questioned whether or not I had made the right decision in undertaking a trip like this, but in the end, my fears were eventually laid to rest because we finally made it to the shores of where we intended to go. Thankfully, we persevered the perils of our journey and shortly thereafter, we set our sights on the rolling hills of the Sacramento Valley. Anyway, from what we were told, the odds of striking it rich there were very good. Nevertheless, after stocking up on some supplies in the bustling town of San Francisco, we got our things together, and a short time later, we headed for the Sierra Nevada mountain range with the hope of finding our weight in gold. As a matter of fact, according to the people living in San Francisco County, a relatively unknown place referred to as Sutter's Mill was what we were looking for. Anyway, I didn't doubt for a minute what they were saying about the area. Needless to say, from what we heard, gold had been discovered near a sawmill owned by a man named John Sutter. Anyway, like you might think, we made camp on one of the nearby hills and believe it or not, shortly thereafter, we began panning for gold. As for the rumor, there was an abundance of gold in the area, it wasn't just hearsay. In fact, we literally struck it rich in no time at all. At any rate, with the determination of a raging storm that won't let up when it's hell bent on achieving its goal of a path of destruction, we continued to pan for gold in that area through the fall and well into the next year before we eventually made the decision to move on. Actually, by the time 1849 arrived, people from all over the country were migrating to the area with the intentions of striking it rich, much the same way we had. Anyway, just for that reason alone, the hills of the Sierra Nevada mountain range very quickly came to life as hundreds if not thousands of people rushed to the area to try their luck at panning for gold. Unfortunately, that so-called gold fever was spreading like a wildfire. I hadn't ever seen anything like it before. Everyone was doing the same thing we were and then laying down a claim for the spot they were mining. I guess the only good thing I can say about that is all those claims were legitimate. The area was rich in gold. At any rate, as you can well imagine, it was becoming too crowded for us to continue mining where we'd been over the past eight months, so once again, we got our things together and headed north. The fact of the matter is due to the influx of people hoping to strike it rich, the overall amount of gold we were finding kept getting less and less each day so the logical thing to do was move on. Actually, I don't mean to infer the California Valley wasn't still rich in gold, however it meant there were so many people panning for gold these days that everyone was getting in one another's way. In fact, you might even say, that's when

I realized what a world of wealth will do to a person. It makes them very greedy. Anyway, if for some reason a person was to pan for gold on another person's claim, it would probably get you shot and that was something none of us wanted to deal with. Needless to say, if that happened, everything we worked so hard for since we left the state of Louisiana would've all been in vain. At any rate, not knowing what else to do, at the end of July that year we made the decision to return to the city of San Francisco. It was the only logical thing to do. Captain Smith's plan was to go up the coast a ways in search of a better spot to pan for gold however due to some unfortunate circumstances, things didn't go the way we wanted it too. Well, as fate would have it, shortly after we left the booming town of San Francisco, our crew encountered a bad storm. Anyway, as it turns out, our vessel got swept away in the raging fury of that cursed storm and we ended up being shipwrecked on the northern coast of the Oregon Territory. Obviously, the only good thing I can say about the incident is that we survived the storm. At any rate, with a good amount of luck, we managed to save most of the wealth we accumulated down in the California Territory even though because of the ill-fated way everything unfolded, I didn't think that was going to be possible however we succeeded in doing that as well. Anyway, we were now stranded in an area that had not been settled. That was kind of scary to me because we were literally lost in the wilderness of what would eventually become the state of Oregon. Needless to say, because of what happened, our original plan was no longer doable. In fact, shortly after we made it onto shore, it also became apparent, we had a long hard road ahead of us. Anyway, with nothing at all going in the right direction, it was quickly agreed upon, the best thing to do would be to hide all of our wealth up in the Oregon Territory, and then head back down the coast to the soon to be state of California. If we had tried to carry the money we brought with us back to San Francisco, the burden would've been too great because the coins were very heavy. Even if we had been able to construct a couple of sturdy carts to haul the coins down the coast, it still would have been too hard to do. At any rate, a short time later, one of the men discovered a cave on the side of a cliff, not far away from where we ran into the unfortunate circumstances of running aground. Needless to say, it was an ideal place to hide all of the money we brought with us. Anyway, after an early morning breakfast the following day, Captain Smith suggested we begin the long and tedious task of hauling away the money we accumulated during our stay in the California Territory to the safety of a well-hidden cave we found on the shores of the Oregon Territory. The truth of the matter is if we actually made it back to San Francisco, we could always retrieve the money at a later time so with that in mind, the seven of us worked very hard at getting all that money taken care of and by the time sun set that day, we had succeeded in getting everything stashed away in the cave. Furthermore, in the course of a few hours, our crew had managed to completely cover up the entrance to the cave with a fairly good amount of debris that had been lying around on the ground so there wasn't any way a person would ever know that a cave was there. Anyway, soon one of the men started a fire and we feasted on a little deer meat that one of the other men got for us. Needless to say, it was the end of a very challenging day for all of us and one that didn't come without a lot of hard work. Anyway, shortly after having a bite to eat, we settled in for the night, however not before we reached a mutual agreement not to tell a soul about what we hid inside the cave. Obviously, the plan was to come back and get the wealth we left behind at some point down the road however that was really nothing more than optimistic speculation on our part. Actually, for what it's worth, none of us knew exactly how much wealth was left behind there, however if I were a betting person, it was more than likely enough to make every one of us a rich man. Anyway, no sooner did the sun rise the following day, and the seven of us started the long arduous journey back down the coast to the California Territory. In fact, to be more precise, we were on our way back to bustling city of San Francisco and for the most part everything went very well until a small group of Indian braves ambushed us one night. Needless to say, we did our best to defend ourselves however in a matter of ten minutes, George and Jacob lost their lives to the savages. Like you might expect, we gave them a decent burial and then, we headed on our way again. Anyway, after a couple more days of foraging through the wilderness, the rest of our original group of seven men made it back to the California Territory. At this point, I would also like to say, that was about the time, I began thinking about starting a new endeavor. Needless to say, with all that money buried up in the Oregon Territory, starting a business of my own sounded like a good thing to do. In fact, from the perspective of a future businessman, and due to the booming economy in the San Francisco area, I thought it would be an easy thing to do. The truth of the matter is I didn't have anything to lose, so with that in mind and more set in my ways than I had ever been in my life, I began making plans to go into business for myself as the year of 1849 came to an end."

At this point, Maude looked up from the diary she was reading and rubbed her eyes for a moment. Miracles do happen every now and then, she thought to herself as she began to ponder the first part of the diary. In fact, it was actually amazing that the life story of a man like Charles Winston Kimball I had been preserved down beneath her property for so many years without the least bit of knowledge of its existence. For whatever the reason, you would've thought someone would have known about it, however that obviously didn't turn out to be the case. Anyway, like you might expect, her eyes were beginning to burn a little from all of the intense reading she had been doing over the past couple of hours so she set the diary down upon the table that was sitting in front of her and went into the kitchen to make herself a cup of coffee. Needless to say, a break was in order. At least, a short one was anyway so after brewing a fresh pot of coffee and taking a moment to get a couple of donuts out of one of the kitchen cabinets, she sat down at the table and had a snack. For more than one reason, Maude didn't usually do that during the day but every so often when the urge hit her, she would. Like most women, she was always concerned about her weight, and since donuts were fattening, she didn't normally opt for a lunch of that nature. More often than not, it was something like yogurt or a little fruit. In this particular case, it was nothing of the sort however she kept telling herself a person has to splurge every once in a while and that seemed to satisfy her ego, so everything was fine. Furthermore, right at the moment, Maude had a lot on her mind however that wasn't anything unusual for her. In fact, quite frankly, it was par for the course for her. Not only was she all wrapped up in the reading of this diary, but it just so happens, she had a crush on Ricky Vestellini as well. Actually, what complicated things to some degree was Ricky was a very passionate man. Not that something like that is a bad thing but she couldn't get him off her mind so it was extremely hard for her to concentrate on the diary. On the other hand, the only way she was ever going to find out how all those gold and silver coins ended up down beneath her house was to read on so with that in mind, after a quick trip to the bathroom to freshen up a little, she went back into the living-room to read more of the diary. Actually, with all due honesty, Maude was hoping to finish reading it before supper that evening, so without any further ado, she picked the diary back up, and began foraging through its pages to try and unravel the mystery surrounding the old Kimball mansion.

The diary read as follows: "Anyway, shortly after making it back to the ever-growing city of San Francisco, some more bad luck bit our crew in the ass. In fact, as much as I hate to say it, everything took another turn for the worse when Captain Smith got into a bad argument with one of the members of our crew. Actually, I wasn't there when the incident happened, but I was glad I didn't see the fight because I got along well with all of Captain Smith's men. At any rate, as it turns out, on this occasion what actually saved me from witnessing the unfortunate incident was the fact, I don't like playing cards. Anyway, from what I was told, Captain Smith murdered two of the men over a lousy game of poker. In fact, when I found out about this, it didn't surprise me any because of the nature of a couple of the men. According to the bartender of the saloon where the card game was being played, one of the men tried to cheat Captain Smith out of some money. Well, in my opinion, regardless of who you're playing cards against in a hand of poker, that's not a wise thing to do. Anyway, from what I heard, Stephen took the side of the man who was trying to cheat Captain Smith out of money and as fate would have it, shortly thereafter, it was all over because Captain Smith shot them both dead. Actually, John was the name of the other man who lost his life in that unfortunate card game. In fact, the third individual involved in the card game that night was Thomas, who, according to one of the eyewitnesses at the saloon, ran off down the street in fear of his life and since he was somewhat of a coward, it was highly unlikely we would ever see him again. As for myself, well, I didn't want anything to do with their darn poker game that evening. First of all, I very rarely gamble at anything and secondly, I don't like to play cards anyway. If I had, there was a good possibility I would've come out on the short end of the game too and that would have meant losing everything I own. Needless to say, that's not what I had in mind. In fact, quite frankly, with circumstances as they were, I would've probably lost my life as well. The truth of the matter is the rest of the men in our group were gambling on the premise of they would win some more money and the end result of that was none of them lived long enough to see what they had worked so hard for. At any rate, Captain Smith and I were the only ones left from the original crew of seven men that set sail from the port of New Orleans in 1848 that were still alive now. Actually, believe it or not, it gets even more grievous than that. Anyway, as fate would have it, immediately following that unfortunate game of cards, Captain Smith took to the whiskey bottle that evening and got drunker than a skunk before heading back to his room at the Cheyenne Saloon. Normally, that was something he slept off during the course of the night, but not this time. For some unexplained reason, he must have made a miscalculation on his intake of alcohol because when I went to see him the following day, he was lying unconscious on the floor of his room. At any rate, as you might expect, I immediately checked for a pulse but there wasn't any. In fact, he wasn't breathing at all. Anyway, based upon what I saw, I would say our fearless leader drank too much whiskey and passed away during the night in a degrading drunken stupor. Furthermore, since there wasn't any visible sign of a gunshot wound, I was quick to assume, he drank himself to death. Of course, that didn't really come as any surprise to me because I knew Captain Smith was a very mindless carefree man who often drank too much whiskey even under normal circumstances, so that's more than likely what happened to him. Anyway, upon learning of the unfortunate matter, I made a quick trip over to the sheriff's office and explained to him the situation and also what I thought might have happened however he was quick to point out, things of this nature happen all the time in San Francisco. I guess, due to the steady influx of miners in to the area, it was a very common, everyday occurrence there so he wasn't concerned about what happened. Actually, to be perfectly honest with you, regardless of what the sheriff told me, I had no desire to know any more about what happened to Captain Smith. Granted, it was unfortunate something like this ever came about but it was all water under the bridge now. As for myself, at this point, I had a decision to make because I was the only one left alive from our crew of seven men, so it was up to me to decide what was to become of all the wealth that was buried up in the Oregon Territory. Needless to say, even though there was enough money up there to have made all of us rich, right at the moment, I only had to be concerned for myself. As you might think, in a way that was good, not that I was greedy or anything like that, however it made things a whole lot easier for me because the way things stood now, there wasn't going to be any disagreement as to who gets what when it came time to divvy up the wealth. Actually, I was expecting a problem in that area when the seven of us sat down to do that, however due to recent developments, there wasn't any reason to be concerned about that anymore because I was the only one left to make a claim on the money. It was as simple as that. Anyway, immediately following Captain Smith's death, I began thinking about the situation in more depth. Surely, if anyone knew I had attained so much wealth from mining, I would've been in a very enviable position. Actually, I thought I was the only one who knew about the money stashed up in the Oregon Territory however at this point, I also realized, I hadn't taken everything into consideration. In fact, to be more precise, I made a miscalculation on something. To the best of my knowledge, Thomas Johnston was still living. He was the other man that took part in that tragic card game with Captain Smith. In my opinion, he was a poor excuse for a man because he usually got everyone to do his work for him. In addition to that, as I said before, he was a cowardly man. Why Captain Smith ever chose him to be a part of our crew is beyond me. Anyway, it was my understanding, he was still alive. At first, I was slightly alarmed by that revelation because Thomas Johnston knew where the money up in the Oregon Territory was hidden. If it weren't for that, I couldn't have cared less where he ran off too. At any rate, that's when I remembered what the sheriff told me about the city of San Francisco. He said, gambling, prostitution and murder were all very common occurrences in the California Territory so I looked into the matter through his office and made the unique discovery, Thomas Johnston had been murdered as well. I guess, according to someone who witnessed that unfortunate event, when Thomas fled the card that night, one of the local area miners thought he had a lot of money on him however upon learning he didn't really have any money on him at all, he shot him dead. Of all the possible things that could have happened. In fact, it was damn near unbelievable however I wasn't about to argue with the law enforcement in San Francisco, so I let things be as they were. In reality, I did not have any reason to doubt the sheriff, so I was content with what he told me. In fact, if I were to think about it, had Thomas lived, he was such a poorly structured man, I probably didn't have anything to worry about anyway because if he headed up to the Oregon Territory on his own, he wouldn't have survived the ordeal. I am sure of that. On my honor, he would have more than likely met his match when he was confronted with the perils of the wilderness. Anyway, at this point, I was convinced I didn't have anything to be concerned about, so I made the decision to go ahead with my original plan to venture into a business of my own. Actually, it was something I had been giving a lot of thought too for some time. Anyway, I applied for a loan through a bank in San Francisco and a couple of weeks later, I got the financial backing I needed to purchase a small boat. My objective was to start a merchant goods business. In addition to that, in order to get my business up and running, there was a need to lease building space for the entrepreneurship I was entering into, so I did that as well. Then, after the purchase of another boat so I could move goods up and down the coast, a short time later, you might say, I was officially in business. Actually, I thought the city of San Francisco was an ideal place to get a new business off the ground and unless something proved to me otherwise, that's how I looked at it. Anyway, regardless of how everything eventually turned out in the days ahead, I wanted to try and make a go of it on my own. In fact, quite frankly, I would have been ashamed of myself had I not tried to do so. In this case, I can assuredly say, pride had a lot to do with it, in addition to my strong desire to succeed in life. I have always been that kind of person and it's very likely that will ever change."

"Anyway, one day while I was out taking care of business, I stopped into one of the local saloons in

San Francisco to get something to eat. As it turns out, a very pretty young lady, by the name of Monica Shawl was working there as a waitress. Anyway, as fate would have it, Monica came over to my table that day and immediately struck up a conversation with me. Not only did she take my order for lunch but within minutes of bringing the food back to my table, the two of us were engaged in conversation. Anyway, one thing quickly led to another and before I realized it, I had asked her to marry me. Generally speaking, I am not the kind of person who rushes into anything, nor do I actually believe in love at first sight however in this particular instance, that is what happened. In fact, I was so infatuated with her that she literally blew the socks off my feet in the blink of an eyelash. Needless to say, that led me to assume, there must've been some type of instantaneous combustion between us because it did not take me very long to realize this was the woman I wanted to spend the rest of my life with. Anyway, much to my surprise she quickly accepted my proposal of marriage and agreed to become my lawfully wedded wife. With all do honesty, that was something I hadn't counted on however circumstances as they were, things fell into place really well. In fact, it turned out to be one of the best decisions I ever made. Not only was Monica a very pretty woman but she had a dynamic personality as well. Anyway, from that point on, my heart belonged to her. If she breathed, I breathed. If she smiled, I smiled. She was my reason for living now and I was happier than I had ever been in my life.

At any rate, about a week later, on a very pleasant day in the spring of 1850, Monica and I took our marriage vows. It was the pleasantest of days and I'd had all of a week to think about it so there wasn't a lot of time to do anything. In fact, since, I had a business to oversee now, we chose to make our home up overhead of my merchant goods store so I would be able to keep an eye on things from there. In reality, because the business climate in San Francisco was booming better than ever these days, I thought it was a wise thing to do. Furthermore, I was fairly certain my merchant goods business would do well. Call it a hunch or just a lucky guess, it didn't really matter. The end result would be the same. With gold being discovered to the east of the bustling community of San Francisco, there was all kinds of money in the area. For that reason, I did not think I would run into any problems maintaining my business. As a matter of fact, between what I had for wealth stashed away up in the Oregon Territory and with what I would more than likely be taking in for revenue with my new business, chances are, I was going to be financially well to do in the days ahead. Needless to say, the odds were in my favor for not having to be concerned about monetary issues anymore and I was very thankful for that."

"In other matters, there were a lot of really noteworthy things going on that year. First of all, the gold rush that began a year earlier was still going strong. Most of the miners panning for gold in the Sacramento Valley were still striking it rich. In fact, the area was growing so frigging fast it could not actually accommodate the number of people moving into the area. In addition to that, there was a lot of talk about enacting legislation to make the California Territory a state and it goes without saying, if the legislators back east ever got around to doing that, the people living in the area would benefit greatly. Actually, I thought it was the right thing to do. Of course, like most things in life, there's always pros and cons to a matter but in this case, I thought the benefits of doing that far outweighed the negative side to the whole thing. Anyway, while this was going on in the United States, I concluded, I would not be going back to the state of Louisiana after all. As stated before, Monica was my reason for living these days so my profound desire to return to my parent's home in Louisiana no longer took precedent. Obviously, it would have been nice to see them again however I had other obligations now. In fact, quite frankly, a lot had happened to me since I journeyed out west. Between starting a new business and looking forward to building a new life for myself with Monica, there really wasn't a lot of time to do anything. Don't get me wrong, I didn't have any misgivings about having done either one of those things and I'm certain if my family knew how happy I was here, they would have understood my decision to remain in the California Territory. Anyway, as it turns out, later in the year, the territory became the thirty-first state of the United States. Needless to say, when the law was enacted, there was all kinds of celebrations going on in the area however I didn't participate in any of them because the business I was engaged in kept me busy most of the time. Monica got out and did a little shopping at one of their festive bazaars, but other than that life didn't change any for us. It was business as usual, and we spent as much time together as possible enjoying one another's company. At this point, I changed the name of my company's boat to the Monica Lee. Actually, after giving it a good deal of thought, I came to the conclusion, it was only fitting for me to do that because I loved Monica dearly, and she would be my inspiration in everything I did for many years to come. Anyway, as anticipated, my merchant goods business continued to be a very profitable investment for me. In fact, I had a hunch a business like that would do well in the city of San Francisco and it turns out, I was right about that. It was indeed turning out to be one of the best decisions I ever made. Not only did I not have any regrets about doing that, but with Monica being very supportive of me in everything I did, I could honestly say, I felt really good about myself and what I was doing."

"Anyway, our first child was born in December of 1850, about a week before Christmas, and I have to say, it was the single greatest moment of my life. Monica gave birth to a little boy, and I don't ever remember being any happier than I was that day. As for our newborn son, I got to name him and that was something I was very proud of as well. Well, what can I say? I loved and respected my father very much so after giving it a little thought, I chose to name him Charles Winston Kimball II. Actually, my father's name was Charles and my uncle's name was Winston so I thought combining the two names was only fitting. Not only would the child be named after myself but it would bear the names of the other two men as well. Anyway, as for everything else that was going on at the time, nothing significant happened. With the exception of our child, life had returned to normal for us. I was usually busy at the shop while Monica took care of all those things at home. In fact, it was sort of a routine for both of us. On Sunday mornings, we attended church and in the afternoon we usually went for a picnic at a nearby lake. Those days were some of the best days of my life and I'm sure Monica felt the same way about that as I did. Anyway, in the days ahead, time went by quickly however in the due course of a person's life that really isn't anything unusual. In fact, I'm sure I don't have to tell you time goes by so fast that sometimes it passes us by before we even have a chance to live it. Unfortunately, that's the reality of it all and there isn't any way to change that. In being human, you will live, you'll die and at some point in your life, you'll get buried beneath the earth. That's life! Perhaps, the only saving grace of it all is the seeds you sow along the way, both physically and spiritually. Anyway, as it turns out, over the course of the next four years our family grew threefold. Monica gave birth to a couple more children. To be more precise, she had two girls. We named them Annabel and Rebekah. I guess the only bad thing I can say about that is, with business matters that had to be taken care of from one day to the next, I couldn't spend as much time as I would have like to with them, however a person can't be in two places at one time, and such was the case here as well."

"Anyway, the business I owned (Kimball's Merchant Goods Service) grew with leaps and bounds in the years ahead however by the time 1854 arrived, the gold rush was gradually coming to an end. At this point in my life, I began looking down the road a ways, not being sure of what I was going to do next. Once again, after giving it a lot of careful thought, I made the decision to purchase a small variety goods store. To be honest with you, I didn't need to do that however due to the fact I loved what I was doing, I thought I would expand my operations to include a store as well. Needless to say, it would supplement my already profitable merchant goods service and as a result of doing this, I very quickly realized, it would add even more money to the coffers I was already in the process of putting together for my family. At any rate, one thing often leads to the act of doing another and such was the case this time as well because I began moving more goods up and down the coast of California. The fact of the matter is that's what I originally planned to do anyway, so it fit in really well with the plans I had for my business. Even with the better part of the gold rush having come to an end, business was booming in

San Francisco, and I was soon making money faster than I could take it in."

"Anyway, as time went by, I began wondering whether or not I would be able to find the money that was buried up in the Oregon Territory. In addition to that, I was busier than I would have preferred to have been these days, but with all due honesty, I was trying to look out for my family and what the future held for them. Anyway, with that said, I wasn't certain if I would be able to find the time to go up there and retrieve it. Obviously, that was the only way that would happen, and I didn't have to think about it anymore to realize that. In fact, nearly five years had passed by since I was roaming around in the wilderness of the Oregon Territory. It didn't seem like it had been that long, but it had. At any rate, what complicated matters to some degree was Monica didn't know anything about the money up in the Oregon Territory so without a practical reason for going there, I couldn't justify making a trip up there to get it. In all actuality, without telling her the gods honest truth about the wealth of money that was up there, I was sorely afraid she would think I had another woman so I wasn't sure how I should approach the matter. Now, I would also like to say, I really and truly believe Monica would be better off if she didn't have any knowledge of the money in the Oregon Territory. Like most things in life, money tends to breed greed, jealousy, and eventually power. In fact, it's the reason why I didn't say a word about it to anyone, not even Monica. In her case, I was sorely afraid something might happen to her. If one of the lowlife individuals in the area knew I was rich, it might prompt them to abduct her or one of my kids and hold them for ransom. Needless to say, I didn't want to take any chances on that happening, so I kept my mouth shut about it and bore the responsibility of my actions regardless of whether or not that was the right thing to do. Actually, if I didn't miss my guess, if word ever get around there was that kind of wealth up there and they knew I was the owner of it, there was a very good possibility I wouldn't be around very long. At the very least, it would have been the cause of a lot of problems for me and that was something I didn't want to deal with. Anyway, as I am sure you have already surmised by now, shortly after returning to the California Territory in 1849, I realized rather quickly that I didn't have to travel back up to the Oregon Territory for that money if I didn't want too. Between having a little more luck panning for gold, and engaging in a profitable business of my own, I no longer had any need for that wealth. In fact, quite frankly, at this point in my life, I was so financially well off that I was able to purchase anything I wanted with cash these days, so I didn't have to take out a loan to buy anything anymore. Of course, if I wanted credit, it was always there for the taking but with all due honesty that was an option these days. Needless to say, that left me with a really good feeling inside, knowing I didn't have to ask for credit from a bank anymore. Anyway, before I ramble on any further about something else, I would also like to say, I still wanted to return to the Oregon Territory if the right opportunity ever came along. Obviously, it would be a crying shame not to do something with all that hard earned money that was stashed up in the wilderness there even though most of that wealth never actually belonged to me. At any rate, regardless of the unusual circumstances surrounding my unyielding desire to do that, somewhere down the road, I would have to make a decision on the matter. For the time being, I thought it was best to wait a little while longer before taking on an undertaking as challenge-some as that."

"In other matters, the summer of 1854 was soon all but history and yet another year came to an end. Everything was going really well for me and the business I owned was thriving better than ever now even though the gold rush in California had officially come to an end. Needless to say, for as long as people are around there will always be a need for food, clothing, and shelter so my merchant goods business continued to do really well. In fact, it had everything to do with the reason why I wanted to go into that kind of business in the first place. It was actually a recession proof business and like you might think, with important matters like that, a person should always take something like that into consideration. Anyway, everything was working out very well and I couldn't have been more pleased about that. It was during this period of time that Monica gave birth to our fourth child. It was a boy. We named him William after her father. Needless to say, at this point in our marriage, we now had two boys and two girls. In reality, I wanted to have one more child anyway and having another son fared well with not only me but Monica as well, so it worked out well for us. Obviously, that meant more responsibility for me, but I didn't mind that. I enjoyed being a father so like the old expression goes, the more the merrier actually fit in really well with my personality. I didn't have any complaints and I don't think Monica had any either."

"Anyway, once again, in other matters, I eventually got around to changing the name of my business to an even more prestigious name by calling my business Kimball and Son. It was actually something I had intended to do for some time but because of business obligations, I was not able to do that until now. Like I said before, being in business for myself kept me very busy. In fact, so much so that I had a hard time getting things done around the house. As for the rest of my business ventures, when I expanded my business to include a general goods store, I also built us a much bigger and more comfortable house to live in as well. Actually, believe it or not, I was a carpenter's apprentice by trade before leaving the state of Louisiana anyway so building things came easy to me. At any rate, William was the last child Monica had. Regrettably, even though we both had a very strong desire to have more children, a short time later, we found out Monica wasn't able to have any more kids. Her doctor told us, if we tried to have another child, Monica could very well lose her life so with the saddest of hearts, we took his advice, and decided not to pursue that endeavor any longer. Needless to say, that was extremely disappointing to both of us however neither one of us wanted to take a chance on having something happen, so we let things be as they were and we immediately abandoned all efforts to have another child. Actually, like a true gentleman, if I were to think about it, it wasn't the end of the world. We still had each other, and four beautiful children so I was content, however as disappointing as that news was, Monica took what the doctor told us very badly and from that point on she seemed to be off in a world of her own. Perhaps, I should say, I quickly assumed that was due to her inability to have any more children. If for some reason she was suffering from something other than that, I wasn't aware of it at the time. Anyway, life continued on as usual, and we enjoyed out time together as a family."

"Now, as for what was going on in the world around us, in particularly, the United States, by the time the decade came to an end, the concept of slavery was becoming a major problem in the southern part of our country. Actually, it was my profound understanding that the majority of the southern states wanted to break away from the rest of the United States because slavery was a way of life for them and they didn't have any desire to change that. Of course, the northern states took opposition to that, believing very strongly that slavery should be abolished and even though I was from the state of Louisiana, I thought slavery should be abolished too. Anyway, there was a major difference of opinion on this matter these days. The north and south were divided on the issue, and it looked like there wasn't going to be any solution to the problem unless they went to war over the matter. Out here in California, slavery was prohibited and had been for the past ten years however back east, things were really beginning to heat up because no one could agree on a solution to the problem. Anyway, at no surprise to anyone, shortly thereafter, war broke out in the eastern half of the United States. At this point, the country was literally divided right in two. I really hated to see that happen, but it was undeniably the fate and destiny of this country. As a matter of fact, the whole unfortunate matter rested on the shoulders of President Lincoln. It was obviously up to him to fix the problem although I have to admit, that wasn't going to be an easy thing to do. The goal and objective was to try and keep the United States of America together as a union, however if that actually came about, in the end, it was going to be at the price of a lot of bloodshed. Needless to say, the southern states just simply wouldn't give up the use of slaves, so an awful battle ensued. In fact, not one battle but many. It was definitely a very sad time for this country and all I could do out here in the state of California was to try and keep informed of what was going back east. Needless to say, at this point in my life, memories of my family in the state of Louisiana kept inundating my mind with some of the most pleasant of thoughts imaginable. I was constantly wondering how they were doing these days and because of the war that was going on, I was extremely concerned something might happen to them. Needless to say, I had a family of my own now or I would've probably journeyed home to see them. As a matter of fact, I'd be willing to bet both of my brothers were fighting on the side of the Confederate States, however I didn't have any way to confirm that. It was an assumption on my part. Unfortunately, news was very slow at making its way out to the state of California, so I wasn't sure what was going on in that part of the country. Anyway, as fate would have it, sometime in June of 1865, news reached the state of California that the north won the war. Obviously, it was great news for anyone who believed in freedom and equality. More importantly, thanks to the effort of Abraham Lincoln to preserve the union, we were still the United States of America. Unfortunately, a lot of blood had been shed in order to keep this country undivided and many lives were lost in that horrible cause however in the end, Old Glory prevailed and perhaps, that's all that really mattered. As for me, a month later, I learned that one of my brother's as well as my father lost their lives in that terrible war. It was very disheartening news however there wasn't anything I could have done to change what happened. Actually, according to the letter I received from my sister, Mabel, she said other than that, the rest of my family was fine. Obviously, that was good news as well. At this point, I was beginning to give some very serious thought to going back to Louisiana for a visit if Monica and the kids were up to it. Needless to say, I would get one of the guys at work to look after my business while I was away, and everything should work out fine. Sadly, not too long after that I received more bad news. One day, shortly after getting home from work, I learned Monica had contracted some type of incurable disease. Well, at first, I cried, then I took to banging my head against the wall of my office to see if I could knock some blessed sense into my highly distressed mind however it was to no avail. I couldn't stop thinking about Monica's diagnosis. In fact, you might say, I was hit with a bad bout of despair for the very first time in my life. I was devastated beyond what any words could say because Monica had only two more years to live. At any rate, like a dedicated husband, I supported her every step of the way through her untimely battle with the disease she was fighting however in the fall of 1868, she fell gravely ill and died. There was nothing more I could do however for what it's worth, Monica lasted a year longer than the doctor said she would. That wasn't necessarily a good thing, but it was the reality of what happened. In fact, over the course of the past year and a half, as her health declined, she got terribly thin, and it was painful to see her suffer, but that was the nature of the disease her body was fighting. As for me, it was a very hard thing to deal with and shortly after Monica passed away, I began feeling a bit lonely for the first time in as long as I could remember but considering the circumstances that was actually quite understandable. Monica and I had been the best of friends for years and even though the kids were still around, it wasn't the same anymore without her. In fact, quite frankly, it was the first time I ever had to deal with death and like you might think, I didn't care for it too much. Anyway, as time went by, I began to gradually withdraw from the public until I woke up one day and realized there wasn't any kind of human feeling left in my body. I was emotionally exhausted, distraught, and even took to drinking alcohol, which was something I very rarely did. At this point, it became apparent, I was going to have to let go of Monica or I wasn't going to be around much longer myself. Unfortunately, some things are easier said than done though, and in this particular case, that's how it was with me as well. Anyway, in realizing this, I finally made a decision on something I had been wanting to do for years. I was going to travel up to the state of Oregon. First of all, it would give me an opportunity to unearth the wealth that was buried there, and secondly, with any kind of luck at all, I would be able to start a new life for myself there too. It was a decision long in the making however if I ever had any intentions of doing that, now was the time to do so. Anyway, with that in mind and with much regret, a couple of weeks later, I put my business up for sale with the intentions of going to Oregon. Actually, had I done this in years past, it would have been to just get what I had for money up there however with circumstances as they were now, I intended to live there."

"Anyway, in the days ahead, I moved my family up the coast a ways to the beautiful state of Oregon. In fact, it was actually something I thought about doing many times over the past few years, however I had decided against it for reasons only known to me. At any rate, since Monica was no longer around, my reason for not wanting to do that had changed so there wasn't anything holding me back from doing that now. Anyway, that's what I set out to do and as anticipated, the endeavor took some time to accomplish and not without some more hard work however from my perspective, it was the only logical thing to do. At any rate, shortly after returning to the area our boat ran aground in 1850, I soon realized no one had found the money that was buried there. For me, that didn't come as any surprise because the money was very well hidden. Needless to say, I knew that when it was buried there nearly twenty years ago. Anyway, like I said before, I had no need for that wealth these days, nevertheless, I still wanted to unearth the money that was buried there. In fact, I planned to leave the money to my children when I passed away, and considering the circumstances, that was the best thing to do."

At this point, Maude paused from the reading of the diary again. Actually, her eyes were beginning to smart a little from all of the intense reading she had done over the past few minutes, so it was necessary she take another break. In fact, if Maude didn't do that, there wasn't any way she would be able to finish reading the diary before dinner and that wasn't what she had in mind at all. At any rate, after thinking about it for a moment or two, she quickly concluded, instead of having another cup of coffee, she would read on, so she picked the diary back up, turned another page and continued reading.

"My oldest son and I built our new home from the foundation up in the summer of 1870. Actually, I put a lot of thought into how I was going to do this, and I came to the conclusion, the house would be built directly over the cave where the money was buried. Admittedly, that made things a lot easier for me. In fact, quite frankly, by doing it this way, I wouldn't need to move the money. As you can well imagine, the coins that were buried there were not light. Furthermore, I could only surmise, due to the overall quantity of coins, regardless of their face value, there must have been thousands of dollars there. Anyway, since, the better part of the area we settled in was still nothing more than a vast wilderness, I thought it would be a good idea to store that wealth in a safe place. Well, that is where I came up with the idea to bury it down beneath the house. This way, not only was the money safe but I didn't have to move it either. Needless to say, I liked the idea a lot, and by doing things this way, no one would ever have any knowledge the money even existed except me and my children. At any rate, it took us about three months to build the house and a little more time than that went into the overall construction of it. In the end, I felt the time that was spent on building it was well worth it. In fact, I'm sure most people would've thought I was off my rocker by doing what I did however in my opinion taking this course of action was a wise thing to do. Needless to say, it would have been way too difficult to explain how I came to own that kind of wealth. Actually, the way I saw that was, too many years had gone by since the gold rush of 1849 happened so I was afraid someone would think I robbed a bank. In addition to that, no one in the state of Oregon knew I had a profitable business back in the state of California so that would only add even more mystery to how I attained that much money. Anyway, for that reason alone, I thought what I did was the best thing to do. I suppose a person could inherit that kind of wealth however that wasn't going to solve any of the problems that would arise from the knowledge I was a very rich man, so I decided against telling anyone about the money. Actually, my oldest son was the only one I really confided in on this matter. Eventually, I made my other three children aware of the wealth I came to amass over the years, but I did not elaborate on how I attained it, nor did I say where it was stored. For all they knew, the money had been deposited in a bank somewhere. As I said before, the less anyone knew about the wealth, the better chance there was no one would ever get harmed over its existence. Anyway, since my oldest son agreed to share the wealth with my other three children when I passed away, I was satisfied. Actually, I made one other request to my oldest son before I died and that was to bury me down beneath the house at the time of my death. Believe it or not, I didn't want to be buried in San Francisco with Monica. Too many fond memories were left behind there for me to do that. Perhaps, that wasn't looking at things the right way but that's how I wanted to do it and that's the way everything was going to end. At this point, perhaps, I should say, there isn't too much more I can say about what I did or didn't do in life, nor how I became such a wealthy man. For the most part, I lived a good life. Neither did I have any regrets about anything I did and I earned every penny of the money I left behind to my children. Other than that, I guess it's fair to say, this is where the story ends for me. The house in the state of Oregon as well as all of the wealth associated with it, in addition to my family legacy, I bequeathed to my oldest son, Charles Winston Kimball II. Like I have stated before, I left it entirely up to him as to what he did with the money however he promised to share everything with the other three kids, and I didn't have any reason to think he would do otherwise. Needless to say, my oldest son is a very trustworthy man so I had all the faith in the world in him to see to it that his younger siblings were looked out for as well. Now, as much as I hate to say it the time has come to say good-bye. Anyway, with the heaviest of hearts, and with great regret, I leave this world behind so this is my last and final entry into my diary. I really and truly hope all of the wealth I attained through the years is used wisely. Regrettably, I have fallen into ill health these days, much the same way my dear sweet wife Monica did. At any rate, without having any other options available to me, at this point in my life, I bid my children, the rest of this world and the individual who reads this diary farewell. Sincerely, Charles Winston Kimball I."

It was the last entry made into the diary of Charles Winston Kimball I. By now, she felt a justifiable urge to shout with glee at having figured things out as she glanced over at the clock on the living-room wall to see what time it was. It was a little after the hour of five o'clock. Almost supper time, she thought to herself. As always, the afternoon had gone by very quickly but being engaged in the reading of the diary had given her reason to remain relaxed for a good part of that time. In fact, it had actually allowed her to finish reading the diary. At any rate, she was starting to get hungry, so she set the diary down upon the table next to her easy chair and headed into the kitchen to find something for supper. Fortunately for her, there was some left-over pizza kicking around in the refrigerator, so she didn't have to cook anything up for supper. As a matter of fact, in case this wasn't stated before, pizza was one of her comfort foods anyway so she feasted away on the remains of her well received lunch. Tomorrow, she would more than likely fix up a good meal for herself however in the meantime, her hunger had to be satisfied so that's where a couple slices of pizza came in. Anyway, once lunch was all taken care of, she began thinking about the diary of Charles Winston Kimball I. Not only was it an interesting story but it also shed light on how everything at her newly acquired estate came to be. It appears, Charles Winston Kimball II had a son or possibly, a daughter and then passed away before they had a chance to tell anyone in the family about what was buried beneath the house. Furthermore, since, the house was referred to as the old Kimball mansion by everyone in the area, one would assume, the house remained in the family throughout the years. In fact, it was more than likely the reason why Charles Winston Kimball III or another member of the family didn't have any knowledge of anything. It was also most probable, Charles Winston Kimball II had a son, and not only would his name been Charles Winston Kimball III, but he would have also been literally sitting on a gold mine he didn't know existed. Of course, that was speculation on her part but that's what the diary seemed to indicate. Furthermore, whoever this person was, they more than likely made their residence there without any knowledge their grandfather was buried there. In fact, from what she could deduce, Charles Winston Kimball II died unexpectedly, because not only was he supposed to bury his father in a tomb beneath the house, but he was also supposed to distribute all of the wealth that was buried there with his siblings. Since that never happened, Maude concluded, Charles Winston Kimball II died unexpectedly, perhaps from a heart attack or from a fatal injury he may have gotten from an unexpected accident. Obviously, no one in their right mind would've left that kind of wealth behind without putting it to good use so Maude concluded, the heir of Charles Winston Kimball II didn't know anything about the coins that were buried beneath the house. Sadly, none of that wealth was passed onto any of the members of the family. That was actually a crying shame but that's how life turns out sometimes. At this point, it's also safe to say, as a result of what Maude discovered beneath her house, she was now an even wealthier person. For the time being, those old gold and silver coins would have to remain where they were however given a little time, she was going to look into how much they were worth. Needless to say, because of the time of day, that wasn't going to happen now though. In fact, with it being late in the day, Maude was going to watch television for a little while and then go to bed. That is what she usually did at this time of the day anyway so with everything seemingly under control and most certainly explained, she took to watching television for a couple of hours. At this point, it should also be noted, her mind was a little restless. I guess between absorbing the contents Charles Winston Kimball III's diary and having a new love interest, you might say, she was mulling things over inside her head some more. Actually, it wasn't anything unusual for Maude to do that however it created problems for her from time to time. At any rate, after keeping up with the local and national news that was on television and taking in a couple comedic sit-com's, she eventually called it a day. Like always, tomorrow would be here a lot sooner than she would prefer it to be so she with that in mind, she headed off to bed to try and get some sleep.

CHAPTER 15

Early next morning, sometime around 8:00 o'clock, Maude was abruptly awakened from her night's sleep, when the telephone next to her bed rang. Startled and half asleep, she began to wonder who was calling at such an early hour in the day. Needless to say, anyone who knew her would have realized she seldom got out of bed before ten o'clock in the morning. Then, all of a sudden, it dawned on her. It was probably Ricky. I wonder what he wants, she mused to herself. At this point, Maude distinctly remembered telling him to call her if he needed something and it goes without saying, this was more than likely one of those things. At any rate, at no surprise to her, she soon found out Ricky was the one who was calling her. Anyway, this time he wanted to know if she wanted to spend the afternoon on his yacht. Actually, she was hoping he would call again however she didn't think he would call so early in the morning. Needless to say, after that absolutely divine evening the other day, she was really looking forward to being with him again. Initially, she thought their relationship may end up being a one-night stand however thanks to his follow up interest in her, it appeared that wasn't going to be the case after all. At any rate, at this point, it was just a question of whether or not he was ready for marriage. Maude knew from past experience that most men don't like to be tied down and as much as she hated to say it, there was not any reason to believe he was any different from all of the other men she knew at one time or another. Anyway, for that reason alone, Maude was uncertain about how things would work out between them in the days ahead. The truth of the matter is she was head over heels in love with a man she barely knew however most people would have looked at what she was experiencing as infatuation. Obviously, that isn't necessarily a bad thing however when you're seriously thinking about getting married, that wouldn't be a good thing to factor into the equation. Anyway, Maude thought she was in love and perhaps, that's the only thing that really mattered. All she knew was whenever she stood in his presence, she wanted to succumb to his every want and desire. At this point, she closed her eyes and imagined Ricky making love to her. Needless to say, it was such a pleasant thought, she couldn't stop thinking about him. In fact, he was the first man who seemed to care enough to make her feel like a woman. In the past, the men she knew only appeared to be interested in two things. A piece of her ass and money, neither of which Maude cared to give out any more than she had too.

At any rate, while she listened to Ricky explain how he came to inherit his boat as well as everything else for that matter, Maude couldn't help wondering how things would go in the days ahead. Needless to say, some things in life change on a moment's notice and perhaps, stated best as not always the way you want things to go. For that reason and because he was a good-looking man, she was afraid she would lose Ricky to another woman. That had happened before and she was extremely concerned, it would happen again. Anyway, on this occasion, with the thought of being out on his yacht with Maude, he was in a very talkative mood. In fact, she soon learned he spent numerous hours a week at sea, either getting some fishing in or doing some bird watching. Occasionally, he would do some whale watching too however the bottom line of it all was, Ricky loved spending time at sea.

Anyway, on this occasion, she also came to learn he discovered some uninhabited islands on one of his fishing excursions some time ago and now, it was turning out to be one of his most favorite places to go whenever he was out on his yacht. Granted, those islands were quite a few miles away from the mainland of the state of Oregon however he assured her his yacht was more than capable of reaching those islands in a few hours, so it was where Ricky headed whenever he wanted to get away from the reality of everyday living. In fact, if she understood him correctly, those islands where the closest thing to paradise so he kept going back there every chance he got. At any rate, the invitation he gave Maude that day was to join him on his yacht for the afternoon only and she didn't see any harm in doing that. Granted, Maude loved being near the ocean, not on it however since it was a good opportunity to see if she liked being at sea, she quickly agreed to go with him. Besides, she wanted to spend more time with him anyway, so it seemed like the only logical thing to do.

At this point in their conversation, being long-winded and all, he went onto suggest they take a cruise out to one of the islands sometime and camp out under the stars for the weekend if that was something she might be interested in doing. Well, like you might think, she was really receptive to the idea just as long as she could get used to being at sea. Actually, in her eyes, the most important thing of all was it gave them more time to be together, so you might say, Maude looked favorably upon doing that. Anyway, not long after the idea of camping out on one of the islands was mentioned to her, their telephone conversation came to an end but not before a lot of very important ground was covered. At any rate, once she got off the phone with Ricky, Maude made a quick trip to the bathroom to freshen up a bit. Then, with everything apparently in order, she had a bite to eat from a few leftovers that were kicking around in the refrigerator, and shortly thereafter, she went over to Ricky's house in anticipation of enjoying the afternoon at sea.

By the time they were out on the waters of the Pacific Ocean that morning, it was close to the hour of noon. Maude was dressed in jeans and a blouse while Ricky wore a polo shirt, a pair of khaki pants and a seaman's cap. He was also sporting a two day's growth of beard on his face as well however in her opinion that made him look even more handsome. Yes, he was certainly a very dashing, debonair, and well-mannered young man and she was completely mesmerized by it all. In fact, between admiring his stately appearance and having what she discovered beneath the old Kimball mansion on her mind, you might say, Maude was a bit reflective on those things that afternoon. First, she wasn't absolutely certain telling Ricky about what she found down beneath her house was the right thing to do and secondly, she wanted to get the coins appraised. It was as simple as that however after thinking about that and looking to start a family of her own, she was a little preoccupied with things that afternoon. At any rate, she eventually concluded, she would tell Ricky about the coins sometime. She just wasn't sure when that would be, that's all. For the time being, it would remain a secret. In the meantime, she had to track down a numismatic coin dealer in order to find out how much those old coins were actually worth.

At any rate, they could not have asked for a better day to be out to sea. In fact, with calm winds, blue skies, and lots of sunshine, in most respects it was a picture-perfect day and certainly theirs to enjoy. Anyway, it turns out, the sea was favorable to her liking so Maude told Ricky she would go fishing with him sometime. In addition to that, much to her surprise she liked being at sea better than flying in an airplane. Needless to say, that was something she wasn't sure of until now however the case had proved itself because within an hour of being out on his yacht, she felt good about things and in Ricky's eyes, that's all that really mattered. Anyway, once he knew she didn't mind being at sea, weather permitting, he suggested they go camping on one of the islands next weekend, which was mutually agreed upon in literally no time at all. The truth of the matter is, it would give her another opportunity to spend some more time with Ricky, so it fit in really well with her plans for the following week. Furthermore, since Ricky already had the camping gear they needed, it would be just a matter of getting things in order and they would be ready to go. He did go onto say, they could always sleep in the cabin of his boat if she wanted too but he quickly inferred, she would probably enjoy herself more if they camped out beneath the stars on one of the islands. Well, that sounded fine to her, and because Maude was actually interested in seeing the islands anyway, what better reason did she have for going. Between an abundance of sunshine, palm trees and god only knows what else, Maude quickly formulated a picture of those islands inside her head, and it added up to only one thing, paradise. Yes, from her perspective, it sounded like a great place to be, in addition to the fact, she would be spending the weekend with the best-looking guy in the state of Oregon so it looked like a great adventure was shaping up for them in the days ahead.

Anyway, they spent the better part of the afternoon and the early hours of the evening out on Ricky's yacht. In fact, it wasn't actually until sometime around 7:00 o'clock before they made it back into shore. At any rate, upon returning to Tierra Del Mar, Ricky proceeded to tie his boat up securely to the dock and then, after sharing a very affectionate kiss with her, they parted ways and she went home. Needless to say, it had been an absolutely delightful afternoon and since he gave her his promise, they would do it again sometime, she was more than satisfied with the way everything went. Actually, she was a little disappointed at not seeing the inside of the lighthouse however they could always do that another time. Anyway, with these thoughts planted firmly in the back of her mind, Maude had already decided to go to bed a little earlier than usual so upon returning home, she headed upstairs to her bedroom and after a quick shower to freshen up a bit, she called it a day.

CHAPTER 16

Shortly after breakfast the following day, Maude headed off to the living-room for a few minutes. Actually, her first and foremost thought was to find a numismatic coin dealer that might be interested in purchasing the coins that were down beneath the house so with that in mind, she picked up a local telephone directory and began thumbing through its yellow pages with the hope of finding a numismatic coin dealer. In fact, it was the only way she was ever going to be able to unload all those old coins, so it was obviously the best way to proceed. Furthermore, she thought it would be a good idea to have the individual go through the coins and appraise them. Needless to say, that would more than likely accomplish two things. First of all, she would be paid a good, fair price for the coins because a coin dealer would know how much they're worth and secondly, it would give that individual an opportunity to make them available to the public. Anyway, with that said, just as she was about to expand her search outside the Tierra Del Mar area, she found a coin dealer right in the community of where she was living. Now, she wouldn't have to travel to Portland or somewhere else to see if the coins were worth something. It was just simply a matter of convenience because in reality, Maude didn't mind traveling somewhere if she felt good. This time, like so many instances in the past, Maude didn't waste any time looking into the matter and a few minutes later, she was on the phone with the coin dealer listed in the telephone directory. I can further state, she knew it was going to be necessary to get the coins appraised, so rather than procrastinating about it any longer, she tried to get things taken care of now. Neither did it come as any big surprise to learn he wanted Maude to bring in a sample of the old coins to his place of business so he could take a look at them. Needless to say, it was the only way he would be able to tell her how much the coins were worth if anything at all. Anyway, within minutes of having spoken with him, she made an 11:00 o'clock appointment for that morning and not too long after that their conversation came to an end. At this point, she headed back down beneath the house to take a sample of every coin she could find. Obviously, it was going to take a while to do that but it would more than likely pay off in the long run. As for the remains of Charles Winston Kimball I, they weren't going anywhere. In fact, after the coins were sold, she did not plan on going back down beneath the house anyway so why should she excavate his remains. Let the poor man rest in peace.

At least, that's what Maude thought she would do anyway. As for getting all those old coins appraised, it was the only way she would be able to determine their worth. If it weren't for that reason, she would probably let the coins set where they were. In reality, she didn't need the money anyway, however it would be foolish of her not to do something with the coins. Besides, they were very interesting to look at so Maude thought if she was able to sell them, it would give someone who was into the hobby of coin collecting an opportunity to own them. In fact, chances are, it would turn out to be a win, win situation for everyone involved. She would obviously get compensated for the coins and in a relatively short period of time and someone else would get to expand their coin collection. As to what it would cost someone to do that, she really didn't know however if she were a betting person, those coins would make someone who was in the hobby to collect coins a very happy individual. Anyway, with that in mind, Maude spent as much time as she possibly could in getting things together so Mr. Robinson would have a good representation of each coin. Finally, after spending a good hour or more going through all those old coins, she put the spoils of her search into a small tote and headed out to her car. Seconds later, she was on her way to Robinson's Coin Mart. Anyway, as it turns out, about fifteen minutes later, she pulled into the parking lot of his business. Fortunately for Maude, in a small town like Tierra Del Mar, most things were easy to find, and Robinson's Coin Mart certainly fell into that category as well. As for who she was supposed to meet, well, that would be Matt Robinson. He was the proprietor of the store as well as part owner, and she could immediately tell by the tone of his voice that he was the one she spoke with earlier in the day. Anyway, on this particular occasion, she could see he was just finishing up some business with another customer when she entered his store. Now, it would be just a matter of introducing herself so with that in mind, she walked ever so casually over to the counter and began looking at some of the coins he had in his showcase. Actually, for most people, it was nothing more than a formality for engaging in business with someone and in this particular case, that's all it really amounted to with Maude as well. Anyway, as I said before, she very quickly assumed the man standing behind the counter was Mr. Robinson and a moment later, her assumption proved to be correct. At this point, he lit up a cigar and walked slowly over to where she stood before going onto ask the inevitable question, "How may I help you, ma'am?" Well, like you might expect, she immediately replied, "Hello, Mr. Robinson. My name is Maude Derringer. I'm the one you spoke with earlier today. I believe I've got some coins from the 19th century you might be interested in. Anyway, if I understood you correctly, you said to bring in a sample of each coin. Well, that's what I did. I will also assume, that's more than likely the only way you're going to be able to determine how much the coins are worth. Anyway, now that I did what you suggested, I'm here with the coins, Mr. Robinson. I hope you will be able to give me a good ballpark estimate of how much they're actually worth. Just so you know, Mr. Robinson, I would really like to sell the coins because I don't have any use for them. Anyway, with any kind of luck at all, I was hoping it will turn out to be something you can help me with." At this point, she pulled out about twenty coins from her purse and spread them out on top of the counter so he could see them. This is the moment of truth, she thought to herself. Anyway, within seconds of having laid the coins down on the counter, he reached down into his shirt pocket and pulled out a small magnifying glass. Then, Mr. Robinson methodically looked each coin over, studying them for obvious signs of wear because that was one of the only ways a numismatic coin dealer could determine the coins worth. Furthermore, in addition to the overall condition of the coin, its value is determined by the date and mint mark of each coin. Actually, the scarcity of each coin adds to its value as well. Anyway, as expected, Mr. Robinson did not have any problem recognizing the different types of coins she had from years of buying and selling coins with his clientele. Then, I believe, not totally unexpected from her perspective, he took a few minutes to explain how coins use to be minted. Needless to say, most of what he told her was interesting but she wasn't able to absorb everything he said. If Maude understood him correctly though, the further a person went back in time, more often than not the coins were individually struck from dye cast molds, one at a time. In addition to that, most of the coins minted in those days were spent out of necessity so that made them all that harder to find and also even harder to attain one in really good condition. For that reason, most of them were actually quite valuable to a coin collector. Anyway, after ten or fifteen minutes of time elapsed by, he came to the conclusion, the coins she brought in for him to look at, were indeed worth a lot of money. Just exactly how much money would depend upon how many of each coin she actually had. In fact, if Maude understood him correctly, most of her coins were the bust half and flowing hair designs of the early 1800's and ranged from a penny to a dollar. Needless to say, that didn't mean anything to her because she was totally illiterate when it came to coin collecting. "Well," he said, "based upon the coins you brought into me today, I'd say, they're worth a lot of money Ms. Derringer. Out of curiosity, about how many coins of each design do you have ma'am? You must realize that's the only way I can give you a good ballpark estimate of how much the coins are worth." At this point, she thought about what Mr. Robinson said for a moment or two because she had no idea how many of each coin she had. In fact, if she were to make a piece count of every coin that was literally buried beneath her house, it would be some time before she would be able to give him an exact answer. Finally, with some reluctance, due to the lack of knowledge of what he wanted to know, she replied, "I'm not actually sure how many of each coin I have, Mr. Robinson.

Unfortunately, the unusual circumstance's surrounding my ownership of these coins is a little out of the ordinary. In fact, quite frankly, you'd more than likely find what I had to tell you so bizarre that you'd probably never believe me anyway. I'd like to say one other thing though, and that is I didn't rob anyone to get them. Believe it or not, these coins just happened to come with the property I purchased in Tierra Del Mar. It's the gods honest truth, Mr. Robinson! Take my word for it! I didn't do anything criminal to attain them!" At this point, he replied back to her, "I believe you, Ms. Derringer but I still need to know how many of each coin there are. It's as simple as that. There isn't any way I can give you an overall estimate of their worth until you are a little more precise about the quantity of coins you have." Needless to say, with that said, she thought about what Mr. Robinson said for a moment or two, and then she replied, "I don't know what I have for coins, Mr. Robinson however if I had to make a guess, I would say, somewhere between fifty and a hundred thousand coins, ranging from a penny to a dollar. I apologize for being so vague about that however that's as precise as I can be." "You've got to be kidding, Ms. Derringer," he exclaimed! "Do you realize coins like this are worth many thousands of dollars to a numismatic coin dealer. I would not even be surprised if they are worth upwards of a million dollars, ma'am." "Actually, I thought you may say something like that, Mr. Robinson," she quickly replied. "Well, now that you have the information you need, how do I go about selling the coins?" At this point, he paused for a moment to think about what she said. "I don't have the financial resources to buy them from you, Ms. Derringer but I can find a buyer for you. I'm absolutely certain of that. It may take me a couple of days to do that but if you aren't in any hurry, I'll see what I can do. Give me your telephone number and I will call you just as soon as I know something." With that in mind, Maude proceeded to write down her telephone number on a small piece of paper Mr. Robinson had given her. Once that was taken care of, she gathered up the coins that were sitting on his counter and put them back into her purse. Then, she thanked him for taking the time to look the coins over, and a moment later, she departed from his place of business. Obviously, if the matter could be taken care of in a couple of days that wouldn't be bad she thought to herself. In fact, that would be easy enough to deal with. At this point, Maude got into her car, shifted it into gear and sped off down the road with the intention of taking the rest of the day off. In fact, unless Ricky gave her a reason to do otherwise, she was going to relax for a little while in the comfort of her living-room by reading a book. Needless to say, that was one of the things she liked to do most when things got really stressful for her and with no other business matters to attend too, it seemed like the only logical thing to do.

CHAPTER 17

As anticipated, a couple of days later, Maude received the telephone call she was looking for. Shortly before 9:00 o'clock in the morning, Mr. Robinson called, only this time he had some good news to share with her. If she understood him correctly, he found a coin dealer down in the Los Angeles area that was interested in purchasing her coins. Needless to say, that's what Maude was counting on so at this point, it had become quite apparent, she was going to be able to sell all those old coins after all. Originally, she wasn't sure that's the way everything would turn out but it was clear now, that was indeed going to happen. Actually, the irony of it all was, the company she would be dealing with was based in the same part of California she used to live in however if a person lived in the Los Angeles area like she did, they would quickly realize, a lot of business's made their home there as well. At any rate, the most important thing of all was Mr. Robinson did in fact find a buyer for her coins. If he hadn't been able to do so, Maude wasn't certain what she would do with the coins because they weren't legal tender anymore and she had no use for them. In realistic terms, the coins she had were only worth something to a numismatic coin collector so there wasn't any sense of saving them unless she intended to become a coin collector herself and you might say, that's not what she had in mind. Anyway, for that reason, the only logical thing to do was sell them so that's what she planned on doing. Actually, on the plus side of it all, Maude would get a little compensation in return, so it was unquestionably the right thing to do. Besides, it was an opportunity to give someone who collected coins the opportunity to own them, and she didn't see that as a bad thing at all. In fact, in her opinion, it was by far the better thing to do, so she was more than content with her decision to sell the coins. Needless to say, it's always nice to see a happy face anyway and if she didn't miss her guess, whoever became the new owner of the coins would more than likely be as happy as a person could be in owning them.

At any rate, not long after receiving the phone call from Mr. Robinson, he gave her the name and telephone number of the coin dealer she would be doing business with and went onto say, "The company that's interested in your coins will be giving you a call shortly, Ms. Derringer. I'm absolutely certain of that. The Dearstone Company is a very reputable business, so if I don't miss my guess, you will hear from them later this afternoon. Believe me, they're very interested in your coins, ma'am so I don't think you'll have long to wait before you hear from them. In the meantime, if you have any questions, you may get a hold of me at my place of business. Now, as for the company you will be dealing with, I'm all but certain, they'll be able to help you. In fact, I do business with them quite often so I can easily vouch for their reputation. It's impeccable but if for some reason things don't work out for you with this company, I'll find you another one. Do not worry about that. There are all kinds of them out there. It would be just a matter of finding a company that's interested in coins of the late 19th century, that's all. In particularly, United States coins. Actually, a lot of coin dealers only buy and sell foreign coins, so a company of that nature probably wouldn't be interested in your coins, Ms. Derringer. Anyway, enough said about that. I am sure you will be happy doing business with the company I found for you. Now, with regards to this conversation, Ms. Derringer, due to other business obligations, it is necessary I cut it short so I bid you a good day and I sincerely apologize for any inconvenience it may cause you," he finished saying. "That's no problem at all, Mr. Robinson. In fact, I thank you for calling," she stated. "I'll be looking forward to speaking with you again sometime." With that said, Maude hung up the telephone and went back into the living-room to think about Mr. Robinson told her. At this point, she quickly deduced, it would be a good idea to hang around the house for a little while just in case the coin dealer from Los Angeles called later that afternoon. The truth of the matter was she hated sitting around with nothing to do but in this instance, she thought it would be a good idea to hang around the house until the Dearstone Company called. Actually, she was hoping the matter would be all taken care of before the weekend arrived. Obviously, with plans to go camping with Ricky, she did not want things to interfere with that and with any luck at all, that's how everything would go. At this point, she took a moment to glance over in the direction of the clock on the living-room wall and noticed it was only 10:00 o'clock in the morning. What on earth was she going to do with herself until the company from Los Angeles called? Needless to say, she could always find a book to read however she eventually concluded, she would watch television for a while. At any rate, no sooner had she done this, and the telephone began ringing off the hook again, only this time Ricky was the one who was calling. Anyway, at no surprise to her, he was checking with her to make sure their plans for the weekend were still on and as far as she was concerned, unless an unexpected catastrophe happened, they were. In fact, quite frankly, Maude intended to spend the entire weekend with Ricky so she quickly gave him her reassurance she would be there. At any rate, it was a short conversation and directly to the point of what they would be doing on the weekend and after about fifteen minutes, she thanked him for calling and within seconds of having done that, their conversation came to an end. Needless to say, if things went as planned, she would join him for their camping adventure on Friday.

In the meantime, a very impatient, Maude Derringer waited ever so patiently for a telephone call from the Dearstone Company. Actually, as Mr. Robinson told her a little while ago, she anticipated a call later in the afternoon, so the rest of the morning was spent watching television. Sometime around twelve or one o'clock, she had lunch and was just about to sit down to try and read a book when the phone rang again, only this time it was the call she was looking for. Anyway, much to her surprise, she soon found out the Dearstone Company was more interested in her coins than she ever expected them to be, however that was fine with her. Now, she would be able to get rid of the coins down beneath her house and that's really all she wanted to do. At any rate, Michael Johnson turned out to be the man representing the Dearstone Company and after a fairly long, in depth conversation, a 1:00 o'clock appointment for the following day was agreed upon. Needless to say, that time fit in really well with her schedule, so she didn't hesitate making plans for that hour. In fact, believe it or not, what came as somewhat of a surprise to her was, she didn't have to describe the coins in detail to him however Mr. Robinson had more than likely already done that. Anyway, by now, it looked like she was going to find out how much those coins were really worth.

In the meantime, after having gotten off the phone with Michael Johnson, she went back into the kitchen for a few minutes to deduce how much food she would need to buy at one of the grocery stores in the area.

Needless to say, by now, she had decided to use the rest of the day for shopping purposes. First, she would buy herself some new clothes and then, she would purchase some food. Then, she would come back home and restock the refrigerator and kitchen cupboards with a fresh supply of items for the coming days. Actually, it was something that had to be done anyway so she figured there wasn't any better time than the present to do that. At any rate, with that in mind, Maude grabbed the keys to her car from the kitchen countertop and took off out the door to take care of some shopping matters while she had the time to do so.

CHAPTER 18

As expected, the next day the gentleman from the Dearstone Company arrived at Maude's house around 1:00 o'clock. In fact, much to her surprise, Mr. Johnson was actually right on time, unlike so many of the other businessmen she had dealt with at one time or another over the years. Generally speaking, from personal experience, she would be the first one to admit, most men had a tendency to keep her waiting, when it came down to dealing with business matters but this man didn't do that to her so you might say, it was a pleasure to do business with him. At any rate, Mr. Johnson was quite punctual and that's all that really mattered. Anyway, with business matters in mind, after speaking with him for a moment at the door, she asked him to come inside. It was a short walk to the living-room and within a few minutes time, they were engaged in conversation over the coins she had to sell. Anyway, like you might think, one thing led to another and about five minutes later, she had Mr. Johnson follow her over to where the fireplace in the living-room was so she would be able to take him down the secret passageway and onto the chambers below. Of course, at no surprise to her, Mr. Johnson's initial reaction to the hidden stairway was one of absolute total astonishment, nevertheless, he followed her down the stairs with only one intention in mind that was to make Maude an offer for her coins. He did say, if the coins were as good of a find as he thought they were, he would purchase all of them from her, no questions asked. In the meantime, they proceeded down the secret passageway until they came to the first room. If you remember correctly, this was where some of the chests of gold and silver coins were. Anyway, at this point, she walked around the room and lit all of the lanterns inside the chamber and within a few seconds time, Mr. Johnson's eyes lit up brighter than a fireworks celebration on the fourth of July. At any rate, the moment he saw the coins, he turned to Maude and said, "It's unbelievable! In all my years of being in this line of business, I have never seen anything like it! Boy, you sure as hell weren't kidding when you said you had some old coins to sell, ma'am. I can also tell you some of those coins are worth a lot of money. I really mean that, Mrs. Derringer." At this point, she replied back to him saying, "Believe it or not, there're more coins in the other room." Then, Maude pointed in the direction of the other chamber, where there were even more coins that had been stored over the years. Well, like you might think, Mr. Johnson was speechless. Actually, it wasn't really the sort of thing he usually dealt with in the due course of taking care of business so you might say, Mr. Johnson was at a complete loss for words. At any rate, after taking a moment to regain his composure, he went onto say, "If what you tell me is true, Ms. Derringer, then I will have to take an overall estimate of your coins rather than doing a per piece estimate. I would not know of any other way to do it. There are just simply too many coins here for me to individually appraise every one of them. I really and truly apologize for the inconvenience however that's the nature of the business. Anyway, if it's all right with you, I will give you a good ballpark estimate for the entire lot of coins. I have a lot of experience in the numismatic field, so I won't have any trouble doing this for you. Don't worry about a thing, Ms. Derringer. I will give you a good fair price for your coins. You have my word on it!" At this point, knowing darn well she didn't have to give that any thought, Maude replied, "That's fine with me, Mr. Johnson. I probably shouldn't say this, but I am not actually short on money so the actual dollars and cents you come up with doesn't make any difference to me. I would just like to get those coins off my hands, that's all. Do whatever you think is necessary to make that possible. As I am sure I've said before, I don't know a thing about coins, so a good fair estimate of what they are worth is fine with me. Shall I assume we have an agreement," Maude finished saying. "Yes, you may assume that ma'am. I'll do my best to give you a good deal," Mr. Johnson stated. "Now, I must get busy, or I won't ever get this appraisal done." At this point, with only one thing in mind, he walked over to where one of those chests of coins sat and began looking it over with the small magnifying glass, he brought with him. Needless to say, it was the only way he could determine their worth, and at no surprise to him, the coins certainly lived up to their billing. At any rate, he proceeded to give the coins a thorough going over as he looked closely at their dates, mintmarks, and the overall condition of each coin. Anyway, after a few minutes, the man could see the coins were worth a lot of money. In fact, after years of experience in the numismatic field, he could quickly identify which coins were worth a lot and which coins had value only by the content of the coin, so it didn't come as any surprise to Maude when she learned they were worth a lot of money. At any rate, after about three and a half hours of going from one chest of coins to the other, Mr. Johnson got out a small pocket-sized calculator from his pocket and after doing a few calculations and satisfied in theory with the figure he came up, he turned to Maude and gave her his best offer. At this point, he was quick to say, "I'm willing to make you an offer of two million dollars, ma'am. I realize that isn't much money for someone like yourself, but it's all I dare offer you without appraising each coin. In my opinion, it's a good offer however if you want to think about it for a while that's fine with me. I am just a phone call away." Needless to say, it was time for her to make a decision on the matter. In fact, without knowing anything about coins, Maude concluded, the offer Mr. Johnson made was a good one however more importantly, she would be able to get all of those old coins off her hands, and of course, that's what she wanted to do so a second or two later, she gave him her answer. "I don't have to think about it, Mr. Johnson," she replied. "I am more than satisfied with your offer. In fact, quite frankly, if you weren't interested in those coins, I'm not sure what I would do. I guess they would just have to sit there until hell froze over and that really would be a crying shame because I am sure there are people out there who would like to add some of those coins to their coin collection." "Then, I assume we have a deal," Mr. Johnson replied. "I'll give you two million dollars for them, ma'am." "That sounds good to me," she replied. At this point in their conversation, he asked Maude how she would like to be paid. Of course, it goes without saying, it didn't really matter to her how she got paid at which point, he said, "If you want cash, I will have to come back another day, perhaps a couple of days from now however if you'll accept a check, I'll make a trip to one of the banks in Tierra Del Mar and have a check made out in your name." "That will be fine, Mr. Johnson," she replied. "I guess I'll be looking forward to seeing you in a little while then." "If everything goes as planned you will," he stated. "Now if I'm ever going to get this matter taken care of today, I really must be on my way. I will see you in a little while, Ms. Derringer." At this point, he bid her farewell and headed off to the bank.

At any rate, just as soon as he left, she went into the kitchen and made herself a fresh cup of coffee. Needless to say, that was one of those things that helped her to relax a little whenever she was feeling a bit stressed or anxious. Whether it actually accomplished that end result or not she wasn't certain but since she thought it did, she had a hot cup of coffee. As for everything else that afternoon, all in all, everything went very well. In fact, she was more than satisfied with Mr. Johnson's offer to purchase her coins so that's all that really mattered. Anyway, about forty-five minutes to an hour later, Mr. Johnson returned with a bank check made out to her in the amount of two million dollars. Actually, even for Maude, that was a very sizable check and the fact this business matter was going to be taken care of in one day also favored her as well. At any rate, in a matter of a few minutes, he paid her for the coins and then, he began the process of loading the chests of coins into his van with a dolly that he brought with him. Obviously, due to the size and weight of the chests, it took Mr. Johnson another hour and a half to move the coins from beneath her house to his van. Anyway, after giving Maude a very diplomatic thank you for allowing him to do business with her, he took off out the door and departed from the house. At this point, there wasn't anything left to be done. Maude had gotten all of those old coins off her hands and made some money doing so as well. Now, she would be able to turn her attention to a more important matter and that was her relationship with Ricky. Anyway, it was time to start thinking about her plans for the weekend, which to the best of her knowledge was going to be deep sea fishing and camping out beneath the stars. Obviously, there were a few other things she would've preferred to be doing however if she had any aspirations of marrying this man, and she most certainly did, then, it was important that she keep Ricky happy. In fact, she intended to give this matter a little more time and if nothing further came of their relationship, she would look for another guy.

Anyway, with the better part of these thoughts racing through her head, Maude went into the den and put the check away inside a small safe she used to keep her valuables in until she got around to cashing it, sometime later next week. Right at the moment, she intended to have a bite to eat and then, she was going to head off to bed a little earlier than usual. Actually, believe it or not, something in the back of her mind told her a little extra rest might do her well because most of the coming weekend was going to be spent on an island somewhere and that favored less rest than sleeping at home. Obviously, she was hoping it would be a fun filled weekend packed with all kinds of adventure however the nature of doing something she hadn't done before was going to create a lot of anxiety for her and the end result of that would probably leave her restless over the weekend. Anyway, putting all that aside and for what it's worth, camping out under the stars and deep-sea fishing were a couple of things she wasn't familiar with so you might say, it would be learning experience for her as well. Anyway, the more she thought about it, the more Maude was convinced she was going to enjoy herself. All she really knew for certain was she wanted to be well rested for the weekend. At any rate, with that way of thinking anchored firmly inside her head, rather than watching television for a little while, shortly after supper that evening, she took the more conservative approach to the weekend and opted to get a little extra rest by heading off to bed a littler earlier than usual even though the well-directed life she was accustomed to living was about to come to an abrupt end. Regrettably, nightmarish experiences happen sometimes, in particularly, when they turn out to be a real-life nightmare and as fate would have it, destiny was about to unload a very memorable one on her.

CHAPTER 19

At four-thirty in the morning, Maude's alarm clock went off, alerting her to the fact a new day had begun. Actually, the sun hadn't officially risen yet however she wanted to be ready to go with Ricky on a well-planned out adventure that weekend, so Maude arose out of bed and headed directly for the shower. Needless to say, four-thirty in the morning wasn't even close to the usual time she got out of bed in the morning however Ricky wanted to get an early start on things, so it was necessary she get up at this time. The truth of the matter is the islands they would be going to were located a ways out in the Pacific Ocean, so it was going to take the better part of a day to get there. In fact, she was certain that had everything to do with the reason why he wanted to get an early start on things and having made the assumption, he knew what he was doing, she trusted his judgment on this matter. If he stated, they would be better off leaving early in the morning as he suggested, then that's what they would do. The fact of the matter is Maude was just happy for the opportunity to spend the weekend with him. Furthermore, the more she thought about it, the more she was convinced, it was going to be a great weekend and at this point, there really wasn't any reason to believe otherwise. Needless to say, even though there were other things she would have preferred doing, right at the moment, she was determined to learn the art of deep-sea fishing as well as how to camp out under the stars. Anyway, while trying to keep all this in perspective, she proceeded to freshen up a bit in the bathroom. Yes, it's time wake up and get going, Maude mused to herself. Unfortunately, like so many times in the past, the moment she looked into the mirror, the haunting scar of loneliness crept back into her mind. Actually, it was the way Maude felt since she dumped her last boyfriend and now, months later, that huge, unmistakable void was still there. Anyway, after looking into the mirror for a moment or two, she eventually got a grip on herself, and then ever so gradually, she began to focus on the reality of the day. First, a little make-up went on and then, she rushed back to her bedroom and got dressed. Once that was all taken care of, Maude threw a few pieces of clothing into a small tote along with some necessary sundries she would be needing over the weekend, then, she headed downstairs to have breakfast. Needless to say, that didn't take her very long. She had a dish of cereal and a full glass of orange juice. Normally, she would've taken the time to have something more appetizing to eat however it was a weekend where time was actually of the essence so that approach was not followed. At this point, it was determined, she was ready to go over to Ricky's however it wasn't without any reservations though as she began thinking about all the things that could possibly go wrong while they were out to sea. Surely, everything would be fine, she thought to herself. Ricky was an old pro at what he did so it was very unlikely anything bad would happen to them. At any rate, with that said, she took one last look around the house to make sure everything was in order and then, she headed out the door. Weather-wise, it was supposed to be a nice weekend and with any luck at all, that is how everything would turn out. Anyway, with things looking better than ever now, Maude made a quick dash across her yard, and then proceeded up the road a ways until she was standing at the backdoor to Ricky's house. In this particular case, she didn't get any further than that because Ricky saw her coming and was waiting to let her into the house, which of course he did upon seeing her. At any rate, within ten to fifteen minutes of having arrived at his house, she soon found herself listening to him explain what they would be doing that weekend. Actually, he thought it was a good idea to do that so Maude would have some way of knowing what to expect while they were out to sea. Anyway, like you might think, he proceeded to give her his complete reassurance that everything would be fine, and it goes without saying, that's undeniably what she wanted to hear. As for the time it would take to get out to the islands, about ten hours.

In fact, if she had her information right, it wouldn't be until late afternoon or early evening before they got there. At that point, they would still have plenty of time to go ashore to set up camp somewhere on the island before dark. From there, they would be able to fish and do whatever they wanted to do for the rest of the weekend. Anyway, since everything appeared to be in order, around fifteen minutes to the hour of 7:00 o'clock that morning, Ricky pulled up anchor and they headed out to sea so you might say, the camping excursion to the islands he loved so much was officially under way.

As for Ricky's yacht, it had all the fine amenities of a really nice apartment and she found that very comforting to say the least. In fact, just for that reason alone, it didn't take Maude very long to see why Ricky loved the boat so much. To begin with, the lower deck was very spacious, which gave them ample room to move around. Secondly, it had a very luxurious bedroom in the rear of the boat, in addition to a well-equipped all-purpose room that served as their living-room. There was also a really nice bathroom adjacent to the bedroom but that just happens to be one of those necessities a person can't live without so that was to be expected. In addition to that, there was also a very well laid out kitchen aboard his yacht too and it had all of the amenities a person could ever wish for. All in all, it was a very luxurious yacht. Granted, it could have been a little larger in size however that falls in line with a little extra space always comes in handy.

Anyway, as you might think, Ricky went onto reassure her that he kept his boat in good running condition so she wouldn't start worrying about the possibility something could happen to them while they were at sea. Needless to say, sometimes, unexpected things will come about regardless of what we do to prepare for something and in this case, that's what he did before they left the state of Oregon for the open sea. In fact, he went out of his way to ensure everything was in good working order because the future of his relationship with Maude was at stake if anything happened to them. At any rate, shortly after they were out on the ocean, she began to gaze down into the depths of the water. It was a normal reaction for anyone who wasn't really familiar with the ocean however she noticed the ocean was deep blue color. The other day when they were out on the ocean, it appeared to be a dark green in color. Of course, she was immediately puzzled by that abnormality, so she asked Ricky about it. He said, believe it or not, the ocean has a tendency to reflect light so if the sky is blue, the ocean will appear blue. On a cloudy day, the sea takes on a more greenish-gray color because it's reflecting light from the sky above. The other factor that determines the overall color of the ocean has to do with the number of algae on the bottom of the ocean and under those circumstances, the ocean will appear green in color. At any rate, she was quick to find this very interesting and that eventually led them into discussing a few other things as well. In fact, after a little more small talk, they went onto discuss safe yachting measures like what to do in the event of an engine failure at sea. Of course, Maude took what he said in like a student trying to learn reading, writing and arithmetic in school because yachting was something that meant a lot to Ricky. Anyway, at this point, he reassured her one more time how unlikely it was they would ever run into a problem at sea and with the National Weather Service calling for sunny skies all weekend, it gave Ricky no reason for concern. Admittedly, that could change on a moment's notice however he told her not to worry about it and that was the end of that.

Anyway, as you might think, they continued on their way. South by southwest they went, hour after hour they traveled and onto the islands they went. Actually, a light breeze was fanning the air from a southerly direction, so it did provide some resistance to their means of travel, but it had little to no impact on what they were doing so there wasn't any reason for concern. All in all, it was a nice summer day and the warm breeze that was blowing in off the ocean only made their adventure that much more enjoyable. At any rate, no problems arose, and things were apparently going as planned as they continued on their way. Finally, around 5:00 o'clock, they caught sight of the islands. Actually, to be more precise, Ricky was the first one to spot land and the moment that was apparent, he didn't waste any time bringing this to her attention. The truth of the matter is, she had been busy sunbathing out on the stern of the deck so she wasn't immediately aware of the situation however within a few seconds time, she came to realize, these were the islands they would be inhabiting for the weekend. Needless to say, that's what they had been waiting for and with their destination having been reached, he had only one goal and objective now and that was to make it a very memorable weekend for her. At this point, everything appeared to be fine. As a matter of fact, Ricky was thinking about some of the memorable experiences he'd had there in years past when he frequented the area to do a little fishing. Anyway, this is where he took a few minutes to explain a little geography about the islands to Maude. Of course, she was all ears for the duration of his informative talk about where they would be staying and also what they would be doing over the weekend. In fact, this is where she learned there were only three islands in the area. One of the islands was much larger in size than the other two, and for reasons only known to Ricky, he chose to head for the larger one of the three islands, which in this case, was the one located directly between the other two and also where they were headed at this very moment. At this point, Ricky began running these thoughts through his head as he carefully steered his yacht in the direction of the middle island, then, without a warning of any kind, a mechanical problem arose. For some reason, the engines located in the stern of the boat began to sputter. Of course, it goes without saying, that wasn't supposed to happen however something was amiss because in the process of trying to bring the boat closer into shore, the engines went dead. Initially, Maude thought he was just trying to slow the boat down a little before they got to shore, but that wasn't the case at all. Something was terribly wrong! At any rate, with some type of engine trouble, he lowered the anchor of his boat into the depths of the ocean and went down below to see what the problem was. After about twenty-five minutes, Ricky came back up on deck and walked over to where Maude stood to explain to her what was wrong. "Well," he said, "just in case you weren't aware of it, we've run into a problem. In fact, by now, I'm sure you've already guessed that, but as much as I hate to say it, I have some bad news to share with you. First, and also on the bright side of it all, there is some good news to our situation, however on the other hand, I'm absolutely certain you aren't going to care too much for the bad news I have to tell you. That's just a hunch, but it's also the reality of the situation we now face so before I go any further, which part of what I have to tell you would you like to hear first?" "Well, seeing that I have a choice, I would begin with the good news," she replied, "because I have a feeling I'm not going to like the bad news at all." At this point, he turned around and looked out towards the open sea. The fact of the matter is, he knew what he wanted to say but with the circumstances as they were, Ricky wasn't certain what the best way to proceed would be. If he told her that he over-looked something before they left home earlier in the day, he was going to get hell. There wasn't any question about that but if he fudged it a little, perhaps, he wouldn't incur her wrath. Needless to say, it was a very difficult decision to make. Anyway, after a few more seconds of time went by, Ricky replied back to her saying, "Well, the way I see it, if I were to look at it from an optimist's point of view, we're still alive. The bad news is, we're going to be here for a long time because we are out of gas. In fact, quite frankly, someway, somehow, we developed a leak in the fuel tank. I really don't know how that could've happened but it did. Furthermore, there isn't any reason to cry about it because that won't change a thing. We've got to deal with matters as they are regardless of what happened. I probably shouldn't say this but in addition to that, for some reason our communications system is not working either. Unfortunately, the battery inside the transmitting section of the radio is dead. I don't know what happened but we're definitely up shit creek without a paddle. We do have the boat but it's not going to get us anywhere now. What I find strange is I just checked the battery a couple of days ago, so it should have been fine. Anyway, regardless of what made the battery go dead is irrelevant now, but just so you know, that was our line of communication with the rest of the world and due to recent developments, that no longer exists. I'm sorry to have to tell you this but it's the reality of the situation now. In fact, under these circumstances, the radio is absolutely useless to us. It won't hold a charge anymore and I can't tell you why that is. Now, with regards to the fuel tank, I had that serviced last week, so it should've been fine. Unfortunately, that's not the case at all. Anyway, I'm truly sorry for the mess I have gotten us into, Maude. None of what happened should've ever came about however there is one thing I'm certain of and that is, we are going to have to try and make the most of a bad situation," he finished saying. At this point, she just stared off into space, shaking her head in disbelief. "Why in the name of Christ did this ever have to happen to us," she asked? "I suppose we're going to die here," but long before he had an opportunity to give her an answer, she went onto say, "You must realize, we're a long ways from civilization out here. Back on the mainland, we could have gone next door and asked one of our neighbors for assistance. Out here in the middle of the Pacific Ocean, there isn't anyone we can go to for help. In fact, we're as good as dead, Ricky." At this point, silence ensued for a moment as she thought about what she was going to say. Then, a couple more seconds went by. Finally, she yelled at him madder than a wet hen, "I am scared to death, Ricky! What you told me a few minutes earlier will probably be our death sentences. In fact, unless I'm overlooking something, we might just as well stick our head between our legs and kiss our ass's good-bye. Well, believe it or not, that's not at all what I had in mind when I consented to come out here with you. Surely, you could have been less negligent with the maintenance of your boat! Look what you've done! You must have had your head stuck up your ass to have overlooked something like this! Do you realize the situation you've gotten us in should never have happened? How could you have been so blatantly careless of my well-being? Well, don't just stand there, dig the finger out of your ass and do something about it! Get us out of here!" Unfortunately, there wasn't really too much he could do. He did try his darndest to think of something he could say that might comfort her a bit but nothing came to mind. Finally, after mulling things around inside his head for a moment, he said, "First, we need to keep a good positive attitude about this unfortunate little matter. Sooner or later, something will turn up. I'm certain of that but you're going to have to be patient. Most things don't happen overnight, and some problems take time to resolve. In the meantime, we're going to have to do the best we can with the situation as it now stands." At this point, she began to cry. Needless to say, the whole unfortunate mess was more than she could bear. Not knowing what else to do, he took her in his arms and gave her his reassurance they would eventually find a way off the island. It would take a little time to do that however like a man of his word, Ricky promised he would find a way to get them back to the mainland. Someway, somehow, he would persevere in that endeavor. Just exactly how that would come about he didn't know but with any luck at all, perhaps, somewhere down the road that would happen. In the meantime, there would be some difficult challenges ahead and it would probably be some time before that changed.

Anyway, the early evening hours of the day quickly descended upon them as they sat out on the back of Ricky's boat trying to figure out what they were going to do. It hadn't been a very good day. Seemingly everything that could go wrong went wrong and now, they were faced with a very challenging situation. Finally, after giving it some very careful thought, Ricky said, "Let's get the life raft out and head into shore. Sitting here on the boat won't accomplish anything. We will be a lot safer on shore if the weather takes a turn for the worse at some point in the future, so we need to make camp on the island like we originally planned. Besides, it'll be dark soon so we had best get busy. In fact, because I no longer have the use of our radio, there isn't any way I can tell what the weather's going to be. In other words, as much as I hate to say it, Maude, we are on our own. That means, we have to prepare for the worst and hope for the best. That's actually all we can do. Anyway, come on. Let's get moving. I would like to set up camp before it gets dark and sitting around here feeling sorry for ourselves isn't going to accomplish anything. I think, if we remain vigilant, somewhere along the way, someone will come along and rescue us but in the meantime, it would be a good idea to head into shore." With that said, Maude reluctantly agreed to go ashore with him. In fact, she even took a moment to acknowledge he was right about that. They would indeed be a lot safer on the island than where they were now, so she agreed to do as he suggested. At any rate, they got a few things together, and shortly thereafter, they made their way into shore. As for priorities, the first thing they did was find a spot where they could set up their camping gear so after making a quick check of the area, Ricky thought it was best to put up the tent on the shore of the lagoon. In truth, at this point in the day, there wasn't a lot of daylight left anyway so rather than trying to deal with the interior of an island that he wasn't familiar with, they chose on the beach of the lagoon they came in on. Actually, she thought the area he selected to make camp in was in an ideal location but he was quick to point out that wasn't necessarily the case. Ricky said he would've preferred a more sheltered area but the spot he chose would do for the time being. The truth of the matter is, there were cliffs on both sides of the lagoon and with a heavily wooded forest directly behind them, in some ways, they would have been hard pressed to find a better spot to make camp. All in all, it wasn't a bad location and in all likelihood, it would give them with an ample protection from most weather-related issues. Actually, the lagoon itself was the only vulnerable spot to the location and there was an ever so slight possibility, they were far enough away from the open sea so it wouldn't be a problem anyway. At any rate, for the time being, that important matter was seemingly resolved so they were now at liberty to try and focus on some other things. Of course, first and foremost, they had to come up with a plan of survival. After that, if there weren't any other pressing matters that had to be taken care of, a little rest was in order. Needless to say, it had been a very long day for both of them and with the stress of their situation literally biting them in the ass, that probably wasn't a bad thing to do. At this point, he took a few minutes of his time to make Maude aware of the fact, there was an outside possibility there might be wild animals on the island, so he urged her to use caution whenever she wandered away from where they made camp. From what he could remember, there were only a few small rodents and some tropical bird's native to the island, so she more than likely didn't have anything to worry about. Anyway, after their tent was all set up and shortly before sunset, they took a few minutes of their time to feast on some of the food they brought with them. Needless to say, what they had in the way of food obviously wasn't going to last forever but it would sustain their lives until they found some natural food substances on the island. In the meantime, they had to live on what they brought with them for food. As for the rest of what they talked about that evening, not a hell of a lot more was said between them, however sometime the following day, Ricky planned on building a make-shift fireplace so they would be able to cook food safely without dealing with the fear of burning the island down with an uncontrolled fire. In addition to that, he told Maude he would look the island over good to make sure there weren't any changes to the islands overall natural habitat since the last time he was there. In truth, that was something that might adversely affect their survival so Ricky wanted to stay on top of that. In the meantime, without making the situation sound any worse than it already was, he made her aware, they only had two emergency flares. That meant, they were only to be used if they were certain there was someone out there to rescue them, which in this case would entail a boat or a plane and either one would certainly be a justification for using one. In fact, quite frankly, it was the only hope they had for being rescued from the island.

Anyway, a short time later, she conceded defeat and opted to try and get some sleep while Ricky stayed up all night long to keep an eye out for a passing ship. Actually, it was decided, the following night their roles would be reversed. He would try to get some rest while she stayed up through the long hours of the night. It wasn't much of a plan, but it was undeniably the only one they had. As for their first night on the island, not anything too bad could be said about it except they were in a very undesirable situation and the possibility of being rescued from the island was very unlikely. Needless to say, their future looked very bleak indeed, however on the bright side of it all, the weather was cooperating and since they weren't starving to death, I guess their sorry state of affairs could have been a lot worse. Anyway, she tried to get some sleep that night while he kept watch for a ship or a plane however for obvious reasons neither one of them got any rest. In fact, it was a dismally frustrating night for both of them and what they did that night became a nightly ritual over the next few days, while their plans for spending a fun and enjoyable weekend together had now turned into the worst nightmare of their lives.

Part IV

CHAPTER 20

Day 1: Their first night on the island was a really difficult one to get through. Between listening to the sounds of birds and animals they weren't familiar with and not being able to get any sleep, you might say, it wasn't the best night either one of them ever had. Actually, Maude spent the better part of the night thinking about how they would get off the island and of course, that only added more misery to the predicament they were in. At any rate, for that reason alone, when she arose that morning, she was tired and still deprived of sleep. In fact, at no surprise to her, she was struggling with the reality of what they were up against. Realistically, with no hope of being rescued, it was a very dismal situation to say the least but just in case something on the positive side turned up, like a passing ship or plane, it was their intention to keep a nightly vigil. Anyway, since Ricky stayed up all night long the previous night, it would be her turn to do that the following night. In fact, until they came up with a better plan, that's the way they would do things.

Needless to say, on the outside possibility a ship or plane passed by the area, perhaps, it was a good idea to do that and with any luck at all, maybe their effort to get off the island would eventually pay off.

At any rate, it turns out, their first day on the island was a nice one. There wasn't a cloud in the sky and with a pleasant breeze blowing in from the ocean, the day was a lot more bearable for them. Under normal circumstances, if the weather wasn't good, it wouldn't have mattered to them that it was a nice day however because they were stranded on an island out in the middle of the Pacific Ocean, it was very important to them. Obviously, if by some chance, a tropical storm passed through the area in the days ahead, it might deliver a devastating blow to their survival, so they were extremely grateful for the good weather they received that day. Hopefully, everything would continue to go that way. Not only did it make the day more pleasant, but it would also aid them in their effort to find a way off the island as well. In the meantime, with only limited food supplies available to them, it was imperative they find some natural food substances on the island before they starved to death. In fact, it was what they would need to do next however right at the moment, she wanted to see how Ricky was doing so shortly after sunrise, she emerged from their tent and went over to where he sat on the left side of the encampment and checked on him. As it turns out, he was in good spirits, so she gave him a kiss on the cheek and asked how he made out last night. Needless to say, that's where she learned Ricky had the resolve of a lion that wouldn't accept defeat but that was a characteristic of his that she wasn't familiar with. At any rate, it was a good sign because if he gave up the cause of trying to survive on the island, then, it would only be a matter of time before she did also. In fact, quite frankly, if that point was reached, it would be all over for both of them. Anyway, he very quickly replied in the affirmative that he was fine, but he was also quick to point out someone had to keep an eye out for a boat or plane during the night however that wasn't anything she wasn't already aware of. Then, he apologized for being so hard-nosed about the whole thing, however he said it was in their own best interest to do that for as long as possible because any chance they had of being rescued would depend on that. At this point, they had a bite to eat from some of the food they brought with them from the state of Oregon. It wasn't anything too elegant however it wasn't meant to be. Actually, the concept of camping out beneath the stars isn't supposed be anyway so not any more than that was expected from their meal. At any rate, as anticipated, Ricky suggested they look the island over good for possible food substances they would be able to eat in the days ahead. Of course, Maude thought that was a good idea and she told him she was ready to go whenever he was. Anyway, as it turns out, not long after they finished having breakfast that morning, he retrieved a hunting knife from their tent, and they went in search of food. Actually, besides that, they also needed to find a good source of drinking water as well so you might say, that was high on their list of priorities too. At any rate, with that ulterior motive in mind, they headed for the interior of the island.

Thankfully, their search for edible food substances turned out well. In fact, in a matter of two or three hours, they managed to gather up some well ripened bananas, a few coconuts and at least, a dozen or more papayas as well. Finally, things were beginning to look up for them. With the discovery of edible food, they wouldn't starve to death. Furthermore, there appeared to be an abundance of those fruits so they quickly deduced, they would be able to survive for an extended period of time on the island if their effort to be rescued failed. In addition to that, there would be fish from the ocean as well, so it looked like they were going to be okay for a while. Needless to say, after the unfortunate stroke of luck befell them the day before, things were finally heading in the right direction. Granted, those measures to find a good edible source of food wasn't going to get them rescued however it would help them survive their ordeal for as long as it was necessary. At any rate, by mid-afternoon, they brought the spoils of their labor back to where they had made camp. At this point, Ricky and Maude proceeded to unload all of the food they gathered up from their backpacks, then after taking a short break, they headed off to the interior of the island again, only this time they went in a different direction. In fact, to be a little more precise, they headed for the mountainous area of the island, where according to Ricky, they would be able to get fresh water. Anyway, as it turns out, his hunch proved to be correct so they would have a fresh supply of water to drink as well. Needless to say, that was a good omen, and they didn't waste any time filling up their canteens. Furthermore, the distance they had to walk to get water wasn't far from their camp either so that was a positive aspect to the whole thing as well. At any rate, it turns out the pond of fresh water they discovered was fed by a waterfall that cascaded down over the right side of a small mountain located near the interior of the island. Of course, being an investigative kind of guy, Ricky wanted to look into the matter further. The truth of the matter is, had they not been able to find water, they would've had to boil some ocean water as a means for survival. At any rate, it wouldn't be necessary to do that now and with that problem considered solved, Ricky proceeded to follow the small stream of water to see where it went too. As for Maude, while he was off investigating the area for future sources of water, she quickly disrobed from her clothes and went for a swim in the pond. About twenty minutes later Ricky returned from his excursion, only to find Maude swimming around in the pond of water with her beautiful body glistening in the sunlight. Needless to say, he was immediately taken back with awe of such a beautiful sight, and he began to admire every square inch of her body. Finally, after another fifteen minutes went by, she got out of the water, dried off and got dressed however in the meantime, he couldn't stop thinking about Maude. She was a masterpiece in every sense of the word and not unexpectedly, his hormones apparently began to kick in because he was getting hornier by the minute. At any rate, by the time she realized he had been admiring her body, you might say, Ricky had a strong desire to make love to her. Of course, by this time, she just happened to notice that unmistakable look in his eyes of I want to get laid in the worst possible was literally tattooed across his face in the most obvious of ways, so she nudged him in the side and said, "Do you realize you have been admiring my ass for the better part of an hour now?" "Well, I suppose it looks like that," he said. "Actually, if you don't mind me saying so, you are a very beautiful woman." "Yes, it seems you mentioned that to me before, Mr. Vestellini," she remarked. "Well, I'm very flattered however if you have any serious intentions of laying me, I suggest you get busy. Neither one of us are going to live forever, so would you please dig the finger you of your ass, and make love to me, Ricky." At this point, he couldn't contain himself any longer, so he took her in his arms and proceeded to kiss her passionately on the lips until she was literally gasping for air. Then, after gazing deeply into her eyes and admiring the absolute stunning beauty of her body, he proceeded to say, "Well, it just so happens, it would be really and truly be an honor to make love to you, Mrs. Derringer!" "My aren't we formal with our words," she replied. "You may call it what you like but that's the way I see it and that's what I would like to do," Ricky stated. "Then, don't just stand there, fuck the hell out of me, Ricky," she exclaimed! "Actually, I was hoping you would say something to that effect," he quipped. At this point, with really nothing left to be said, Ricky quickly shuffled her up into his arms and carried her over to a small meadow next to the pond, where a moment or two later, Ricky made love to her in the splendor of the grass. Yes, for a few minutes in time, the nightmare they were living was completely forgotten.

Anyway, a little while later, probably late afternoon, they made their way back to where their camp was set up, fully rested and totally at ease with their sexuality but it was also a day of uncertainty for them even though they had accomplished a lot. At any rate, with a little daylight left to their day, Ricky wanted to build a fireplace for their cooking purposes on the beachhead of the lagoon. By doing so, not only would they have a good way to cook food, but they would also have a good way to generate some light for themselves after it got dark. In fact, that would allow them to see things that were within a few feet of where they set up their tent. Obviously, it was a win, win situation for them because there was always a possibility that a passing ship or perhaps, even a plane would see their fire and take a closer look at the island to see what was going on. It might even end up saving their lives. Anyway, supper that evening consisted of some of the food they brought with them from the state of Oregon as well as some of the fruit which was gathered up earlier in the day. All in all, it wasn't a bad meal however more importantly, their appetite had been satisfied for a while. At any rate, shortly after supper that evening, Ricky made a path from where they made camp all the way up the right side of a fairly dense thicket, which led to the top of a cliff that overlooked the lagoon. Needless to say, from that observation point, they would be able to shoot off one of his flares if the opportunity came along for them to do that. Hopefully, at some point along the way that would happen, and they would be rescued. In the meantime, night was nearly upon them and this time, it was her turn to stay up all night. Obviously, someone had to keep watch for a boat, or a plane and it was her job to do that this evening. Anyway, with that in mind, she gave Ricky an inspirational kiss to convince him it was time to get some rest, and a moment or two later, he headed into the tent to try and get some sleep while she sat down on top of the large rock that was located on the side of their encampment. From there she would be able to keep an eye on things while he slept. The next evening their roles would be reversed, and she would try and get some sleep while he kept the nightly vigil of keeping an eye out for a boat or a plane. In the meantime, she had an opportunity to think about a few things. First of all, she had decided to keep a diary about their adventure on the island so if good fortune were to come their way and they actually made it back to the state of Oregon, Maude would have another idea for a book. Actually, she saw it as all in a day's work, although she had a feeling Ricky was going to tease her about what she intended to do. In reality, Maude had not written anything for a couple of years so if everything went as planned, her next novel may actually turn out to be a challenge. Anyway, without dwelling on it too much, that's what she planned on doing if they ever got back to the state of Oregon. In other matters, Maude wanted to talk Ricky into marrying her however she thought it was best to not pressure him into doing that. The fact of the matter is she wanted a family of her own and since she wasn't getting any younger, that was something she couldn't put off too much longer. Of course, now that they were stranded on an island in the Pacific Ocean, it goes without saying, that might not be possible. At this point, it was a question of whether or not Ricky was going to be the lucky guy that married her however unless they found a way to get off the island, it wasn't going to matter anyway. For the time being, that matter was up in the air, but all indications pointed to a future marriage between them. As for the possibility of being rescued from the island, the odds of that happening were slim to none however she refused to give up. In fact, Ricky looked at it the same way she did and with a good positive attitude in the day ahead, I suppose there was always a possibility that would pay off for them and they would have a chance to get married and live happily ever after.

CHAPTER 21

Day 2: Early next morning, Ricky was awakened by the first rays of sunlight to reach the island however as bright and enchanting a day it was, he was still concerned about Maude's well-being. Needless to say, the past forty-eight hours had been particularly hard on her so Ricky was worried about how she was doing, in particularly, how she managed to get through the night. Of course, when either one of them stayed up all night long, sleep wasn't thought of. They just kept watch for something that might be able to help them and got through the night. At any rate, since it was Maude's responsibility to keep watch for a boat or plane last night, he thought it would be a good idea to make sure she everything was fine with her. Actually, Ricky was sorely afraid the stress of what they were up against may have gotten to her because a lot of responsibility was on her shoulders during the nights, she kept watch. Anyway, with that in mind, he went to check on Maude this morning to see if anything materialized during the night. Unfortunately, the moment Ricky saw her propped up against a palm tree, sound asleep, he had his answer. At this point, he quickly surmised, she must have fallen asleep sometime during the night because she was totally oblivious to everything around her, including Ricky. His first thought was to let Maude rest for a while however he also quickly deduced, that wouldn't be the best thing to do. Anyway, with that said, he proceeded to tap her lightly on the shoulder in an effort to wake her up, which did in fact work well however she was a bit startled by the sudden appearance of Ricky standing next to her. At this point, she realized what happened. Anyway, within a few seconds of having regained her composure, Maude felt combatant to defend the mistake she made because she should have been keeping an eye out for a boat or plane however rather than making a spectacle of the situation, he just simply gave her a little praise for trying to be so vigilant in their effort to be rescued and then he brushed the matter aside. Actually, that's not at all what she thought he was going to say. She would have guessed; he would've been madder than hell at her for falling asleep during the night but that wasn't the case at all. He was cool, calm, collected and the nicest person a person could ever wish for. At any rate, she was extremely relieved he didn't lower the boom on her for being so negligent because she thought a lot of him and circumstances as they were, what happened to her could have happened to anyone.

Anyway, as it turns out, they were soon discussing some other matters, least of which had to do with the fact, they were trying to conserve what little food they had in case they were stuck on the island for an extended period of time. Needless to say, that was very quickly agreed upon because there really wasn't any way of knowing if they would even be rescued in the days ahead, so food conservation was obviously the right thing to do. The truth of the matter is, even though they found edible substances in the way of different kinds of tropical fruit, it would still be a very good idea to conserve what they had for food just simply because there future was up in the air. I grant you; things were beginning to look up for the first time since they learned that Ricky's boat wasn't capable of going anywhere however that was still the wisest thing to do. Sadly, there was not too much of anything they could do because his boat was out of gas and there wasn't any way Ricky could fix the leak in the gas tank. In other words, they were going to be on the island until someone came along to rescue them and as I said before, the prognosis of that happening was not very good. In the meantime, it was decided, they would go look for some more fruit. At the very least, if nothing else, it would keep them alive for a while. Besides, maybe they would get lucky and find another source of food in addition to what they found growing abundantly on the island. Anyway, they both agreed, it was the best thing to do. As for their plan of action regarding food, they intended to supplement their diet with what the ocean had to offer in the way of edible food, which in this particular instance, meant they would be eating a lot of fish and perhaps some other things like oysters and crabs as well. One way or another, if they did that, they would more than likely be able to survive on the island for as long as they were there. In addition to that, common sense told them, there was an outside chance they might even be able to get some meat from one of the birds on the island because Ricky kept a small handgun on the boat. Obviously, his fishing gear would give them an opportunity to catch some fish, so their situation wasn't as bleak as they originally thought.

Anyway, breakfast that morning consisted of nothing more than a few stale donuts and a cup of instant coffee although Ricky had already made plans to catch some fish for supper. As a matter of fact, after a bit of small talk regarding their current state of affairs, he told Maude what his intentions were, and true to his word, a short time later, he took the boats life raft and headed back out to his yacht to do a little fishing. Needless to say, from there, he spent a couple of hours doing that in an effort to catch some fish for dinner. Furthermore, it just so happens he got more than what he bargained for in the way of fish, so they had enough fish for a couple of meals. At any rate, that meant they would be eating well today so Ricky gathered up the spoils of his labor and a few minutes later, he headed back into shore. In addition to that, Ricky also took the time to bring some more of their belongings into shore in case a bad storm came along and destroyed his boat or cut it loose from where it was anchored in the lagoon. In fact, there was a possibility what he did might actually turn out to be an important move on his part because his boat was the only lifeline they had to the mainland of the United States as well as the rest of the world for that matter. Actually, most of their camping gear was still on the boat anyway so it stood to reason, it would probably be best to haul what he could into shore. The truth of the matter is, if something were to happen to his yacht, they would be up shit creek without a paddle, boat, or anything else so he opted to take this course of action. It obviously didn't hurt to be on the safe side. Not only would that help ensure the preservation of their lives, but it would also help facilitate his effort to make their existence on the island as comfortable as possible for as long as they were there.

At any rate, as it turns out, the morning and afternoon went by rather quickly that day but with regards to being human, time goes by very quickly anyway. In this particular case, while he was out on his boat catching fish, she gathered up all the fruit she could find over much the same path they followed the day before. In fact, all that actually amounted too was more bananas and coconuts however it was enough food to sustain their life and that's all that really mattered. The day had gone well and that was very important as well because they had a couple of good meals lined up for them now. Anyway, on this occasion, he made make it back to camp before she did and by late morning, with everything under control and with ample food for both meals already planned out, Ricky fried up the fish while she prepared the rest of the meal. Obviously, it wasn't the best meal either one of them ever had but they didn't have a lot of options available to them, so they were content with what they had. The most important thing of all was the meal satisfied their hunger which of course, meant they weren't going to starve to death. At any rate, once that was taken care of, the rest of the day was spent talking about different things, none of which was as important as how they intended to survive on the island. Needless to say, sometimes, dreams run deep within our imagination however the reality of what we live is sometimes not even close to our expectations because there are times when a situation speaks for itself. In this case, that is what can be said about them as well. At any rate, with their best meant intentions gone awry and with not too much more of anything they could do, the better part of the rest of the day was spent sitting beneath the palm trees, catching a breeze every now and then while the tropical winds that had a tendency to caress the island from one day to the next continued to blow in from the ocean giving them relief from the intense heat of the sun. Anyway, by days end, it was time to start on their nightly vigil one more time, however it was his turn to stay up while she got a little rest, so after she went to bed, Ricky watched for a passing vessel while she tried to get some sleep.

CHAPTER 22

Day 3: The third night on the island turned out to be a better one for Maude because she was able to get a little restful sleep however since they weren't going anywhere for a while, there were still a lot of unanswered questions lingering in the back of her mind. Of course, Ricky was having much the same problems she was with regards to getting an ample amount of rest as well as being concerned about where their next meal would come from. Perhaps, what benefited him a bit more than it did her was he had a higher tolerance level for physical stress and other factors so he was able to absorb the unfortunate situation they were in a lot better than she could. At any rate, by this time, she had finally come to terms with herself about the possibility they may have to live the rest of their lives out on the island. Needless to say, it wasn't a very pleasant thought, however that was the reality of the quandary they had been thrust into after their boat wasn't able to go any further. Anyway, now, there were other things to be concerned about as well. What if one of them became ill or got injured? Obviously, with no doctors or hospitals around, they were at the mercy of mother nature. Then, there was always the concern for bad weather in the way of a storm that might do damage to their environment on the island so badly that they may not even be able to recover from the aftermath of it even if they survived the storm. In fact, as it turns out, that was the next thing they had to deal with because the great weather they were enjoying over the weekend had disappeared. Sometime, during the night, dark gray clouds rolled into the area, leaving the skies mostly overcast. It appeared some type of storm was headed their way and that was obviously a reason for concern. At any rate, with that thought eating away at the back of her mind and now fully awake, Maude went to check on Ricky that morning and once again, she had the good fortune to find him in good spirits even after he had been up all night long. Anyway, in a matter of a couple of minutes, she conveyed to him her concern over what appeared to be a bad electrical storm headed their way. At this point, as much as he hated to admit it, they might be in danger because the skies were beginning to look quite formidable, so Ricky was quick to suggest they abandon all of their food gathering routines that day in favor of temporarily dismantling the tent and storing it away in a nearby cave until the storm passes by the island. Needless to say, if they encountered a really bad storm with high winds, it would save their tent from destruction as well as save all of their supplies and personal belongings too because they would put those inside the cave also. The truth of the matter was, if the impending storm was more than a tropical rain shower, they would be in big trouble if they didn't abandon their plans to continue making camp on the shore of the lagoon. In fact, by the look of things, it was probably going to be a bad storm so rather than taking a chance on riding it out anywhere near their encampment, they would seek shelter from what mother nature was about to unleash upon them inside a cave located on top of one of the cliffs overlooking the lagoon. At any rate, the way everything unfolded that day, after all of their belongings as well as the tent were relocated to the interior of the cave, he took a few extra minutes to go out to his boat one more time to make sure it was anchored into the coral reef that it was sitting upon. Needless to say, it's where his yacht came to rest the other day and with any luck at all, that's where it would be sitting after the storm. Actually, from what Ricky heard, just the sway of the oceans waves alone were usually strong enough to make an anchor let go and of course, if that happened, it would deal another devastating blow to their survival but there was nothing else he could do. It would have to ride the storm out on its own. The truth of the matter is, Ricky loved that boat more than anything in the world with the exception of Maude, so it was going to be hard to part with it if his boat didn't survive the storm. In addition to that, there was a good possibility he might be able to use the wooden planks from the yacht to build a house on the island somewhere in the days ahead. Granted, Ricky wouldn't be able to put one together the conventional way with screws and nails, but he could always use a few vines to hold the wooden planks together. Anyway, the idea certainly had a lot of merit to it, and Ricky thought that might work well for them, so if his boat wasn't destroyed in the storm, he would think about doing that. For the time being, they had other things to be concerned about. First of all, a storm was headed in their direction, and secondly, there was a possibility they might be rescued at some point along the way. Obviously, that wasn't likely to happen, nevertheless, it was the only realistic way they could look at it, so he wanted to see how things went for a while before deciding to dismantle his boat.

Anyway, regardless of what Ricky may or may not be able to do the reality at hand was a storm was on the way and after doing what he could to preserve his boat, they both headed off to the safety of the cave. They would try and ride out the fury of the storm there and by the look of things, the action they took wasn't a moment too soon because by early in the afternoon, the rain was beginning to fall lightly however a very short time later, it turned into a torrential down pour. Then, as anticipated, high velocity winds came in and an hour later, the island was assaulted with all the fury of an unrelenting hurricane. In fact, it was lucky they sought shelter in the cave when they did because the storm showed no mercy, and it continued to pelt the island for several hours.

Finally, along towards the time night usually set in, it looked like the storm had shit itself out right to the point of looking like the following day would be fine. It would be just a question of how much destruction it did, that's all. At this point, with it being late in the day, it was easily decided, they would spend the rest of the night inside the cave. Tomorrow, they would assess the damage it had done, and then if there was any way possible, they would resurrect their tent back up on the shore where they had it before. In the meantime, a little while later and shortly before they called it a day, Ricky and Maude began discussing what they would do if they ever got back to the state of Oregon. It was then that she finally got around to telling Ricky about the coins she found down beneath her house and how she eventually sold them to an investor who would more than likely market them somewhere within the numismatic field. Then, she went onto tell Ricky the entire story from beginning to end. Of course, it took Maude some time to tell him the whole story however right at the moment, time was something they had a lot of. Anyway, as you might think, he was really and truly amazed at how something like that ever came about however Ricky also realized, she wasn't the kind of person to fabricate a story so even though the story was a bit on the unbelievable side, he didn't doubt the authenticity of the whole thing for a minute. At this point in their conversation, she gradually went onto another subject and told him about her recent trip to France. Until now, Maude had not taken the time to do that either because she wasn't sure what direction their relationship was headed in however now they were stranded on an island out in the middle of the Pacific Ocean, there was not any reason not to tell him everything. Anyway, for the most part, he appeared to be extremely interested in everything she told him about France. In fact, much to his surprise, she even went as far as asking him if he had ever given any thought to living there, which of course was the furthest thing from his mind. At this point, Maude went onto tell him how much she liked being in France, in particularly, the southern coast of that fine country. Anyway, long before either one of them had an opportunity to say any more than that, Ricky was quick to suggest they move there if that's what she wanted to do. Well, as you might think, Maude didn't expect to get that kind of a response from him, but he quickly stated that was contingent upon her marrying him. Needless to say, she was flabbergasted. Maude knew he was interested in her and all indications pointed to the fact he liked her really well, but Maude wasn't certain whether or not he wanted to get married. As for moving to France, she never thought that would be anything of interest to him. In fact, one of the reasons why she didn't mention her trip to France to him before was because she didn't think he would agree to go there if she expressed a desire to live there. At any rate, silence quickly ensued while Maude thought about what Ricky said. A few seconds went by. Then a few more. Finally, she gazed into his eyes and said, "You know, I was hoping you would come to that conclusion but with all do honesty, I didn't think you would ever agree to do either. Do you feel all right?" "Yes, I feel just fine," he replied. "In fact, I would follow you to the ends of the earth, if that's what you wanted to do. I love you, Maude." By now, she was in a state of shock. Granted, she wanted to get married and raise a family, and Ricky was an ideal candidate, but everything was so sudden that even she was taken back by his statement. "Well," she replied, "give it some thought. Both marriage and moving to France are life changing events. I would hate like hell for you to be unhappy with either situation." "I most certainly realize that however I would still like to marry you," he answered. "It's just that at this point in time, that's impossible. It will have to wait until we get off this frigging island." "Then, let's try and look at this optimistically and perhaps, if we ever get away from here, we'll have an opportunity to do that," she answered. "Right now, I think it would be a good idea to try and get some rest." "I totally agree," Ricky replied. "I've got a feeling tomorrow we'll be busy trying to get our camp site set back up. In fact, it will be a question of how much damage this storm did to the island." "I here you, Ricky," she stated. "I was thinking the same thing myself." "Then, get some rest and I will talk to you in the morning," he answered. At this point, with nothing left to say, a few minutes later, they rolled out their sleeping bags inside the safety of the cave and were soon sound asleep. Needless to say, the next day would probably be another challenging day for them as the uncertainty of their situation continued to haunt the hell out of their minds. In truth, all they could actually hope for was to be given the chance to live another day on the island and then if by some frigging miracle someone were to come along and rescue them, perhaps, all the things they wanted to do would become reality. In the meantime, a little rest was in order due to the undeniable fact, they had a lot of work ahead of them in the days ahead.

CHAPTER 23

Day 4: As anticipated, when the next day arrived, it was quickly noted, it was going to be a nice day. The sun was back out shining brightly, and the skies were blue again. In fact, now, a day later, everything appeared to be fine. Other than a few downed trees here and there about the island, life had returned to normal. Perhaps, to an outside observer, they would've thought it was just another day in paradise there however that really wasn't the case at all for Ricky and Maude. Every day was a struggle for them, and it wasn't very likely that would change anytime soon. At any rate, with the tropical storm that ravished the island out of the area now, it was time to assess the damage that was done so shortly after sunrise, they emerged from the cave and set off for the shore of the lagoon. Initial estimates of the damage to the area was less than what they originally thought however the path of its destruction was still quite visible. Anyway, as unbelievable as it may be, Ricky's boat was spared any major damage so that was a good sign. In fact, it was still anchored out in the lagoon and that wasn't at all what they thought would happen. The truth of the matter is, if they were on the island long enough, he intended to use the wood from the boat to build a house somewhere on the island so the fact his boat survived the storm was good news. At any rate, after the initial assessment of the damage from the storm was done, the remainder of the morning was spent setting their tent back up and reestablishing their camp on the beachhead of the lagoon. Of course, that meant making more than one trip from the cave to the shore of the lagoon however by the first of the afternoon, that was all taken care of and all of a sudden, Ricky and Maude felt like they were back in the good graces of god. In reality, there really wasn't any basis for them to make that claim, nevertheless, it's how they looked at it and perhaps, that is all that really mattered in the end.

Anyway, with everything seemingly in order and with their food supply running a bit low, their brunch, lunch or whatever the hell you want to call, consisted of nothing more than bananas and coconuts that morning. Unfortunately, what little food they brought with them from the state of Oregon had been depleted so from this point on, they had to survive on what the island had to offer in the way of food substances. In this particular case, that meant they would be eating a lot of bananas, coconuts, papayas, and mangos in addition to some seafood. At any rate, they would do whatever it took to survive on the island. In the meantime, as part of their daily routine, once again, they went in search of food that afternoon. So far, they had plenty of luck doing that so at this point, there wasn't any reason to think that would change. Actually, Ricky said, if they were there long enough, they might have to take some of the seeds from the papayas and mangos that had become a part of their diet, and plant them somewhere on the island in order to replenish the abundance of the plants. Needless to say, even though Maude didn't know a thing about planting anything, that made all the sense in the world to her, so she was in favor of doing that. In fact, he had already taken the initiative to plant a few apple seeds from the some of the fruit they already had so there was a good possibility they might have another food source to eat in the days ahead. In fact, there wasn't too much else they could do but if Ricky came up with some other ideas that increased their chances of survival, they would do whatever it took to seize upon the opportunity. Right at the moment, it was too early to be concerned about that because there was still a chance they might be rescued. Perhaps, that was wishful thinking on their part however as long as there was a glimmer of hope of being rescued, they would not abandon ship and they would hang onto everything they thought might be able to help them. Needless to say, it was the only way to look at it and it was how they got through each day. In fact, they both had a good positive attitude and perhaps, with any luck at all, maybe that way of thinking would get them through the unfortunate debacle they were going through until someone came to their rescue.

At any rate, after an early afternoon lunch that day, he got out his pistol and they went in search of a wild boar or some kind of bird they could eat. Perhaps, even a rabbit. As of yet, they hadn't spotted anything like that on the island however Ricky was still fairly certain, if they kept looking around, sooner or later, something would turn up. In fact, quite frankly, the odds were in their favor for that happening sometime. In this particular case, nothing turned up however there was always a possibility somewhere down the road, it might. Actually, the way things were right now, they still had plenty of natural fruit they could eat in addition to whatever they caught in the way of seafood. Obviously, it was not a good situation, however things could've been worse. In the meantime, and certainly by late afternoon they headed back to camp, which as I stated before was located on the shore of the lagoon. Anyway, from there, Ricky grabbed his fishing gear and went back out to his boat to do some fishing while Maude took care of the fruit they gathered up a little while earlier. At any rate, like all of the other days on the island, he had plenty of luck in catching something, and a short time later, good fortune had them feasting on more fish and fruit from the island. Actually, it wasn't a bad meal although they were both getting tired of eating the same thing every day. In fact, it's the reason why they went in search of some game earlier in the day however nothing came of it so they would have to eat some more bananas and coconuts.

Anyway, by now, early evening had arrived again and like usual, they took to discussing a few things that were first and foremost on their mind. In this particular instance, Maude began the conversation by telling Ricky how much she loved the palm trees and the white sand beach's that adorned the island even though they both wanted to get off the island if an opportunity to do so arose. Of course, that got an immediate response from Ricky however he expressed the same desire to get off the island that she did. In fact, they both loved the natural beauty of the islands however neither one of them wanted to spend the rest of their life there. At any rate, after being engaged in their conversation for a little while, they eventually began discussing what they were going to do when they got back to the mainland. Needless to say, that entailed a lot of promises, most of which they would hopefully have an opportunity to go through with at some point in the days ahead. Then, not unexpectedly, the subject of moving to France came up again and Maude reiterated herself saying, she would like to live there for a while and see where everything went. Well, as stated before, Ricky had no objections about doing that so she was quite pleased that he would even consider living there and of course, Ricky said he would live there if that's what she wanted to do. Actually, that projected supposition was based on the fact, they would be rescued from the island at some point along the way and when that happened, upon returning to the state of Oregon, they would get married. Anyway, if things went well and they made it off the island sometime, the plan was to get married and move to France. At least, that's what Maude wanted to do anyway. In the meantime, there was a lot of work to be done on the island. If things went as planned, he was going to build them a permanent place to live somewhere on the island which would provide them with a necessary shelter to live in. As for exploring the other two islands in the area, that was something he planned on doing as well. In fact, there was always a possibility, there might be some other edible food substances on those islands too so Ricky thought it would be a good idea to investigate that as soon as possible. Needless to say, it wasn't very likely that was the case however circumstances as they were, it was in their own best interest to look into it sometime because there was something there that might be useful to them. Perhaps, with a little luck, they might even find a better place to build a house. It's true, Ricky had been to the islands many times before however in each instance, his time was spent in the waters around the islands, not on shore. At any rate, for that reason, he wasn't really that familiar with the other two islands so if nothing unfortunate befell them, he would check them out sometime.

Anyway, as it turns out, they carried on a conversation for an hour or so before what they were talking about began to get old. It wasn't that either one of them actually thought discussing future plans was a trivial matter however there is only so many ways, you can look at something. In this particular instance, they weren't going anywhere, anytime soon so the subject was brought to an end a short time later. For as long as they were alive, there would always be another day so it was a lot more important to concentrate on the matters at hand, rather than speculating on what may or may not be in the days ahead. Of course, as long as they were on the island, there would always be challenges ahead of them like making sure they had food to eat so it was decided, they would talk about something else for a while. Furthermore, by this time, the day was all but done, so after a little more small talk about this, that and everything under the sun, Ricky began getting the urge to make love to Maude again. First, there was a kiss. Then, a very long passionate kiss ensued. Time continued to go by however both were oblivious to the outside world again. Little by little, Ricky pursued his conquest of Maude until he reached the point where he was caressing every square inch of her body. Needless to say, she immediately heeded to his advances in light of the approaching darkness and soon they were rolling away in the grasp of love. In fact, in the eyes of god, it was the perfect ending to a perfect day for them. At any rate, fairly typical of the way a person feels human emotions through the act of physical touch, the ecstasy they had been enjoying was very short lived to say the least and shortly thereafter, the sun retreated down upon the horizon, signaling the end of another day. Then, ever so gradually, the jewel, laden sky lit up the heavens above bringing to an end another day while the peace and serenity of the night spoke their names softly through the presence of mother nature. In fact, not much more than the sound of a hoot owl could be heard off in the distance. Needless to say, they were sexually gratified in every sense of the word even if it was only for the moment and never to happen again. Surely, it was life the way it should be with the exception of where they were. At any rate, a few minutes later, after having enjoyed themselves in a brief respite of ecstasy, they called it a day. In truth, it was at this point in their routine of doing things each day that they headed off to bed anyway and with all the necessary thing having been done, they were content to get some rest. Actually, with all do honesty, another day had come and gone a midst some of the most punishing days of their lives however the most import thing of all was they were still alive. Anyway, as you might think, a short time later, without giving any more thought to their less than desirable situation, the night sky above exploded into the most heavenly paradoxical sky imaginable and soon they drifted off to sleep in the comfort of one another's arms.

CHAPTER 24

Day 5: On the morning of the fifth day of being stranded on an island they would've just as soon forgotten about; they both arose from their night's sleep in good spirits although nothing in the way of hope of being rescued had materialized yet. As for their nightly vigil of keeping an eye out for a passing boat or plane, that was given up in favor of getting some sleep and that was the first time that had happened since making their unfortunate arrival on the island. The fact of the matter is, the only plan they had for getting off the island wasn't getting them anywhere, so it was eventually concluded, what they were doing was a waste of time. Realistically, it more than likely wouldn't have made any difference anyway because they were too far out in the middle of nowhere for anyone to find them. In fact, circumstances as they were, the odds of being rescued were slim to none so the previous night was used to get a good night's sleep.

Anyway, this day started out pretty much the same way as all the other days on the island did with the exception of one thing. Instead of going in search of food, Maude chose to go for a swim in the ocean. Usually, her time was spent gathering up fruit while Ricky fished the lagoon however not this morning. On this occasion, after thoroughly letting go of the idea they might be rescued from the island sometime, once their appetites had been satisfied with a few bananas and coconuts, Maude took off her clothes with the intentions of taking a dip in the ocean. Of course, like usual, Ricky was far more interested in what she was doing than anything else, so he spent a few minutes watching her beautiful body glisten beneath the early morning sun. Needless to say, there wasn't any need for modesty on the island so swimming in the nude was obviously the only way to go. He was disappointed about one thing though and that was Maude totally disregarded his warning about being attacked by a shark and went swimming out in the lagoon anyway. The truth of the matter is she didn't like being told what to do however she promised not to swim too far out into the lagoon, and that seemed to satisfy his demands so nothing more was said about it. Believe it or not, her only thought was if for some reason she were to run into a shark, she would cross that bridge when she came to it. Realistically speaking, it was quite possible she could lose her life by taking a dip in the ocean however regardless of that fact, she was determined to do so. Until now, she spent most of her leisure time swimming in a small pond of water located a half a mile inland so there hadn't been any reason for concern. Anyway, this time, Ricky was watching her swim about the lagoon and perhaps, it was a good idea that he was because if a shark were in the area, he might be able to spot it ahead of time and it goes without saying, that might save her life. In fact, it was moments like these that he realized just how lucky he was to have her and of course, that made him appreciate her even more. At any rate, after swimming about in the depths of the lagoon for a while, on her way back into shore, Ricky noticed that she was reaching down in the water to pick something up. At this point, he wasn't aware that she found a pearl. In truth, he had been daydreaming a bit about how he could make their lives better on the island so Ricky didn't immediately pick up on what she was doing. Anyway, after a moment or two of assessing the situation, he walked over to where Maude stood on the shore of the lagoon. At this point, he could see why she was so excited. Maude was in possession of a great big pearl, and it glistened brightly in the sunlight. Actually, Ricky didn't think she would find anything like that so close to shore however much to his surprise, she had. At any rate, within a short period of time of having made this unique discovery, they began scanning the bottom of the ocean to see if they could find more pearls. Well, as fate would have it, sure enough, they began finding one pearl after another. In fact, not only did they have the pearls, but they also had some oysters to eat for their next meal as well.

Anyway, as it turns out, they spent the next hour or so gathering all the pearls and oysters they could find until it became apparent, there wasn't any more to be found. At this point, Ricky suggested they call it quits however by this time he could no longer control his urge to make love to her again. In fact, as usual, he was awestruck by her mesmerizing beauty, in addition to being overwhelmed by the passion of the moment so without hesitating another second, Ricky took her in his arms and began kissing her passionately on the lips. Anyway, like with most things of that nature, one thing quickly led to another, and before either one of them realized it, he had planted his feet firmly into the sand on the shore of the lagoon, and with her legs wrapped tightly around his thighs, Ricky made love to her. Not once or twice but three times and in the process of doing so something good actually came out of it all. As a matter of act, while they were engaged in the exhilarating thralls of passion, a fishing vessel was passing by the island. Of course, at this point in their moment of passion that discovery hadn't been made yet but within the next few minutes, that was all about to change. At any rate, as fate would have it, Ricky just happened to look over his right shoulder in the direction of the open sea, when he spotted a ship on the horizon however he didn't immediately say anything because he thought it was his imagination. Anyway, for that reason, he didn't pay any attention to the ship that was passing by the island at that very moment. A few more seconds went and then, like being struck by a bolt of lightning or by a great idea that suddenly comes to light, something inside his highly meticulous mind clicked and at that point, it became obvious to him that a ship was indeed passing by the island after all. It can also be noted that Ricky was more than likely experiencing what most people call systematic shock or perhaps, better stated as stunned disbelief. Anyway, regardless of how you look at it, Ricky wasn't totally convinced he had seen a ship, so he looked out to sea one more time to try and reassure his mind he wasn't seeing things. Well, it turns out, there really was a ship passing by the island, and like you might think, Ricky was now beside himself at learning this. At any rate, it was undoubtably the time to act so he pushed Maude aside and pointed to where the ship was. At first, she didn't have any idea what he was all worked up about because she was facing the interior of the island however a second or two later, the reality of the situation sank in. It was a chance to be rescued and it goes without saying, that was something neither one of them thought would happen. As a matter of fact, it was the opportunity they had been waiting for and barring another catastrophe, a godsend miracle was about to take place. Anyway, one thing quickly lead to another and seconds later, they began jumping up and down in excitement at the hope of being rescued. At this point, the only logical thing to do was to go back to where they made camp and get his flare gun. Time was of the essence because a ship was unquestionably passing by the island, so it was imperative they signal the vessel before it left the area. In reality, neither one of them would have ever been able to live with themselves if they let the vessel slip away without at least making an effort to let whoever was out there know they were stranded on the island, so after a very quick inspection of the gun to make sure it was loaded, he raced back to the edge of the shore and shot off one of the flares. At this point, it's safe to say, they did everything they could to try and get the attention of the passing vessel so there wasn't anything they could do now but wait and see if their attempt to be rescued form the island turned out to be successful after all. In the meantime, uncertainty tore away at both of their hearts in not knowing whether or not they had succeeded in their endeavor to make the passing ship aware of their dire need to get off the island. At this point, they were at the mercy of whoever was out there. They had done everything they possibly could do and now, their lives were in the hands of the crew of the ship that was passing by the island. Nothing else really mattered! If they were going to be rescued, you might say, it was now or never for them in every sense of the word. Either they would go home to the state of Oregon shortly or they would remain stranded on that island forever and the latter alternative wasn't anything to get too excited about.

CHAPTER 25

"Jim, have you got a minute," the first mate of the Roxie Anne asked? "I think you might want to take a look at what I've zeroed in on over there on that island." Then, not sure what he'd found, George passed the binoculars over to Captain Jim Melendez so he could take a closer look at what he had been so focused on for the past fifteen to twenty minutes. Anyway, as it turns out, while the rest of the crew aboard his fishing vessel was hard at work, trying to bring in the catch of the day, George had been preoccupied with something else. In fact, it just so happens, he was observing the distant island through his binoculars. Obviously, he wasn't following the standard operating procedure of the ship however George, being a lazy sort of individual was hard at work with his binoculars, trying to take in the beauty of the islands. At any rate, while he was engaged in the process of doing this, he made an interesting discovery. Over on the distant horizon, while eyeing the landscape for wildlife, George had the good fortune to spot a couple of people making love in the sand upon the shore of the island they were trolling around. Of course, in this case, it was Ricky and Maude. Furthermore, the way everything unfolded that day, after a short series of events, George spied one of their emergency flares shoot across the morning sky. Normally, that meant someone was in some kind of trouble, and even though George was a little slow, mentally, even he could tell someone was in trouble on that island. Anyway, one thing very quickly led to another and like a dedicated person to a cause, George brought the matter to Captain Melendez's attention. Needless to say, after a moment or two of assessing the overall situation on the island, Captain Melendez concluded, someone on the island needed their assistance. "Why in the name of Christ didn't you bring this to my attention sooner," he exclaimed! "Obviously, someone's in distress on that island or they would not have sent an emergency flare up into the sky. In fact, as much as I hate to say it, it's fairly evident, they need help. What were you doing when that flare made itself known to this fishing vessel? You weren't shirking your hired duties as a fisherman, were you?" "Well, as a matter of fact, sir," George stammered, "I was doing some bird watching when I noticed a couple having sexual intercourse on the shore of that island. Actually, I admit, I wasn't doing what I was supposed to be doing but the beauty of the islands are very intriguing to me. Anyway, I sincerely apologize for not mentioning this to you sooner however there was not any reason to believe they were in trouble until a moment ago. I swear to god, I would have said something if that had been the case." At this point, Captain Melendez shook his head in absolute total disgust at George, knowing darn well he was screwing off on the job again, instead of doing his job. "Well, now you know something is wrong," Captain Melendez replied in disgust. "Let's get busy and go see what we can do for them. I have a feeling their situation may be a lot worse than I originally thought. Needless to say, there is only so many hours in a day that a person can utilize to their benefit so if we're going to give them assistance, I suggest we do it right now." A moment later, after giving George a very disapproving look for his carefree laziness, the captain of the ship gave the order to change directions and soon they were headed directly for the island. As for the situation of the couple on the island, there was no way to be certain of what was going on but Captain Melendez was certain the islands were uninhabited so chances are something was wrong. Hopefully, they would be able to give them some assistance, if not, perhaps, at the very least, he would be able to find out what their circumstances were that had them where they were. In fact, in thirty years of operating a fishing vessel on the open seas, he never ran into a situation like this. Anyway, for more than one reason, time was of the essence, so they pressed forward as quickly as possible with the sole intention of coming to the rescue of the individuals that were in distress on the island that was now directly ahead of them.

Meanwhile, back on the island, Ricky and Maude noticed the ship had turned around and was heading in their direction. Needless to say, that was an unbelievably great turn of events and certainly not at all what they thought was going to happen. Of course, they hadn't been officially rescued yet however it appeared to be only a matter of time before that happened now. Anyway, as it turns out, about ten minutes later, the ship was close enough to shore for them to see it was a fishing vessel however that didn't come as any big surprise to Ricky because he knew the waters around the islands were abundant with fish and other kinds of seafood. What was truly amazing was someone had actually found them alive on a deserted island out in the middle of the Pacific Ocean and it goes without saying, the odds of that happening were slim to none. Anyway, with a lot on their mind and perhaps, the only chance they would ever have to get off the island, Maude and Ricky proceeded to get dressed in anticipation of being rescued by the fishing vessel. It was nearing the moment of truth and with excitement, wonder and every possible wonderful feeling a person could imagine for a pleasant and enjoyable life together in the days ahead taking shape in their minds, the future looked promising again. In fact, challenges not yet met would be given a chance to happen now and that was undoubtedly a frigging miracle. Anyway, as fate would have it, in the late morning hours of another day on an island out in the middle of the Pacific Ocean, a small dinghy was eventually sent into shore as two or three individuals from the crew of the ship came to their rescue. Hope had finally arrived and in many respects, not a moment too soon. To say what they had been experiencing was a nightmare was a major understatement, however like so many things in life, when a person gets pushed to the far-reaching extremities of their physical and mental endurance, they usually find a way to do the unbelievable and the impossible in order to survive, and such was the case for them as well. Nevertheless, at this point in their rescue, the most important thing of all was they were going to rescued. In fact, quite frankly, as things stood now, they would more than likely be back on the mainland of the United States in a few hours or at the very least, sometime the following day. Anyway, things continued to progress along rather nicely and as it turns out, by mid-afternoon, Ricky and Maude were aboard the fishing vessel and ready to depart for the state of Oregon. The ordeal that neither one of them sought was now over so with Ricky's yacht tied up behind the fishing vessel, shortly thereafter, they were on their way back to the mainland. By contract, Captain Melendez said, his fishing vessel was supposed to go back to the port of San Francisco however do to the extenuating circumstances of their situation, an exception would be made in the best interests of everyone involved so he agreed to take them to Portland, Oregon instead of sailing to the port of San Francisco. As for Maude Derringer and Ricky Vestellini, just as soon as they arrived in the city of Portland, they would go about making arrangements to return to the community of Tierra Del Mar and with any luck at all, not too long after that they would be able to resume their usual everyday activities at home. In fact, it looked like life was about to return to normal however a little ways down the road, it would turn out that wasn't the case at all.

Part V

CHAPTER 26

Anyway, now, on their way back to the state of Oregon, the weight of the world had been lifted off their shoulders. Needless to say, they would be home soon and it came with great relief to know that. After spending five stressful days on an uninhabited island out in the middle of the Pacific Ocean with little to no sleep, they were ready to set their feet back on the mainland again. At any rate, that unfortunate nightmare was behind them now and that gave them reason to begin thinking about a future together in the days ahead. Actually, it can be noted, they both were very adamant about that however Maude was a lot more outspoken in favor of getting married than he was. In fact, it was obviously the direction everything was headed in and surely what they would be discussing when they got back to Tierra Del Mar.

In the meantime, they had an uneventful trip back to the state of Oregon. The skies were clear, the weather was good and everything seemingly went well. Of course, after living through the worst week of their life on an uninhabited island in the Pacific Ocean for nearly a week, they were ready to resume their daily activities again. Perhaps, even something as simple as having a good conversation at the dinner table without any stress attached to it would turn out to be a very pleasant experience for them. Who knows although at this point in their lives, they were ready to welcome any kind of normalcy with open arms again! At any rate, by the early morning hours of the next day, Captain Melendez had brought his fishing vessel into port in the harbor of Portland, Oregon. From there, not a moment was wasted in their effort to return to Tierra Del Mar as they hired a taxi to take them home. In fact, the way everything unfolded, an hour or so later, shortly before sunrise, the person who was chauffeuring them to their residence pulled into the driveway of Maude's estate. Actually, out of necessity, Ricky's boat was left behind in the city of Portland for maintenance repairs however once the matter was all taken care of, he would pay someone to have the boat brought back to him in Tierra Del Mar.

Anyway, as you might think, upon returning to Tierra Del Mar, Ricky and Maude headed off to bed just as soon as they got home. The truth of the matter was, after suffering from a lack of rest over the past few days, sleep was attained rather easily that morning although in this case, they both slept through the better part of the morning in their own homes. Actually, the plan was for Maude to go over to Ricky's house later in the day and since that met his approval, that is the way they did things. At any rate, it wasn't until sometime late afternoon before they were sitting down together in a couple of lounge chairs in his backyard. At this point, once again, they began discussing their future plans. Anyway, as stated before, they were in absolute total agreement on one thing and that was their intentions to get married. As to just exactly when that would happen was up in the air however they both thought as soon as possible wouldn't be a bad place to begin. Now, with regards to moving to France, they compromised. It was decided they would purchase a home on the southern coast of France with at least intentions of spending winters there. In fact, probably somewhere near the city of Monte Carlo, while summers would be spent in the state of Oregon at Ricky's estate. It sounded like a good viable plan, and they were both looking forward to doing that in the days ahead. As for Maude's estate in Oregon, it was her intentions to sell it. Needless to say, without having been there long, there weren't any personal feelings attached to it there wasn't any reason to keep the property but with regards to her property in California, she planned on keeping that. In fact, she was actually hoping to move back there sometime however at this point in her life, you might say that wasn't in her immediate plans. The truth of the matter is, Maude loved that home, so she wasn't in any hurry to part with it. Besides, if for some reason her relationship with Ricky didn't work out for her, she had something to back up on. In addition to that, with regards to attaining more wealth through profitable business endeavors, they thought it would be a good idea not let it ruin the future of their projected marriage. In reality, nether one of them needed any monetary assets anyway so it had the makings of a marriage made in heaven. Actually, Ricky was already well to do from what he inherited from his parents so there wasn't a need for more money. In fact, he owned the lighthouse, his home, and a boat in addition to some other monetary assets as well. On the other hand, she owned the Kimball mansion, as well as the property in California plus monthly royalties from all the books she had written so neither one of them was in dire need of money. Admittedly, she had some other assets as well but for more than one reason, she didn't want to disclose the full extent of her wealth because in past relationships, she had been used badly. At any rate, in other matters, if at all possible, they would try and raise a family together and on that subject, she was unyielding. She wanted children. It was simple as that. It would be just a question of how many kids they had, that's all. Actually, believe it or not, they had already gotten off a good start on that during their stay on the island but as totally naïve as Ricky he was, he had no idea that was the case. In fact, at this point, she didn't have any way of knowing that either. Obviously, that was something that would make itself known in the days ahead but in the meantime, there was a lot to be done before they got to that point in their lives.

Anyway, as it turns out, after discussing these matters with Ricky for the better part of an hour, regardless of how much she enjoyed being with him, Maude said she had to be on her way. The truth of the matter was, she had some things to do and if she sat around and discussed things with him, nothing was ever going to get done. In the meantime, he was already in the process of planning the rest of the day out for them so just as she was about to leave for home, he asked her to join him for dinner that evening. Of course, there wasn't any way she would ever miss out on something like that, regardless of what she had to do so an 8:00 o'clock dinner was agreed upon. In fact, in this particular case, Ricky said it was in her best interest to be there, which sort of told her, he must be up to something because a future together hinged upon everything they did now. At any rate, he very wisely inferred what he had to tell her later in the day would directly impact both of their lives, but he wouldn't elaborate any more than that. Actually, based on what they'd been discussing, she had a pretty good idea what those plans of his were, so she quickly accepted his invitation for dinner and left. Needless to say, she assumed, he was going to make an official proposal of marriage to her later that evening. If that was the case and something in the back of her mind told her it was, then, everything was headed in the right direction for her.

Anyway, the first thing she did upon returning home that afternoon was to make a list of things that had to be done. As stated before, Maude still had some business to take care of. First, she had to make a trip into town because she wanted to cash the check Mr. Johnson wrote out for her with regards to the old coins that were down beneath the house. Secondly, while she was in town, she wanted to purchase some new clothes and get her hair done. Then, if everything went well, she planned on dropping by the real estate agency's office to put up estate in Oregon up for sale. Of course, that was based on the speculation she would be going to France shortly. Finally, last but not least, if everything went as planned the following day, she would speak with a travel agent about making reservations for a flight to France. Obviously, if she was able to take care of that business ahead of time, she would be able to get a first-class seat for both of them and as you might think, that's what she wanted to do. Actually, she didn't mind flying coach, however if she took the initiative to make reservations ahead of time, Maude would probably be able to get what she wanted in the way of preferred seating so she had decided to take care of this matter ahead of time. Besides, if she had her information right, she would be getting married soon and when that happened, she wanted to be ready to go to France.

At this point, she was lost in thought again. Needless to say, that wasn't anything unusual for her because Maude was a very deep person spiritually and intellectually. At any rate, she was in her favorite recliner in the living-room mulling over some of the things she intended to do. In fact, quite frankly, a lot of her thoughts were focused on marrying Ricky and until that happened, she probably wouldn't be able to get that thought out of her mind. In reality, he was very good at organizing things and if she didn't miss her guess, Ricky was already in the process of doing that right now. That meant, later this evening, he would more than likely propose to her and then, she would be able to move onto some other things. In this particular case, that would probably entail writing another book. After that, she wasn't sure how things would go however with any luck at all, she would be in the beginning stages of raising a family.

Anyway, once her business matters were all taken care of, upon arriving home, she went upstairs and took a shower. Needless to say, she wanted to freshen up a bit before going over to Ricky's house and with plenty of time to do so, that's what she did. At any rate, with everything going according to plan, Maude slipped into a pair of tight-fitting blue jeans and a low-cut blouse that accentuated her perfectly formed breasts, then, after a quick look in the mirror to make sure everything was in order, she concluded, it was time to give Ricky a call. At this point, there was not too much more she could do to make herself presentable that evening, so it looked like it was time to join Ricky for dinner. The truth of the matter is, she would have dressed up in an evening gown for him, but they weren't going out anywhere, so it really wasn't necessary. At any rate, by the time she got around to calling Ricky that evening, he had already begun preparing supper for them, so everything was going as planned. Anyway, Ricky didn't see any reason for delaying the inevitable any longer, so he told her to come over whenever she was ready. The plan was to have supper at eight o'clock and the way everything was going, it looked like that's how things would turn out after all. Anyway, after speaking with him for about ten minutes, she hung up the phone and headed off to the kitchen to have a cup of coffee before going over to his house. Needless to say, once that necessity was taken care of, she made one last trip to the bathroom and then, like a person who won't accept no for an answer, Maude headed over to Ricky's house with a world of optimism running wildly through the back of her mind.

CHAPTER 27

As anticipated, after a short walk over to his house, destiny found Maude standing at the front door of Ricky's estate. Of course, no time was lost in letting her in and the moment Maude looked into his eyes, all the anxiety she was experiencing quickly dissipated into thin air. Ricky had a very charismatic personality, in addition to being a good-looking man so she couldn't help but fall in love with him. Anyway, for that reason, you might say, Maude enjoyed spending time with Ricky every chance she got however on this occasion, that was even more apparent because she was expecting a proposal for marriage. In fact, quite frankly, anything less than that and she would look around for another love interest regardless of her feelings because she wanted to find someone to raise a family with. Granted, Ricky was an ideal candidate for marriage and if he did what she thought he was going to do that evening, everything would be fine. Needless to say, the suspense of that highly desired thought continued to float around inside her head as she followed him through the living-room and into the dining room of his house. Once again, it was like time had come to a complete standstill as Maude contemplated a life together with this man. Yes, this is it, she thought to herself. After months of searching for a person to share her life with, she had come to the conclusion, Ricky would make a fine husband.

At any rate, the evening she was so anxiously awaiting for had finally arrived and just as soon as she stepped through the door and into his house, she could immediately see the measures he had taken for making it another very memorable night for her. As always, the house was very neatly kept, and the dining room table was adorned with Ricky's finest dishes. Needless to say, it appeared he was going to officially propose to her this evening. At least, that's what Maude was counting on anyway and from all appearances, that's what it looked like he was going to do. The atmosphere for the occasion was definitely right and a sixth sense inside her head kept telling her this was it. In fact, once this formality was over, they would be able to go on with their lives as a happily married couple and it goes without saying, that's what she wanted.

Anyway, it wasn't long before Ricky asked her to sit down and have supper with him. As they did, their conversation shifted to buying a home in France, however much to her surprise, he appeared to be looking forward to the whole thing instead of giving her the song and dance about why he didn't want to move there. Actually, the fact he was madly in love with her may have had something to do with it but there wasn't any way to know that for certain. The truth of the matter is she was just content knowing he had decided to go to France with her after they were married. Anyway, by and by, the main course of their meal was served. It was a pork roast seeped in rich aromatic spices with fresh vegetables and a side salad. Like always, Ricky had out done himself again and it wasn't an understatement to say, the meal was delicious. At any rate, by the time he went to serve dessert, she could hardly contain herself from laughing because Ricky was literally tripping all over himself. Needless to say, he was obviously a little nervous about something but as to just exactly what that was remained to be seen. At this point, he told her, dessert would be served next and on this occasion, he had decided on chocolate mousse so Ricky excused himself from the table and went into the kitchen to get it. Since, it was prepared ahead of time, it didn't take him very long to retrieve it from the refrigerator and shortly thereafter, Ricky came back out into the dining room with a very ornate covered dish that he sat down directly in front of her. By now, her mouth was literally salivating at the thought of sampling some of that chocolate mousse he had prepared for them. First of all, she loved anything sweet, and secondly, Ricky was a very good chef, not to mention a very good sweets maker as well. Anyway, after placing the mousse in front of her, he took a seat at the table and waited for her to take the cover off the dish. Little did she know this was the moment she had been waiting for. At any rate, there wasn't too much left to the imagination now because the moment she took the cover off the chocolate mousse, she found one of the most pleasant surprises of her life sitting directly in front of her. Not only did it explain the reason why Ricky was so nervous that evening, but it was also turning out to be what she thought he was going to do. Anyway, one thing quickly led to another, and in the due course of the next moment, she realized, there was a beautiful diamond ring sitting where the chocolate mousse was supposed to be. Son of a gun, she mused to herself. Ricky was going to propose to her after all. Needless to say, Maude was speechless. At first, silence filtered through the air but after a couple seconds went by, she regained her composure. Then, as their eyes seemed to lock in a mesmerizing stare, Ricky said, "I realize this is a very awkward way of doing something but with circumstances as they are, I would like to officially ask you to marry me, Maude? It seems to me, after having spent all of that time with you on the island, I don't believe there's any way I can live without you anymore. My nights are restless, my chest is breathless, and my heart aches to be with you every second of my life now. I need you as a permanent fixture in my life, Maude so I beg you in the name of humanity, accept my most sincere proposal of marriage, and become my lawfully wedded wife." At this point, silence filled the air again as she tried to find the right words to convey her feelings to him. Of course, she wanted to marry him however the mystique of the moment had also caught her off guard. At any rate, after relishing in her heart felt emotion for a second or two, she answered him back by saying, "I would love to be your lawfully wedded wife, Ricky. In fact, quite frankly, it would be the greatest honor of my life to be married to you. Neither is there a person in the world I would rather spend the rest of my life with so I guess that pretty much says it all." At this juncture, both Ricky and Maude became very emotional with the situation and within seconds of having accepted his proposal of marriage, Maude rushed into his arms and kissed him passionately on the lips. Needless to say, by this time, everything was very quickly falling into place as the passion of the moment soon overwhelmed them. In fact, it was as if time had come to a complete standstill as they stood there looking deeply into one another's eyes. Finally, Maude replied to back to him saying, "Just in case there's any question about it, I want a baby, Ricky but first I would like to buy a house in France, and after we get settled in our new home, we'll raise a family together. Do you think that's something you'd be happy doing? I don't intend to settle for anything less than that with the man I plan to marry. I just want to be up front with you about that before we get married. This way you will know what you're getting in to, and hopefully that'll prevent any unexpected surprises from happening in the days ahead." At this point, Maude wasn't really certain what Ricky's response would be, so she held her breath in anticipation of what Ricky was going to say. Anyway, much her relief, seconds later, Ricky very casually replied, "Well, as it turns out, it just so happens, I am looking for the same thing you are in a marriage. In fact, quite frankly, you may rest assured, I would also like to raise a family and it would be an honor to do that with a woman like yourself. Actually, just so you know, I would like to have a daughter at some point along the way so you might say, I'm looking forward to the moment that happens. As for moving to France, if that's what you want, then that's fine with me. Believe it or not, the sun rises and sets wherever you are. I can't stop the feeling, Maude, neither do I have any desire to put an end to the something so wonderfully felt. I will follow you to the ends of the earth if need be because I want you to be a part of my life forever. I love you, baby. I mean that with all my heart and soul. Anyway, let's go into the living-room and sit down for a few minutes so you will have a chance to think about what I said." At this point, she responded back to him by saying, "I don't need any time to think about it, Ricky. You're the guy I want to spend the rest of my life with. It's as simple as that. In fact, if you haven't guessed that by now, I would say, you're living in another world. Shall I say more?" "No," he replied, "that won't be necessary. I can see we both have the same goal and objective. Actually, I've got an idea. Why don't we get married right now? Like this evening! If you give me a few minutes, I will see if I can get a clergyman to come over. I realize that's a very short notice but it's highly probable I'll be able to find someone who can legally unite us in holy matrimony tonight because I will offer a good sum of money to whoever's willing to do this for us right now. Anyway, if you'll be patient for a few minutes, I will see what I can do." "That sounds like a plan to me," she replied. "As a matter of fact, just in case there's any question about it, I've never been so sure of anything in all my life." "Well, that settles it then," Ricky quipped. "Just sit tight and we'll be married shortly." Then, like a man on a mission, he proceeded to pick up a telephone directory that was sitting on one of the tables in the living-room and began looking for a number to call that would make this possible. Anyway, after a moment or two, he found what he was looking for. He found a listing for local area religious services. Of course, a justice of the peace would obviously be able to do the same thing for them however for more than one reason, if it was at all possible, he wanted to get a man of the cloth to unite them in holy matrimony. Perhaps, that was being a little childish about the whole thing however that was still the way he wanted to do it. At this point, he asked her what religious denomination she would prefer to be married with. Since Maude didn't have any religious preference, he suggested a Baptist minister and that was quickly agreed too. At any rate, once that was decided, Ricky proceeded to call the minister of a nearby Baptist church with the hope he would come right over and marry them. Anyway, one thing lead to another, and in a matter of ten minutes, Ricky had thoroughly convinced the minister of the nearby church to unite them in holy matrimony that night. Actually, in this particular case, money had a lot to do with it however in a situation like this, a few hundred dollars was well worth the investment. Anyway, a very short soliloquy ensued, where Ricky proceeded to give the clergyman directions on how to get to his house, and then after his conversation with him was finished, he ventured back into the living-room to join Maude. Needless to say, at this point, it was only a matter of time before the inevitable happened.

In the meantime, it was decided, they would take their marriage vows up inside the turret of the lighthouse. Actually, it was Ricky's idea however she said it sounded like a very romantic thing to do so it was agreed, that's how they would get married. Anyway, about a half hour later, destiny found Reverend Nelson knocking at Ricky's front door. Needless to say, that's what they were waiting for. At any rate, one thing quickly led to another and long before Maude realized it, Ricky was making the formal introductions that go along with meeting a new person. Then, after a brief, it's nice to meet you, handshake, he asked Reverend Nelson into the house. At this point, Mr. Nelson took a moment to eye the couple ever so inquisitively with the keenest of interest, but it wasn't every day someone got married on this short of a notice, and stranger still to request the wedding vows be taken inside the turret of a lighthouse. Anyway, such was the case, and shortly before the hour of ten o'clock, they headed out to the lighthouse. Once there, they proceeded to climb up the seemingly endless flight of stairs until they finally reached the top of the lighthouse. Then, after a brief interlude while Ricky showed Reverend Nelson how the inside of a lighthouse worked, they appeared to be ready to take their marriage vows. At any rate, a moment later, the minister got out his bible and proceeded to administer the oath of marriage to them. It didn't take very long. In fact, it was the basic of ceremony's if you want to call it that, but more importantly, the end result of what they were doing served the purpose. In the eyes of god, they were married and that's all that really mattered. At any rate, once their vows were taken, Mr. Nelson went onto wish them both the very best of luck in their endeavor, and then he headed down the stairs of the lighthouse and went home. His job was finished there so there wasn't any reason to hang around any longer. Needless to say, he wanted to uphold the institute of marriage, so it was best for him to be on his way. Actually, had that not been the case, he probably would've stayed a little while longer to get to know the individuals but with circumstances as they were and because of the late time of day, he left them to enjoy the rest of the evening on their own.

Anyway, just as soon as Reverend Nelson departed from Ricky's property, they made the short walk back to the house. Actually, there were other things to be done so after a quick trip to the bathroom, she headed into the dining room to give Ricky a hand clearing off the table. Once that was taken care of, they went into the living-room to have a drink before doing the inevitable upstairs in Ricky's bedroom. Actually, that was the first place Ricky ever made love to her so it was only fitting they should spend their wedding night there too. As for an official honeymoon, Ricky said they would do that another time. Right at the moment, he was a lot more concerned with banging the hell out of his newly found bride and as tacky as that may sound, even Maude was looking forward to the moment of his conquest that evening. Believe it or not, during their time on the island, very little love making was actually achieved. Most of their time was spent looking for food as a matter of survival. Anyway, now back in the beautiful state of Oregon any love making they did could be done in the comfort of their own home. Needless to say, any way you look at it, where they were now was a far cry better than trying to do it on an island neither one of them cared about. Anyway, as stated a moment ago, after having a couple of drinks, with nothing left to be discussed that evening, shortly thereafter, they went to bed to enjoy the rest of the night upstairs in Ricky's bedroom. At any rate, after some very intense love making, destiny found them drifting off to sleep in the comfort of one another's arms on the wedding night. As a matter of fact, from Maude's perspective, it felt like she had just walked through the pearly gates of heaven, and with nothing better to do now than to enjoy being his lawfully wedded wife, they spent the rest of the night together beneath the sheets of his bed.

When morning arrived, Maude arose from her night's sleep just long enough to close the bedroom windows so the cool night air wouldn't disturb their rest and then, dedicated to the end in her cause to provide Ricky with the love he desired, she went back to bed. Seconds later, with perhaps, only the longing to listen to each other's heartbeat, Maude proceeded to wrap her arms around her newly acquired husband, much the same way a snake would wrap itself around their victim. That wasn't meant to be a tacky statement and perhaps that isn't the best way to word it however the truth of the matter is, she was hopelessly in love with Ricky and that's probably the best wat to describe what she was doing. Anyway, regardless of the nature of her feelings or by giving it any additional thought, while Ricky slept soundly, her body rested in peace next to his. Yes, it was an evening to remember in every sense of the word and Maude was at peace with the world as a result of it. At any rate, a few minutes later, she fell back to sleep herself immersed in the deepest thoughts imaginable with regards to what she perceived as the beginning of a perfect marriage. Perhaps, it wasn't a match made in heaven. She wasn't actually sure but she was still confident everything would work out for the best in the days ahead. In the meantime, she could only hope her marriage would stand the test of time and that they would live happily ever after.

CHAPTER 28

A couple of months later, after a slight delay in their plans to move to France, they finally got around to doing what they wanted to do and of course that was to move to the French Riviera in Europe. Actually, for a couple different reasons, there was a slight delay in their departure, but it can also be noted, that was directly attributed to some business matters that needed to be taken care of first. At any rate, once those business matters were tended too, Maude made reservations for them to fly aboard a wide-bodied jet plane and a short time later, they were on their way. The flight they were on was to take them to Paris, France via two stops along the way with one being in Chicago and the other being in New York City. Actually, it was a direct flight, and because of the distance they had to travel, there was plenty of time for them to talk about things that were in need of discussing. In this case, that entailed everything from what they were willing out to each other in case something happened to one of them. In fact, it came was somewhat of a surprise to

322

learn, Ricky was leaving her the property in Oregon in the unlikely event something happened to him, which of course was speculation on his part about something that may never happen, yet he felt it was important to do so. Furthermore, without having any brothers or sisters, any monetary assets in the way of cash as well as the yacht he loved so much would go to her as well. Believe it or not, he felt it was the only logical thing to do. Of course, that all could easily change on a moments in the days ahead but for the time being, that's the way he wanted it. At any rate, while Ricky took care of that legal work, she began working on a plan to get them all settled into a new home in France. Her last will and testament was made up shortly before they left for France also and her way of thinking was fairly similar to his. Obviously, there were some minor differences to her legal work but as stated before, her property in Oregon was up for sale and her property in Beverly Hills would remain with her for as long as she was alive. Of course, if something were to happen to her that would change the entire complexion of things because in the unlikely event of her death, Ricky would get everything including millions of dollars in cash. At this point, the biggest concern they both had was the success of their marriage. If for some reason things didn't work out between them, there would be a lot of headaches associated with their legal paperwork that was theoretically already taken care of. Anyway, neither one of them was overly concerned about these matters and it was eventually decided, they wouldn't worry about it until something actually happened. In the meantime, there was a lot to be done and a great future ahead of them so rather than speculating on what may or may not happen, they moved onto some other matters like trying to find as much information as possible on the country of France. Needless to say, if they were successful in doing that and both of them thought they had done a pretty good job with that, when they got there, they would have a much easier transition adjusting to everyday life. It can also be said, that's when Maude learned Ricky wanted to make their home on the outskirts of Paris. Well, you might say, that wasn't exactly what she had in mind. It did not have anything to do with not liking the city of Paris but it had everything to do with the fact, Maude wanted to buy a home on the French Riviera. At any rate, she told Ricky she wanted to make their residence on the southern coast of France somewhere near the city of Nice. In fact, Maude said she would not agree to doing anything less than that so Ricky gave into her desire to live on the French Riviera. Actually, just in case there's any question about it, she was a very persuasive person and for that reason alone, she won out on the matter. In this case, the temperate climate the southern coast of France had was the reason why she wanted to live there. Had she not gotten her way about that, she wouldn't have been happy and Ricky had no intentions of making her unhappy. Besides, the southern coast of France was on the Mediterranean Sea and once Ricky put a little more thought into it, he concluded, it would be better to move to the French Riviera after all. In truth, neither one of them disliked being near the ocean anyway in addition to the fact, Ricky liked being on it too so moving to the southern coast of France was undoubtedly the best thing to do. Anyway, at no surprise to him, Maude said he would fall in love with the city of Nice the same way he fell in love with her and from that point on, he didn't pursue the matter any further. In fact, Ricky was more than satisfied knowing where they were headed would make a great place to live and in the end, that's all that really mattered.

Anyway, that was the current state of affairs of Ricky and Maude and certainly what they were discussing as they continued on their way to France on board their flight to the magnificent city of Paris. Until now, it had been a relatively uneventful trip, and everything was going better than either one of them expected, when all of a sudden, without a warning of any kind, the plane they were flying on began to shake violently, alerting them to the possibility something might be wrong. At this point, she just happened to be lost deep in thought again so the sudden movement of the plane was totally unexpected. To add even more uncertainty to the situation, the overhead lights came on, warning everyone aboard the plane to fasten their seat belts. Needless to say, she immediately nudged Ricky in the side in an attempt to alert him to what was going on inside the plane however it wasn't necessary. Ricky had already come around to his senses from the nap he was taking after having conceded defeat in their discussion over where to make their residence in France. Apparently, once the plane started making some strong jolting up and down movements, he realized something was wrong. As a matter of fact, it felt like the plane was going to break up into little pieces. Anyway, over the course of the next few minutes, everyone on board the plane braced for the worst as they continued to experience some very bad turbulence. Needless to say, it was unsettling to say the least but shortly after the plane actually ran into a problem, the pilot's voice could be heard on the intercom system of the plane, informing the passengers aboard, they were experiencing some strong winds associated with an abrupt temperature change. At any rate, the pilot didn't waste any time reassuring everyone aboard, they would be all right. Obviously, it wasn't the best possible experience anyone aboard the plane could have encountered however the problem that mitigated itself a few minutes earlier was soon history and their flight continued on its way to France.

Thankfully, time went by very quickly that day, but that was actually a blessing because neither one of them were really fond of flying. At any rate, during the remainder of their flight, they discussed a few more things, like how they would travel down to Nice once they got to the city of Paris. In fact, she was very adamant about that as well as she insisted they take the train. Actually, he was more intent on renting a car and driving down to the French Riviera, but Maude won out on that matter as well. Furthermore, at no surprise to Ricky, she took a few minutes to describe the countryside to him. In the end, nothing was lost or gained by listening to what she had to say and like before, in not wanting to get their marriage off to a bad start, Ricky agreed to go by train. In reality, they had already decided to move to Nice so the only question remaining had to do with how they would get there once they arrived in Paris. Anyway, since that was all settled now, there was nothing holding them back from enjoying the rest of their flight to France. As always, time went by quickly, and with the remainder of their flight being good, they arrived in the city of Paris later that evening. At any rate, with that part of their journey behind them, the first thing they had to do when they arrived at the airport terminal in Paris was to find a place to stay so with that in mind, after a short ride from the airport terminal to a hotel on the outskirts of the city of Paris, they settled in for the night. At this point, it was easily decided, they would get some rest. Tomorrow was another day, and it stands to reason it would be best if they got started on things after a good restful night of sleep, so that is what they chose to do. Then, if everything went as planned, after a well anticipated train ride down to the city of Nice, they would start their search for a new home. At any rate, it turns out, much to their delight, they fell asleep that night amid the love and romance that went along with being couple of newlyweds in the city of Paris. In fact, what they were now in the process of doing could be looked at as a belated honeymoon. Actually, Ricky was the first one to mention that, and after Maude thought about it for a minute, she totally agreed with him on that. Anyway, with circumstances as they were, one could easily assume the following day would be the beginning of a brand-new chapter in their lives and they were both anxiously awaiting its arrival. Yes, a world of adventure and excitement was waiting for them in Nice, in addition to all of the things that went along with marriage commitments and business matters, but if anything went wrong with their attempt to make a life for themselves in the country of France, it would more than likely be Ricky's fault because even though he was a very caring person, his good-looking, charming personality acted like a magnet to most women and it goes without saying, that very often leads to promiscuity. Anyway, for that reason alone, perhaps, the future they were destined to live together might not work out for them after all. As always, the chances we take in life aren't always successful however that just happens to be one of the things we can't foresee and such was the case with Maude as well.

Part VI

CHAPTER 29

Early next morning, they woke up to find, their first night in the magnificent city of Paris was an absolutely delightful one after all. Thankfully, they weren't having any issues with jet lag and that was actually quite remarkable considering the overall length of their flight. In fact, quite frankly, the way everything unfolded, Ricky was unusually invigorated that morning. Perhaps, it was due to their intense love making from the night before, but Maude was quick to attribute that to the overall atmosphere of being in the city of Paris. At any rate, regardless of what lead Ricky into being full of life that day, it was an unusually warm day in Paris in the midst of early autumn however neither one of them actually minded that. Anyway, as planned, they took the train down to Nice. When they got there, a place favorable to their liking was found on the very outskirts of the city and once again, they settled in for the night. In fact, with business matters to take care of the following day, Maude wanted to get another good restful night of sleep, and then, they would look for a new home. At least, that's what the plan was anyway. In fact, it was very unlikely that would change because they needed a place to live and with intentions to raise a family, that was a necessity they couldn't live without and certainly a step in the right direction for doing that.

Anyway, as it turns out, shortly after rising from their night's sleep the next day, they got dressed and went downstairs to get something to eat. Fortunately for them, they were staying at a hotel that had a small cafe downstairs, so breakfast was going to be a rather easy thing for them to take care of. Anyway, as you might think, they sat down at a table inside the cafe and ordered something to eat. In this particular case, all that really amounted to was a good serving of bacon and eggs. In fact, they both ordered the same thing. Actually, to be more precise, he had orange juice with his breakfast while Maude opted to have a cup of coffee. Once that was taken care of, the time had come to go in search of a new home. For the time being, they planned on renting a car for a while so they would have a means of transportation around the city of Nice but that was only a temporary fix. They would be purchasing something to drive just as soon as they got into a new home. Right at the moment, their first priority was to find a place to live. After that, other things would be taken care of.

At any rate, the way everything unfolded that day, by the time late afternoon arrived, they found what they were looking for in the way of a home, so arrangements were immediately made through a local banking institution to buy the property. Furthermore, since, their monetary assets had been transferred ahead of time, they didn't have any problem purchasing the home. Anyway, a good, fair, equitable agreement was reached with the owner that afternoon so the rest of the day went rather well. In fact, with the house being purchased as a cash sale, things moved forward a lot quicker than it would have taken them if they went the route of a loan although there was still a lot of paperwork that had to be done over the course of the next few days. In this case, because the property was purchased outright and because they gave the owners a little extra money on the side, they were able to move right into their new home. Usually, permission to do something like that isn't granted to the buyer until the paperwork conveying the warranty deed of the property to the new owner is completed however the current owner of the property was very anxious to sell and with circumstances as they were, you might say, they didn't have to wait to enjoy their new home. In fact, the moment cash was offered for the property, the real estate broker very quickly said, they could move into their new home at their earliest convenience. Anyway, thanks to the way everything was taken care of, they wouldn't have to take up residence in a hotel for a while. Needless to say, that in itself was a blessing. As for the scope of the area they were moving into, it appeared to be a very nice neighborhood, so they didn't have any misgivings whatsoever about moving to the location they were headed too. Of course, time would tell whether or not they had made the right decision about doing that, but everything seemed to point in the right direction.

Anyway, the way everything unfolded that day, by the time an agreement to purchase the house had been reached, the real estate broker handling the sale of the property took a moment to inquire where they were from. At this point, Maude could see where this was leading too and as you might think, she very quickly caught onto his line of questioning. In this particular instance, since they were from the United States and spoke very good English, it was fairly obvious to the real estate broker, they weren't from any country in Europe. Anyway, before she had a chance to tell him what part of the United States they were from, the man from the real estate agency could see that Maude was the author of a couple of his wife's favorite books. Well, as you might think, within seconds of having made this unique discovery, he proceeded to make some of the longest hints imaginable for Maude to drop by their house sometime. In fact, he stated very clearly that his wife would love to meet her, which of course, meant an autograph and in all probability, one or two picture taking sessions as well. Needless to say, over the years, Maude had become quite accustomed to doing this sort of thing so she said that wouldn't be a problem. Actually, in most instances, she would've preferred to do things a little differently, however the politer side of her personality surfaced and she agreed to do it. Besides, there wasn't any way she could say no. It would be too rude of her to do that. As a matter of fact, it was individuals like this who actually bought her books so Maude always tried to be as cordial as she could whenever a situation such as this arose. Needless to say, some things have a way of paying off in the long run and this just happened to be one of them. As for Maude, by now, she had gotten use to the process of dealing with the news media and signing autographs. Perhaps, that whole undeniable turn of events had something to do with the fact, she was getting older or maybe she finally came to terms with her identity. Who knows? I suppose there's more than one explanation for that coming about but in the end, the most important thing of all was Maude wasn't a shy person anymore.

At any rate, the house they purchased was a two-story home with six large bedrooms and three full baths. In addition to that, the upstairs had intricately designed woodwork with walkout verandas in all of the bedrooms which added extra distinction to their residence. In fact, with the house being located near the Mediterranean Sea, not only could you see for miles around in most every direction, but you could also gaze out into the waters of the Mediterranean Sea if the desire to do so arose. As for the first floor of the estate, it had a spacious kitchen with an elegant dining room that was fit for any occasion. In addition to that, there was a very large living-room, a den, a laundry room, and a huge basement with an ample amount of storage space. Last but not least, the property sported five acres of land as well. Of course, with it being located in a hilly section of the community on the outskirts of the city, you might say, they were in an ideal location to not only raise a family, but they were also near everything they wanted to be as well. There were all kinds of schools and churches in the area and a short distance away, there were a couple of malls explicitly designed for the shopper in mind. Needless to say, a person could purchase everything imaginable there. As for the business district of the city, it was not far away and certainly within driving distance. All in all, they were satisfied with everything their new property had to offer them. Anyway, at no surprise to Maude or anyone else for that matter, she liked her new home so much that she wanted to stay in France. Of course, that meant making permanent residence there however their plan to spend summers in Oregon would suffer that decision though. As a matter of fact, believe it or not, Ricky didn't want to go back to the United States while Maude still harbored the desire to go back to the coast of Oregon during the summer months. Needless to say, perhaps, only time itself would be able to decide what they did in the days ahead. There are too many variables in life to look at it any other way. The reality of it all is one or the other could always change their mind about things and if that happened, a lot of well laid plans for a future together would turn out much differently than originally planned.

Anyway, things moved along rather quickly, and long before either one of them realized it, they were settled into their new home. Thankfully, the transition to living in the city of Nice went very smoothly and like most people, they made new friends in literally no time at all. That in itself was actually a blessing because a really good friend is an asset that can't be weighed out in dollars and cents. At any rate, as you may think, that helped them adjust to everyday living in Nice and that's all anyone could really ask for. Anyway, as stated before, both Ricky and Maude were well to do so neither one of them had to work for a living but shortly after getting all settled into their new home, Ricky took a job as a concierge at a nearby hotel. In this particular case, he was so impressed with the city of Nice that he told Maude there wasn't any way he could just sit around and admire the city. He wanted to get out and experience it, so like a man dedicated to a cause, he took a job that he was capable of doing and one that he liked really well. Anyway, she didn't have a problem with him doing that and since it didn't interfere with their life at home, she didn't have a problem with that just as long as it was something he wanted to do. As a matter of fact, rather than criticizing him for taking a job he didn't need to take, Maude actually applauded him for doing so. Of course, with any luck at all, not only would the job work out well for Ricky but under these circumstances, perhaps, their marriage would work out well also. Granted, what he did wasn't at all what she thought he was going to do however Maude didn't see how it would interfere with their intentions to raise a family so nothing more was said about the matter. As for what she did in the way of keeping busy, she began writing again. Actually, in recent months she hadn't put any time into doing that however it was something she enjoyed doing so there was not any reason for her not to write another work of literature. Anyway, from a bird's eye perspective, everything appeared to be going well and life was good. He liked his job really well and she was moving forward with the writing of a new book. In fact, they were seemingly the perfect couple. When an opportunity came along to enjoy some aspect of life, they always took full advantage of the moment. Yes, not only did they appear to be head over heels in love with each other but with lots of time to spend together on the weekends, there wasn't any reason to think they would ever run into any marriage problems.

Anyway, another three or four months went by. Things continued to go well for them and like you might expect, not only were they all settled into their new home but also into the city of Nice as well. Actually, part of the smooth transition they made from the United States to France could easily be attributed to the end result of falling into a good predictable routine however she gave credit to her overall love of the area for being able to adjust to living in another country so well. At any rate, at this point, she was already halfway through writing another book and Ricky adapted to his new job in literally no time at all. In fact, quite frankly, things couldn't have been any better than it was now, and everything was apparently headed in the right direction for living a long and happy life together.

About this time, more good news arrived at the Vestellini residence. Maude was going to have a baby. In fact, for more than one reason, it was only fitting that would be the case because Maude and Ricky had been working on that for a while now. At any rate, be so as it may, Maude thought that might be the case because she had missed her period earlier that month, however she didn't immediately look into it because she was too wrapped up in everything else that was going on at the time. At any rate, after a short consultation with her doctor, she found out her first child was due in a few months and you might say, that news was well received by both of them. It was what she had been hoping for and now, it looked like her desire to raise a family would become a reality in the days ahead. Anyway, shortly after finding out she was going to have a baby, Maude brought the news up with Ricky. "Mr. Vestellini, do you remember being stranded on that island out in the middle of the Pacific Ocean," she asked? "Of course, I do," Ricky stated. "How could anyone forget an experience like that? As a matter of fact, it just so happens, I spent some of the most memorable days of my life there. Not that I wanted to live on that island the rest of my life but the time I had with you there was unforgettable." "Well," Maude replied slowly, "just so you know, that's where our child was conceived. In fact, I think it was the day we were rescued from the island. Remember, I was swimming in the lagoon when I made the discovery of some pearls in the shallows of the waters and then, you made love with me just before we noticed the fishing vessel passing by the island. Well, if I don't miss my guess, that's where it happened. Of course, I could be wrong about that however the way I see it, all that really matters is I'm going to have a baby." "I couldn't agree with you more," Ricky replied. "In fact, it's the best news you could've ever told me. I absolutely ecstatic about learning I'm going to become a father. Let me know if there's anything I can do for you." "I will," she answered. "Right now, there isn't a lot you or I can do other than wait and see how everything turns out." Actually, by now, she was giving him all of the details of what her doctor told her, which in this particular case, didn't really amount to much more than telling him when the baby would arrive. Actually, sometime towards the end of next May was when the doctor said she would have the baby. At any rate, he had every intention of following her pregnancy closely to ensure there weren't any complicating problems that might have an adverse effect on the final outcome of the delivery of the child. Obviously, since Maude was in good health, everything should be fine. It would be just a question of whether or not their first child turned out to be a boy or a girl. Of course, in the due course of a pregnancy, there was always a slight chance their child might have a birth defect of some kind however neither one of them wanted to think about the possibility of that happening. As for the sex of the child, Maude was hoping for a boy while Ricky was very adamant about having a girl. Needless to say, it was probably fairly typical of what most couples wish for at some point in their marriage, however in the end, they both agreed, if Maude had a good, healthy child that was all that really mattered. In the meantime, there wasn't any sense of worrying about it so nothing more was said about it for a while.

Anyway, as you might think, with the passing of time, Maude very gradually began doing less and less physical work each day until she was doing nothing except engage herself in writing another work of literature. At any rate, while she was doing that, Ricky took some time off from his job so he would be at home with Maude in case anything went wrong. Needless to say, every possible effort was made to ensure she had a problem free delivery and Ricky was the one whose keen eye kept a watch over things during her pregnancy. The truth of the matter was, Maude was an optimist at heart so she didn't think she would run into any complications before or during the pregnancy. In fact, quite frankly, she would be greatly surprised if things didn't turn out that way although she had already made up her mind to deal with things if it became necessary to do so.

As for the holiday season that year, it was literally knocking upon their door a lot sooner than expected. Naturally, like most things in life, the splendor of the season crept on them very quickly and long before either one of them realized it, the season had come and gone. Actually, it was their first Christmas together and with nothing more than the most pleasantest of thoughts imaginable bouncing around inside their heads, it turned out to be a very good holiday season for them. Ricky purchased her a couple of new dresses and an exquisite necklace while she went to a motorcycle dealership and bought him a new motorcycle. In this case, it was what Maude had been meaning to buy him for some time now however between writing another book and making plans for their first child, she hadn't actually gotten around to it. Anyway, she could immediately see it was a good decision on her part because Ricky took an immediate liking to the motorcycle. In fact, he was out riding around on the roads in the area long before the holiday season was over that year and it goes without saying, that made her feel really good inside that she had gotten him something he liked for Christmas. As for Ricky, not only was he enjoying his time in France, but he was also adjusting to life there a lot better than expected. Obviously, time would tell whether or not everything would work out for them there however for the time being, neither one had any complaints.

Anyway, a few months later, towards the end of May, while Maude was in the process of putting the finishing touches on a new book she had written, she gave birth to their first child. In this particular instance, Ricky got what he was wishing for and that was a baby girl. Anyway, he immediately took it upon himself to name the child, Vanessa Ann Vestellini, which just happened to be after an aunt he use to idolize when he was a young boy growing up in the state of Oregon. At any rate, since she liked the name Ricky chose for the child, the name, Vanessa Ann was very quickly agreed upon. In truth, there were all kinds of good names they could have chosen for the child however Maude was satisfied with that one. As for being a mother for the first time in her life, she took a liking to that as well. Needless to say, she had more responsibility than ever now, but she didn't mind that. The truth of the matter is, she wanted to raise a family anyway so what she was in the process of dealing with did not disenchant her at all. In fact, she grew accustomed to all of the things that went along with motherhood very quickly. Even Ricky was ecstatic about having a new member of the family around and that was something she originally wasn't all that certain of. Anyway, much to her surprise, Ricky took his parenting responsibilities seriously and within a day or two after the child was born, he could be found helping her take care of their new daughter. Actually, there really wasn't any other practical way to look at it and since that fit right in with her plans for a future together, she was all the happier for it. In the meantime, she found herself busier than ever taking care of their newborn child. Of course, that meant, being up at all hours of the night and not getting much sleep but she quickly adapted to that new way of life and everything continued to go well. In fact, with Ricky's request for leave approved, whether it was getting a meal or taking care of the dishes, he was always right there for her. Actually, it was his intentions to stay at home for as long as it was necessary for her to make a smooth transition into motherhood and since his employer was a very understanding man, Ricky had more than enough leeway in doing that. At any rate, at this point in their marriage, she would've been the first one to admit, every dream she ever dreamed in her life was coming true in France. She had wanted a family of her own for some time now, and with everything headed in the right direction, that's all she could really ask for.

CHAPTER 30

The following months very gradually evolved into some of the best and most memorable years of their life. One day rolled into another and all of a sudden, it felt like time had come to a complete standstill. Every day was a brand-new adventure for them and life could not have been treating them any better than it was now. Maude bought herself a new Ferrari and Ricky bought himself another yacht. There was literally nothing to want for. In fact, they were both as content as a person could be. At any rate, during those days most of their time was spent cruising up and down the southern coast of France on Ricky's new yacht. Of course, their daughter, Vanessa Ann went everywhere with them but that was to be expected because she was so young. Actually, due to the fact, there was all kinds of space on the boat anyway, it didn't pose any problems for them. As a matter of fact, the way Maude looked at that was they were a family so it made all the sense in the world to stay together as a family. Obviously, they could've hired a babysitter to take care of Vanessa Ann while they were out and about doing things however circumstances as they were, they both agreed, it was best to take their daughter with them. Perhaps, at some point in the days ahead they would change their mind about that however for the time being, that was the way they wanted to do it.

Anyway, long before either one of them realized it, the best summer of their life was soon behind them. Autumn had arrived and the decision to go back to the United States was tabled for another year. Ricky's excuse was, he didn't want to fly, however she thought it had a lot more to do with the fact, he had no desire to return to the state of Oregon so they weren't going anywhere anytime soon. In fact, believe it or not, as much as Maude liked living in Nice, France, she still missed living in Beverly Hills. At any rate, in realizing they wouldn't be returning to the state of Oregon or anywhere else for that matter, she dismissed the thought and began giving a few other things some attention. Actually, first on the list was her estate in Oregon. In fact, as coincidence would have it, a short time later, she received a call from the real estate broker in Tierra Del Mar, telling her the sale of her home in Oregon was all taken care of. Needless to say, for Maude, that was good news because she wanted to sell the property. Obviously, if summers were to be spent in the state of Oregon, like they originally planned, it would be at his estate anyway. Like I said before, it was Ricky's wish for Maude to have his house so she thought it was best to sell the old Kimball mansion.

Actually, had she not done so, it would have been one too many properties for her to keep an eye on anyway. At any rate, after this matter was all taken care of, Maude went on to publish, yet another book, and once again, like so many times in the past, that course of action treated her well. In fact, it produced even more revenue for her, however Maude's attention was soon diverted to other things as the holiday season quickly descended upon them. Thanksgiving was the first holiday to arrive in all its grandeur and then, two or three weeks later, the magic of Christmas took root in everyone's heart as well. Of course, this year, with a new edition to their family, Vanessa Ann was with them too. Well, what else can a person do but give their child the very best of everything so that's what Ricky and Maude did. Anyway, it was during that holiday season that year, the decision was made to have another child. Like you might think, that's what they both wanted to do, so shortly thereafter, they began working on that endeavor. Thankfully, things went as planned because by the time spring arrived, she was going to have another baby. At any rate, the news was received really well by both of them however Ricky wanted to go back to work. Realistically, there wasn't anything wrong with that however she questioned his reason for wanting to do that. Ricky told her he had too much time on his hands and that he was getting bored with his everyday routine at home. Obviously, there isn't anything wrong with that, but in the back of her mind, Maude was sorely afraid he was getting tired of being around her and their daughter, Vanessa Ann. The truth of the matter is, she was hoping Ricky would stay at home for a little while longer however that's not what he had in mind. In the end, she conceded defeat and accepted his decision to go back to work. Actually, she thought he might have an ulterior motive for wanting to do that however she gave him the benefit of the doubt and said she would support him in whatever he decided to do. Anyway, Maude tried to make the most of the situation in the days ahead, however she wasn't very happy with his decision to go back to work as a concierge. Admittedly, life isn't meant to be perfect, and most people would probably agree, being human is a testament to that statement however Ricky was determined to work a little more so there wasn't any sense of discussing that matter any further. In fact, looking at it from a positive perspective, perhaps, everything would work out for the best in the days ahead anyway. In the meantime, she kept telling herself, give it some time. Surely, Ricky would eventually get tired of working as a concierge and when that happened, that would logically put an end to his desire for employment. At least, that's what she thought would happen anyway. At this point, there wasn't any reason to believe another woman was involved so she thought it was just a simple matter of Ricky wanting something to do. At any rate, she eventually concluded, that's all he wanted to do so for the time being, she didn't intend to worry about it and soon Ricky returned to his old job as a concierge.

Anyway, because Maude was expecting another child, they put off retuning to the United States, yet another year as they waited for the baby to arrive. Finally, after months of a good deal of anticipation waiting for that special day to arrive, her second child was born in October of that year. It was a little baby girl and she was quick to name her Margaret Jean. Actually, the way all this unfolded, little did she know, this was actually the turning point of her marriage. The fact of the matter is she didn't approve of Ricky's desire to go back to work, so they weren't conversing together the way they should have been, and it goes without saying, that would eventually be one of the deciding factors in their soon to be failed marriage but for the time being, things continued to go well for them, and life was good.

At any rate, by now, time was flying by faster than ever before and soon another year had come and gone. Actually, they were a family of four now and with Ricky working again, Maude was busy taking care of the children. In fact, she didn't mind doing that but on occasion, the kids turned out to be a little more than she could handle. That didn't happen too often however if and when it did, she always took the necessary measures to fix the problem. At this point, it can also be said, there was one other good thing that happened that year and that was Maude's mother and father came to visit her during the holiday season. It wasn't an anticipated visit but in not having seen them in a while, it was a pleasant surprise. At least, from her perspective it was anyway. As for how Ricky felt about it, she wasn't sure. These days, he was working so much that she didn't have a lot of time to spend with him. Anyway, regardless of that fact, the holiday season did turn out to be a very special one for her that year. In fact, her parents stayed until the New Year Day's holiday had gone by and then, they went home to the state of Arizona. As for Ricky, he spent all but the week he took off for Christmas at his place of employment during that time span so most of his time was spent away from home.

Anyway, at this point in her life, Maude's marriage to Ricky very gradually began to fall apart. First, it was one thing, then, it was another, and as time went by, he began spending more time at work. In fact, once he began spending every night and most of the weekends there too, it left her a little disenchanted with Ricky. Of course, she didn't have any idea what his reason was for doing things that way however it definitely put a big strain on their marriage. Admittedly, the two of them weren't connecting very well in bed anymore and perhaps, that had something to do with Ricky's continual absence away from home. At any rate, regardless of what had apparently gone wrong in their marriage, they very rarely saw each other anymore. Ricky did his thing and she did hers. It was the worst of times for them, and with very little communication going on, it was not a very good situation. In fact, she knew something was amiss with Ricky, but he would not say what was bothering him so she decided to let things be as they were for a while with the hope everything would eventually work out for the best on its own. Needless to say, that kind of approach to a problem very seldom works, and such was the case here as well. In fact, Maude's marriage to Ricky would turn out to be one of the biggest mistakes her life. Anyway, it turns out their marriage continued to spiral downwards until it became apparent, they were having marital problems. Clearly, from his perspective, it was because Maude didn't appear to be interested in having sex anymore however because Ricky had a very strong desire to get laid every night, that posed a problem. On the other hand, Maude couldn't see that was an issue because in her mind, the most important thing of all was the needs of the children when in fact, she should have been splitting her time between Ricky and the kids. Needless to say, she wasn't doing that and before either one of them realized it, there was an obvious snag in their marriage. In fact, Ricky wasn't any more than secondhand news at home now because the better part of Maude's time was spent taking care of the children while he worked for Mr. Marceau at a nearby hotel.

Anyway, by the time they reached their fourth wedding anniversary, Maude realized their marriage was literally coming apart at the seams however being a little naive, she didn't have any idea why Ricky wasn't spending any time at home. Needless to say, she was desperately seeking an answer to the problem however she had yet to figure out why things were going so badly. For that reason, she felt powerless to change the situation. Actually, most people can usually identify a problem and then address it however in this particular instance, she wasn't able to do that. Call it a flaw in her personality or just plain stupidity, the end result would have been the same. Like I stated before, she was too wrapped up in her children to be concerned about anything else. You could say her attention was diverted too far in one direction however that wasn't going to change anything. As a matter of fact, the damage was done, and Maude didn't know how to make things right again. Furthermore, she didn't want to accept the fact, their marriage had failed. Believe it or not, Maude still loved Ricky very much however because of her shortsightedness, she was not even aware she had done something wrong. Believe it or not, it was her contention, Ricky was at fault for the failure of their marriage, so she didn't know how to go about fixing it. Yes, it was as bad as that.

At any rate, a couple more months went by, and their marriage continued to flounder into absolute total obscurity as Ricky continued to stay away from home and she continued to tend to the children. Something had to change because neither one was speaking to the other at all and a lot of unnecessary tension was building up inside of both of them. At this point, there wasn't any love left in their marriage. In fact, she was actually beginning to entertain the thought Ricky was seeing another woman and that only added to the tension at home. Needless to say, by now, their marriage had all the makings of the biggest disaster known to mankind and in all probability, that wasn't too far away from happening either.

Anyway, as fate would have it, Ricky came home drunker than a skunk one evening, well after the hour of midnight. Somehow, someway, he managed to stumble through the side door of the house and eventually landed in one of the chairs inside the living-room. Initially, she thought there might be an intruder in the house however that fear was quickly dismissed, the moment she saw Ricky all sprawled out in what he called his easy chair. Needless to say, that came as a bit of a surprise for a couple of reasons however she didn't question his motive for being drunk. These days, as long as he wasn't bothering her, she didn't care what the hell he did. At least, as long as he wasn't having sexual relations with another woman. At any rate, as you might think, he came up with some lame brain excuse for coming home drunk so after a little coaxing, he confessed to spending some time in a bar that evening. In fact, from what he inferred, I guess he'd been going there quite frequently in recent days. Not only was it something Maude didn't want to hear but it wasn't what she thought he would say either. The truth of the matter was, Ricky was as drunk as a person could be without being flat on their back, throwing up with the head spins. Anyway, by the look of things, he must have spent a good portion of the evening getting drunk. At this point, it was just a matter of determining what his reason was for doing so. At any rate, he told her that he felt the need to unwind a little before coming home that night so he apologized for his slightly inebriated state although she had a feeling there was a lot more to it than that. In the end, she felt sorry for him so she led him upstairs, got him undressed and helped him get into bed so he could sleep the whole thing off. Unfortunately, that is when Maude detected the undeniable scent of a woman's perfume on his clothes. Suddenly, she wanted to cry out in agony in the worst possible way because that meant he must be seeing another woman after all. Not only would that explain the scent of perfume but it would also explain why he was coming home late every night as well. At this point, Maude's suspicions had been confirmed however Ricky was way too intoxicated to bring the subject up at this time. If she did, he probably wouldn't remember anything anyway so the matter would obviously have to wait until he was sober. In the meantime, Maude had a tough decision to make. She didn't know whether it would be best to play dumb and pretend this didn't happen or if it would be better to try and work things out with him because it was obvious, Ricky had a girlfriend. Normally, that wouldn't have been any big deal however he was a married man and right at the moment, he was a marked man as well. In fact, Maude even entertained the idea of going after an irreconcilable differences divorce settlement however if she sought the latter, it would also mean her marriage was over and as much as she hated to say it, that might not be the best course of action to take. For the time being, Maude was going to look the other way and let things be as they were.

Sometime the following day, after he came around to the point of being sober again, like she anticipated, Ricky acted like nothing ever happened. Yes, cool as a cucumber and as coy as a boy who got caught with his hand caught in the cookie jar, he just brushed the matter aside. You know, like who me? I haven't done anything wrong! Needless to say, she found it really hard to believe that he could be so far removed from the reality of what he had just done to her, however after giving it a little more thought, she couldn't find any pity or compassion for him anymore. It had actually been a bad situation for some time but it had come to the point, Maude wasn't going to be able to look the other way any longer. Something had to be done! It would be just a matter of deciding what course of action needed to be taken. In the meantime, they proceeded to have a good breakfast together that morning, and fairly typical of all their days of late, not a single word was said about his job or what he was doing at work. It was as if his place of employment didn't exist. He just went through his usual routine of looking at the daily newspaper and went to work. The truth of the matter is Ricky's mind was off in the clouds somewhere and in all probability, it was on a woman. It was just a question of who this woman was, that's all. Anyway, regardless of that undeniable fact, there was one thing she was certain of and that was Ricky's mind wasn't on her or the kids. To the best of her knowledge, he still worked for Mr. Marceau though, and it was very unlikely that would change. Perhaps, with time, if a little more light could be shed on the situation, she would know how to proceed. At this point, Maude was literally at wits end for knowing what to do however after giving it some more thought, she eventually concluded, it was time to act. Come hell or high water, she would find out what was keeping Ricky so busy that he was rarely home anymore.

Anyway, later that afternoon, with a plan formulated in her head, she scooted over to her next-door neighbor's house to ask Freda if she would look after her kids for a while so she could look into a matter of importance. Of course, Freda said she would be happy to do that for Maude so that was quickly agreed upon. At any rate, before heading out the door to investigate Ricky's doings and whereabouts, Maude told Freda she wasn't sure how long it would take her to tend to the business she was in need of taking care of however she inferred it would probably be late into the evening before she got home. Needless to say, that was fine with Freda so rather than getting engaged in a conversation she preferred not to talk about, Maude raced out the door, got into her Ferrari and drove off down the road. Anyway, about twenty-five minutes later, she arrived at his place of employment, and not a moment too soon because Ricky would be getting out of work at six o'clock, and it was now, five minutes before the hour. So far, so good, she thought to herself as she waited patiently for her beloved husband to exit the building. At this point, it can also be said, it was perfect timing on Maude's part because at precisely ten minutes past the hour of six, he emerged from the left side of the building, got into his car, and sped off down the road. It was what she had been waiting for so she quickly put her Ferrari into gear and took off down the road after him, driving as inconspicuously as possible with the hope Ricky wouldn't have any idea she was following him. Anyway, thanks to wearing a pair of sunglasses and by following him from a safe distance behind, she was certain he didn't suspect a thing. At any rate, about fifteen minutes later, Ricky pulled into the driveway of a very nice home in a housing development in the city of Nice. From there, he got out of his car and walked over to the front door of the house and within seconds of having knocked on her door, a very pretty woman with long blond hair emerged in the doorway. Then, after giving him the most passionate she had ever seen in her life, the woman in question, let Ricky into the house. All of a sudden, the mystery of where Ricky was spending his time away from home suddenly came to light. So, this was where the no-good despicable son of a bitch was going, she cursed to herself. In fact, what Maude suspected was true. He was seeing another woman after all. At any rate, regardless of how disappointing it was to learn this, Maude was determined to get to the bottom of this highly unfortunate matter so she got out of her Ferrari and walked inconspicuously over to the door he just went into. Time was of the essence because she wanted to catch him in the act of his own stupidity. Anyway, with that in mind, she made her way over to one of the windows on the first floor of the house and peered inside but there wasn't anyone in the living-room. That meant they must be upstairs, so her next course of action was to go around to the back of the house, where she conveniently found a staircase that obviously lead up to a bedroom on the second floor of the house. Then, after going up the stairs, Maude tip-toed her way across the veranda until she came to a partially opened door that lead into a bedroom. It was more than likely where they were, she thought herself. Now, it was just a matter of deciding what to do next. At this point, she could hear the sound of two people having sexual intercourse. Actually, if it were anything other than that, she would have to say, someone was in a lot of pain however she doubted very much that was the case. Anyway, with no choice left to her but to slip quietly into the house, she proceeded forward. Well, as it turns out, neither Ricky nor the woman he was screwing realized she was there. It was an unbelievable stroke of good luck. That was a good omen, she mused to herself. Needless to say, the element of surprise was to her advantage. At any rate, Ricky was delightfully banging away at the back side of the woman who let him into the house. In fact, they were so engrossed in what they were doing they were totally oblivious to Maude and the environment around them. Anyway, obviously, shaken by the most recent turn of events she tried to collect her thoughts however it was to no avail. What she now saw happening in the bedroom was enough to make a grown woman cry. At this point, she cursed to herself that she ever married the asshole. There wasn't any doubt about that. In fact, in her eyes, Ricky was a scumbag! A first-class piece of shit that betrayed her! Damn, life and everything else that goes along with it, she cursed to herself. Life was never meant to be that unkind. Then, she shook her head and cursed to herself one more time, of all the possible things Ricky could have been doing, and he chose to stick his dick in another woman's vagina.

At this point, Maude was seeing infrared, ultraviolet and every other damn color known to mankind as she quickly contemplated her next course of action. Needless to say, the time had come to lower the boom on her beloved husband, so she took a deep breath of air and walked out into the center of the woman's bedroom. "Hello, Romeo," she stated loudly so there wouldn't be any doubt who was addressing him. "I bet you never expected to see me here!" Needless to say, she had caught him with his pants down in every sense of the word. In fact, quite frankly, he was totally speechless. At any rate, upon seeing Maude walk into the bedroom, the woman he was so delightfully screwing, screamed, and ran out of the room. Needless to say, it was unquestionably time to address the situation. At this juncture, Ricky blurted out, "How did you find me here? In fact, how in the hell did you get in here? You must realize you're trespassing on another person's property!" "Never mind how I found you or how I managed to get in here," she said. "The only thing that really matters is I caught you with your hand in the cookie jar or should I say your dick in another woman's vagina. Well, Ricky, it seems you have stuck that thing between your legs in the wrong hole. How dare you violate our marriage vows! I put my trust in you and turn around and do this behind my back! Well, just so you know, you're an asshole Ricky! In fact, you are a miserable little two-timing turd! Now, what have you got to say about that?" Apparently, he was at a total loss for words because there was a bit of silence inside the bedroom for a moment as he thought about what he wanted to say. Finally, after what seemed like forever, a very shocked and bewildered man by the name of Ricky Vestellini replied, "I'm terribly sorry about this dear, but I have been lonely in recent months. For some reason we don't connect in bed anymore and I was deeply distraught by that. In fact, quite frankly, you've been colder than ice to me for some time now, so I came to the conclusion, I would look for love somewhere else. It's as simple as that. I really don't know what else to say." "What you mean to say is you wanted to find a piece of ass somewhere else," she stated. "Seeing we're married, and you didn't ask my permission to do so, that's despicable Ricky! Did I treat you that badly?" "Well, in my opinion you weren't exactly a great lay in bed," he replied. "When a man has to take care of his personal needs himself, I'd say it's time to move on. In fact, shit happens sometimes." "I guess the hell it does," she exclaimed! "I can't believe you would say something as stupid as that to me! In other words, with regards to our marriage, you've likened it unto a bowel movement. Well, just so you know, that's a horrible thing to say to the person you're married too! Furthermore, think of what your actions will do to our children in the days ahead, and all the good times we had together. I hope you realize you're carelessly throwing all of that away." "Yes, Jesus, call it what you want, but the bottom line of it all is, there isn't any love in our marriage anymore, Maude," Ricky said. "Actually, I don't think you see that, however that's the reality of things now." "Well, screw you," she exclaimed! "You can take whatever you think and shove it right up your ass!" At this point, there wasn't too much left to be said, and thinking better of it, Maude immediately turned around and departed from the house the same way she came in. Then, after crossing the street, she got into her Ferrari and took off down the road in a horrible fit of rage. Needless to say, she wasn't sure how she was going to handle the situation in the days ahead but she was certain of one thing and that was Mr. Vestellini was officially on her shit list now.

Anyway, the moment Maude got home, she immediately tried the self-composure method of telling herself everything would be all right even though in all probability her marriage was all but over. Actually, she had been struggling with that thought for some time however after seeing proof positive that Ricky was screwing another woman, a divorce was inevitable now. In fact, it was just a question of when and where this matter between them would be resolved. At any rate, right at the moment, there were other things that had to be taken care of. First, she thanked Freda for looking after the girls while she was out and after a short dialogue, she went home. Then, she headed upstairs to the bathroom to freshen up a little before checking on the girls for a minute to make sure everything was fine. Since they were sound asleep no further action was needed so a moment or two later, she went back down to the living-room and had a good cry. As always, she did most things by priority and such was the case this time as well. Anyway, at this point, Maude got into Ricky's liquor cabinet and made herself a drink before sitting down in the living-room to think about what happened. Actually, there was a lot to consider here so Maude immediately set her mind to work on trying to figure out what the best solution would be to a problem she didn't think she would ever have. Granted, every now and then marriages have been known to fail but in her naive blindness to the simple things in life, she never thought that would happen to her.

At any rate, a couple hours after his confrontation with Maude, Ricky made his less than triumphant return home. Needless to say, he had to face the inevitable sometime, and no sooner did he walk through the door, when she started going up one side of him and down the other. In fact, once again, she gave him a good piece of her mind. Anyway, like you might expect, Maude began yelling at him at the top of her lungs. "You god damn, no good, son of a bitch! How dare you screw around behind my back, Ricky! Actually, I didn't think you would be numb enough to even come back here! Obviously, I wasn't good enough for you in bed. Well, I hope that woman was worth taking a chance on because you just killed the hell out of this marriage." At this point, Ricky replied, "I am sorry, Maude. Believe it or not, I never meant to hurt you." "Then, why in the name of Christ were you screwing the woman I caught you in bed with," she asked? "Surely, you must realize, it hurts me very badly to see you with another woman. I love you dearly, but I regret I ever married you now. Think about what it's going to do to our children. Does that not mean anything to you? I will assume you don't love me anymore." "You assumed correctly," he replied. "In fact, quite frankly, as far as I'm concerned you can shove this marriage right up your ass!" "Well, to hell with you, Ricky," she replied. "How dare you say that to me! As your wife, I deserve more respect from you than that!" "I don't want to discuss this matter any further," he stated. "In fact, I intend to file for a divorce, Maude." At this point, she was silent for a moment as she thought about what he said. Obviously, there wasn't any sense of continuing on with their conversation because any dialogue with this man was a waste of time. "You're hopeless, Ricky," she screamed. "Not only are you a great big loser, but you are a great big asshole too. Now, get out of here! I don't want to ever see you again. In fact, if you don't leave the premises, I'll call the police and have you locked up for domestic assault. I'm sure you would love to spend some time in jail. Actually, I suggest you go back to the woman you've been screwing because you're not welcome around here anymore. I'm sure she will be happy to take you in with open arms. If she doesn't, that's too damn bad. Now, for the last time, leave this house peaceably or I will call the police and have you removed from here. I mean it, Ricky! Get out of here! I've had enough of your bullshit to last me a lifetime!" At this point, rather than trying to reason with Maude any further, Ricky took off out the door madder than a wet hen. The truth of the matter was since she couldn't find a place in her heart to forgive him, there wasn't any sense of hanging around, so he made the fastest exit he could out of their house. Actually, he had been thinking about getting a divorce from her for quite some time anyway, but this incident was the icing on the cake. In fact, their marriage was over. At any rate, on his way out the door that evening, he yelled back at her, saying, "I will have my lawyer draw up a divorce settlement for us, but in the meantime, you can kiss my ass!" "No," she yelled back at him, "you can kiss mine!" Believe it or not, at this point, two grown adult's exchanged middle fingers and a moment later, he drove off down the road in a fit of rage while Maude went back into the house and cried. It was indeed the lowest point of her life. Obviously, nothing could have been more apparent than that however that was the nature of being human and certainly the reality of the situation. Needless to say, what began as the best of times between two people was now a marriage in ruins. She would find a way to go on with her life however nothing between her and Ricky would ever be the same again.

Anyway, shortly after the terrible falling out she had with Ricky, Maude told her children she was going to seek a divorce from their father. Of course, at their age, trying to explain what happened their mother and father's marriage was going to be a hard thing to do however she did her best to let them know their father wouldn't be living with them anymore. Needless to say, it wasn't an easy thing to do and how much they actually understood, she wasn't certain. Anyway, once that matter was taken care of Maude had to come to terms with herself over something else. She was five months pregnant. Of course, Ricky didn't know anything about that however with their marriage gradually going down the drain, she thought it was best not to say anything about it. In fact, she had been entertaining the thought of getting a divorce for some time now anyway so with that matter about to be taken up in a lawyer's office, she realized it was time to move on with her life again. Actually, by this time, Maude realized her marriage to Ricky was a great big mistake. Why she never saw him as a lady's man was beyond her! Granted, he was a handsome man with a lot of personality but those qualities in a man aren't everything and it was regrettable she had to find that out the hard way.

Anyway, at this point, she concluded, a divorce settlement was inevitable. As a matter of fact, the sooner they sat down with a lawyer and worked things out, the sooner this whole cursed nightmare would be over. Furthermore, she wanted full custody of the children. If Mr. Vestellini contested that, it was going to be a problem. As for Ricky's property in Oregon, for some reason he did not want it so if that went in her direction too, she would sell it somewhere down the road. Actually, her first thought was to tell him to shove it up his ass and perhaps that would've been a far better thing to do however she decided against doing that. Maude intended to let things be as they were and hope they would reach a good amicable divorce settlement when the time arrived. In the meantime, there really wasn't too much of anything she could do except wait and see how everything turned out in the days ahead. Hopefully, better days were coming at some point along the way and it goes without saying, if Maude got custody of the children and she didn't have any reason to believe she wouldn't, then in all probability that would be the case.

CHAPTER 31

In the days ahead, Ricky did just exactly what he said he was going to do. After his bad falling out with Maude, he made a couple of telephone calls and found a lawyer who was happy to draw up a divorce settlement for them. Actually, it was the same thing she intended to do but Ricky got to things before she did. Anyway, as you might suspect, a lot of monetary assets were involved in addition to their children and that would more than likely complicate things to some degree. In this particular case, he was more anxious than ever to get everything taken care of so he could move on with his life. The truth of the matter was, Mona Aubert, a very pretty woman was an important part of his life now. She, being roughly the same age as Ricky, appeared to be an ideal match for him. They both were good looking individuals and had pleasant personality's so the odds of having a good relationship together were obviously in their favor. As for Maude, at this point in their lives, she could've cared less what Ricky did however she did condemn the hell out of the woman though. In fact, I believe her exact words to Ricky were, "Mona is a first-class slut with aspirations to be a whore! You ought to be ashamed of yourself, Mr. Vestellini! I really and truly hope you're happy with your newly found trophy." Of course, Ricky was totally oblivious to what she said about his new girlfriend. Needless to say, being extremely dissatisfied with his marriage, he was looking to make some changes in his life. The truth of the matter is, it was the same thing she wanted to do however right at the moment, Maude's biggest concern was getting custody of the children. Obviously, if that worked out the way she wanted it too, Maude thought everything would be all right. It would be just a question of whether or not she stayed in France and whether or not, she made an attempt to rebuild her personal life. Since Maude didn't have any need for monetary support to bring up the children, it was unclear what she would do in the days ahead but there was one thing she was absolutely certain of and that was she didn't want to marry another asshole like Ricky Vestellini.

Anyway, as fate would have it, about two weeks later, destiny found them waiting inside his attorney's office with the sole intention of taking care of their divorce settlement. It was not anticipated to be a pleasant experience and as stated before, she was extremely concerned about getting custody of the children. At any rate, over the course of the next couple of hours most of their personal life was aired out in that office, much the same way someone would air out all of their dirty laundry. Unfortunately, at this point, her highly intellectual mind began to wander off in other directions again as she sat there mired in deep thought. Firstly, her kids never wandered very far away from her mind and secondly, she was thinking about where life may take her in the weeks following her divorce settlement with Ricky. Needless to say, as far as marriages go, she could always find another husband however she wasn't certain that was the best thing to do. As a matter of fact, Maude was very disenchanted by the way men used her in the past so she wasn't in any hurry to get married again. As for writing another book, there was a good possibility that might happen sometime however it probably wouldn't be anytime soon. At any rate, due to the complexity of her mind, thought after thought of how things would go continued to infiltrate her mind. She even began having second thoughts about letting Ricky's attorney represent both of them, however she trusted the man's judgment and in the end, she left everything the way it was. In fact, with regards to their divorce settlement, if Maude didn't miss her guess, she had nothing to worry about. She was fairly certain she would get custody of the children and then she would move on with her life. Anyway, the amount of time that was spent in the attorney's office wasn't really that much however it seemed like forever to her as they proceeded to hash out a few minor details of the settlement. In this particular case, that meant going over their last and testament in addition to deciding who would get custody of the children. A lot of things had changed over the past four years, so a few changes were made to their wills in order to be more compliant with the law in the country of France. Needless to say, it was very important for them to have everything legalized and binding in France because their original will was drawn up in the United States, so the end result of their keen foresight kept most of their discussion right on track. Obviously, had that not been the case, they would have been in the attorney's office for a much longer time, but that didn't happen and everything progressed along rather nicely because there wasn't any major differences between them. In fact, the way everything turned out, no disagreements of any kind had to be dealt with and that's not at all how she thought things would go.

Anyway, time went by very quickly that day, and when everything was all said and done, she could honestly say, things went very well indeed. Needless to say, after a couple of hours of discussion, they came to terms, and she couldn't have been more pleased with the outcome. Not only had they reached a very amicable divorce settlement, but Maude was granted custody of the children as well. Actually, she thought Ricky might contest that particular issue, but much to her surprise, he didn't. Of course, that could've had a lot to do with the fact, he was having an affair with another woman however there wasn't any way to be certain of that. He wouldn't say. Ricky just clearly stated, he didn't want the kids. It was as simple as that. Initially, Maude thought that was something he would contest however he didn't do that. Since he really loved his children, it was her belief the person Ricky was sleeping with didn't want any children so that was probably the reason why he told the attorney she could have the children. As a matter of fact, once upon a time, she thought he loved her too. Obviously, had that not been the case, Maude wouldn't have married him. At any rate, with regards to the rest of their divorce settlement, it was decided, she would get the lighthouse as well as Ricky's home, but that didn't come as too much of a surprise because he didn't want to go back there. In addition to that, she was to keep her home in Beverly Hills and her home in France, plus the rights to the earnings from the books she had written. On the other hand, Ricky only wanted the money he inherited from his parents which probably came to several million dollars however like you might think, she didn't have any interest in that. Her monetary assets were so great she didn't even have to consider fighting for any of his money. He did insist on keeping the yacht he had in France but as far as Maude was concerned, Ricky could shove that right up his ass. It wasn't that she didn't have some good times on the boat however it had everything to do with the fact, Maude wanted to leave behind everything that was attached to Ricky with the exception of the kids. Needless to say, for that reason, she also changed her mind about staying in France. Realistically speaking, she didn't want to live anywhere near Ricky and since, he planned on making his home in Nice, Maude thought it would be best to go back to the United States. In addition to that, there were some other things she had to take into consideration as well however the biggest reason she wanted to leave France was to get away from the memory of her failed marriage to Ricky. Besides, if she went back to the United States, her children had a much better chance of seeing their grandparents. Anyway, to be practical, she set a realistic goal of three to six months for selling her home in France and relocating back to her estate in Beverly Hills. That would more than likely give her plenty of time to make a smooth transition from one country to the other. Of course, that meant she had to begin working on some other things before that could be done. In this particular case, that meant tying up a few loose ends with the lawyer's office as well as selling everything she owned in France. Once those things were taken care of in the due course of taking care of business, Maude would make reservations for a flight back to the United States. As for money transfers, that wouldn't be hard to do so that would logically be left for last. Needless to say, she had everything all planned out right down to the clothing she would wear, and it can be said, that described Maude's personality to the letter T.

Anyway, one thing quickly led to another and before she realized it, Maude was ready to go. Actually, what made that possible was her property in France sold a lot faster than expected. Of course, she wasn't the kind of person to put anything off, if it came down to doing something that directly affected her life and in this case, such was the case here as well. At any rate, Maude was hoping to spend the better part of the spring in Beverly Hills and then, if things continued to go well, she might make a trip up to Oregon in the summer. Chances are she would use Ricky's old estate in Oregon as a summer home or as a place to a getaway from it all when the desire to do so was there but that remained to be seen. At this point, she was more concerned about some other things however seeing that she was the owner of the property now, those were a couple of options available to her. Anyway, when she left the country of France, she did so without saying a word. Actually, that didn't come as any surprise because she didn't want Ricky to know what she was doing, so there weren't any good-byes, teary eyes, or anything else for that matter when she moved back to the United States. She just simply packed up her suitcases and left. It was as simple as that. The truth of the matter is she hated the ground Ricky walked upon, so she had no desire to make him aware of what she was doing. Maybe somewhere down the road her feelings would change about that but in the meantime, that's the way she wanted it.

Anyway, late one afternoon towards the end of the month of April, Maude, Vanessa Ann, Margaret Jean, and the child she was carrying made their triumphant return to the United States. In fact, after having taken the commuter train from Nice to Paris, they had connecting flights to the city of Los Angeles.

From there, the services of a taxi was hired and a short time later, good fortune found her back in the place she would always call home and of course, that was Beverly Hills. Needless to say, she was happier than ever to be back in Beverly Hills. In fact, she didn't realize how much she really missed her old estate until now. As for her children, they obviously hadn't seen their mother's home in Beverly Hills before so pretty typical of most kids, they were very excited to see the place. At any rate, not unexpectedly, at this point, she began to reflect on how things had gone over the past few years. Admittedly, one thing after another had happened to her in that period of time. First of all, she had a family now. With two young girls and a baby on the way, she had more responsibility than she ever these days. Actually, she was a few years older and a hell of a lot wiser than she was the last time she resided in Beverly Hills however she was basically the same person she had always been. On the plus side of it all, she was even more financially well to do and outside of a failed marriage, she wasn't doing too badly. All in all, she was in good health and still had a lot going for her. In fact, knowing her, once Maude got settled into her old estate, chances are she would pick up writing again. Needless to say, that would not be a bad thing because it was something she enjoyed doing. As for her former husband, like you might think, she never wanted to see him again. Irreconcilable differences was how their divorce settlement was filed however due to the fact, he literally dropped her for another woman, she was inclined to believe, the divorce settlement should've been filed as marriage infidelity. In the end, it didn't actually matter what brought an end to her marriage. She was just happy to have had the opportunity to move on with her life and that's all that really mattered. At any rate, now that she was on her own again, it was like having a brand-new lease on life for her. It was also the fourth time she had to deal with a major change in her life since turning twenty-one, however each time that happened, she thought it was best to move on with her life and such was the case this time as well. Needless to say, it was either do what she did or put up with the circumstances of her failed marriage to Ricky Vestellini and of course, Maude chose to do this. Anyway, thanks to feeling at home in Beverly Hills, a short time later, her marriage to Ricky was soon forgotten, and soon she was right back into the swing of things but that was pretty typical of her personality. Yes, Maude had succeeded in making another adjustment in her life, and it goes without saying, she was very happy about having done so.

Anyway, the way everything unfolded, about six weeks later she gave birth to a healthy, little baby boy. It was her third child and even at that young of an age, he looked like his father. In fact, so much so, Maude had a feeling it was going to haunt the hell out of her in the years to come. The shame of it all was, in all probability, his father wasn't ever going to see his son. At least, that's the way everything was supposed to go although believe it or not, Maude named the child after him, regardless of any regrets she may have had about doing so in the days ahead. In fact, if it turned out to be a mistake, then so be it. She was the only one that had to live with that decision so that's the way it was going to be. Anyway, with a little help from her parents, Maude was more than ready to take on whatever life had to throw at her again. The truth of the matter is she had a profession. It may not have been a conventional one but it was one that generated a lot of money for her. It was just a question of whether or not she pursued another relationship, that's all. In the meantime, she had custody of the children and that was the most important thing of all to Maude. Perhaps, the only thing that didn't fit into her plans for a happy and productive future in the months ahead was she would be bringing up the kids on her own. That wasn't going to be an easy thing to do, and one day, shortly after arriving back in Beverly Hills, she began the long process of putting a lot of careful thought into hiring a maid. Obviously, if she were to take the initiative to do that, her children would get the extra attention they needed and of course, it goes without saying, she saw that as favorable situation. Not only would she have someone to tend to the kids, but she would also have someone to give her a hand with the chores around the house as well. At any rate, in the end, Maude concluded, hiring a maid would be a good thing to do but in the meantime there were some other things she had to be concerned with and that was her health. Until now, she had not had any medical issues that posed a risk to her health but that was always subject to change. Sometimes, it doesn't take very long to get things going in the other direction. Needless to say, with every year that went by now, her goal and objective was to stay healthy so with that in mind, she tried to stay more focused on that concern rather than trying to find a new adventure to undertake. The truth of the matter is, Maude wanted to see her children grow up, so she had decided to try and take better care of herself. Not that she hadn't tried to do that in years past however with children now, it was more imperative than ever she do so.

Part VII

CHAPTER 32

To Maude, living in Beverly Hills was life at its finest. There were all kinds of exquisite homes, shops, and boutiques, leaving the residents of the area more than satisfied with their place of residence. In addition to that, she found out very quickly that everything was just a phone call away here and that really typified the word convenience. In this particular instance, that was one of the reasons why she liked living there. Anyway, now years later, she still looked at it the same way. Beverly Hills was where she felt most at home. Even in the days when the news media had a tendency to bother her from time to time, she still loved it there. In fact, chances are she would always feel that way about Beverly Hills even if she were to move onto somewhere else again. I guess, it would be safe to say, this is where her heart was and that pretty much says it all. As for being back in town, everything between her and Ricky seemed like a world away now. Actually, to be more precise, there was a continent and a half between them, in addition to an ocean. Like you might expect, she saw that as a good thing because if he was in the area, she might consider killing the son of a bitch for what he did to her. Obviously, that's a terrible thing to say but it was how she felt. Furthermore, it wasn't that she was unstable in mind however she was emotionally scarred by the whole unfortunate thing that unfolded while she was living in France. One way or another, regardless of what she thought of Ricky's careless actions, she felt better without having him around. In fact, quite frankly, she was finally beginning to enjoy life again now that he was no longer a part of her life. Needless to say, the biggest mistake Ricky ever made was electing to go elsewhere for his sexual needs. At least, that's the way she saw it anyway. Of course, he had an entirely different perspective on the matter, however due to the circumstances of the situation, the only logical thing to do was go separate ways so that's what they did. Actually, Maude didn't have any regrets at all about doing that however she was inclined to believe he did. Whether you call it hunch or just a lucky guess, her intuition told her, Ricky would probably never be satisfied with whoever he was sleeping with. Maude blamed his hot Italian blood for that, however if she didn't miss her guess, that was something that wouldn't ever change. It was in his genes and for that reason alone, his passion for woman would probably never diminish. Anyway, as you might think, she was just thankful for being in good health and getting custody of the children. At this point, Maude realized how much she missed living in the United States.

Needless to say, it's one of those things she took for granted. In fact, it really wouldn't be an understatement to say, home is where the heart is and that expression couldn't have described her feelings any better than that. Actually, now that she had an opportunity to look back on it all, she wondered why, she ever left the United States in the first place. Obviously, it turned out to be a mistake however at the time, it seemed like the right thing to do. Furthermore, that was nothing against the country of France because she liked it there however her love for the United States won out in the end. Sometimes, the grass is greener on the other side of the fence however in this instance, it had more to do with what Ricky Vestellini did to her than anything else. At least, that's how she looked at it anyway. Perhaps, under different circumstances she would have seen things a lot differently.

Anyway, the way everything unfolded, a short time later, Maude found herself a maid. In fact, shortly after Ricky Jr. was born, she put an ad in a local newspaper for a live-in maid. What that actually accomplished was sometime the following week, she went onto hire a stout, middle aged woman by the name of Lisa Ann Hanscom. Both Vanessa, and Margaret took an immediate liking to her, in particularly, Vanessa. Margaret was a little too young to comprehend everything she said however that was to be expected. On the other hand, Vanessa caught onto whatever she said very quickly although if she didn't get her own way, she usually called Lisa a meanie, which of course, she found amusing and in most instances, that harmless comment was laughed off as a part of being a child. Anyway, it didn't take Maude very long to realize the person she hired was not only a nice person, but she was also very good with children as well. As a matter of fact, her maid was the kind of person she was looking for because her children always came first and with Lisa, that wouldn't ever be a problem. In addition to that, what she found really impressive about her maid was she took everything like a grain of salt, regardless of the circumstances, and as you might think, she thought highly of that particular characteristic. More importantly, just as long as her children were happy, she was happy. They were the cornerstone of her life these days and for that reason, it was also very important, they did not want for anything and were content with how they were being treated. Furthermore, Maude thought most of what they did, said or got into was actually quite cute although every now and then, a little discipline had to be used, however, all in all, that was to be expected. Actually, kids will be kids, regardless of how you bring them up. It was also her steadfast conviction; children should have as much freedom as possible so they will grow up to be their own person. Not unexpectedly, her maid held the same belief herself so from a strategist's point of view, Maude hired the right person to take care of her children, and it didn't take her very long to realize that either.

By the time fall arrived that year, Vanessa started school and she couldn't have been more excited about doing so. Unfortunately, that left her younger sister without a playmate around the house and consequently, Margaret was lost without having her older sister around. On the other hand, neither one of the girls missed their father at all because he spent very little time with them when they were living in France. Actually, Vanessa did a little but she had long since gotten over any feelings she had for her father. If you remember correctly, not long after Margaret was born, Ricky began spending more and more time away from home so she never really got to know him during the days they resided in Nice. As for Ricky Jr., his father didn't even know he existed and perhaps, that's the way that would always remain. At this point, there really wasn't anyway to be certain of that although the truth of the matter was, Maude didn't want to see him again. Sadly, it was her contention, Ricky was at fault for the failure of their marriage and in a way she was right about that, because in her opinion, screwing around with another woman was an inexcusable act of marriage infidelity. In fact, it was something Maude had suspected for some time however it wasn't until she literally caught him with his pants down in the comfort of another woman's bed that she came to the conclusion, it was time to move on with her life again. Anyway, as you may have already guessed, at first Maude was totally crushed by the incident, but as time went by, she could honestly say, going separate ways was the best thing she could've done. In fact, a divorce was the only way she would ever be able to get her life back in order, so that's what she did. At any rate, now, back at her home in California, she continued to reflect on the highly undesirable circumstances that befell her in France. Actually, so far, everything appeared to point to the fact moving back to the United States was a good decision on her part, however it was quite possible she made another mistake by having done so. Obviously, time would tell whether or not Maude made the right decision on that matter, but at least for the time being, everything was going well.

Anyway, in addition to the unfortunate falling out she had with her husband, there were a lot of other things running through Maude's head that day. Obviously, time heals all wounds, the only exception to that would be a mortal wound, which of course is physical in nature but Maude didn't have to worry about. Her injuries were in the way of emotional scars, and they can be very hard to heal. In fact, quite frankly, some people never get over things like that. Furthermore, it's my stalwart contention most people say everything in life happens for a reason. Actually, I don't necessarily agree with that, however for anyone who truly believes in love or the positive state of being of the spiritual life within them, chances are, you will more than likely be a happy man or a woman as you journey through life. It really doesn't matter what time of the year you find the love you're looking for but in theory and religiously speaking, love takes root at the beginning of spring and if it's something that's meant to be, it will blossom into a great relationship during the summer months. Perhaps, in the end, what matters most about being human is what we try to do with our lives while we're physically alive upon the earth. The life ever-lasting life that everyone seeks is in the arc of heaven beneath the sky above. In death, you actually go to hell. Believe it or not, it's the life you live while you are physically alive on this earth that counts for everything. It's through the gift of speech and it's the life you make for yourself. Obviously, the life a person creates for themselves is physical in nature and that's having children and raising a family. It's in darkness that you will see light. In fact, sometimes the light of day actually blinds us to the truth of what most people seek in life and if and when you come to realize this, it is very often too late to do anything about it. As I've said many times before, life goes by very quickly and if a person doesn't pick up on this at a young age, they'll more than likely miss out on what life has to offer. Furthermore, to experience life at its finest requires a lot of determination and commitment to be a better person. That doesn't mean you have to go out and be a good deed doer however it does require the spoken word in the light of heaven. Actually, in many cases, it's mankind's intellect that bites himself in the ass because everyone looks at things differently however when it comes right down to living a good life, sometimes, what one person does effects another and when that happens, the heaven on earth you were looking for can literally go right down the drain. At that point, I would say, welcome, to hell! In that case, to be practical, your only chance for a heaven on earth or what most people call, a life hereafter rests in the belief of modern Christianity or any other religion people worship. Anyway, enough said about that. Philosophy on life is very open-ended and it entails a lot of thought so let's get back to the story.

Now, as for Maude, she couldn't have been more satisfied with her decision to have filed for divorce from her husband. Granted, it wasn't an easy thing for her to do however that act of good judgement opened the door to new possibilities for her. So, with that said and with summer having come and gone that year, she quickly began focusing on what was ahead of her. Well, as coincidence would have it, one day while Maude was pondering this highly challenging thought, an old friend just happened to give her a call. Perhaps, that can be better stated as, at one time he was a good friend of hers. Needless to say, that was a few years earlier now but some of the fond memories she had with this man were still alive inside her head, unfortunately, she also distinctly remembered what he did to her as well. Even though they weren't married at the time, it was her understanding that she was the only girl he was seeing, when in fact, that really wasn't the case at all. Anyway, as fate would have it and much to her surprise, Ken Stackford was on the phone. It was actually an unbelievable occurrence because Maude told him years ago, she never wanted to see him again so you might say, he was unquestionably the last person she expected to hear from. Well, as it turns out, Maude was wrong about that because for some unexplained reason, Ken had taken the initiative to give her a call. Actually, as you might think, she wasn't sure how he found out she was back in town however the bottom line of it all was, Ken had and for whatever reason that may be he took it upon himself to look her up. Anyway, like a first-rate detective, she began putting some thought into the matter and concluded, her next-door neighbor was more than likely the one who was responsible for letting the cat out of the bag. Now, it would be just a matter of figuring out what he wanted. As you may recall, Ken saved her life a few years before when she nearly died from an overdose of prescription medication. Needless to say, she was very grateful to him for doing that however at the time, he wasn't ready to settle down yet. As a matter of fact, she found him in bed with another woman. Granted, they weren't married at the time however it was unbelievably heartbreaking to see the person she thought the world of screwing someone she considered to be a first-class whore. Well, as you might expect, it didn't take Maude very long to realize Ken wasn't the right person for her after that unfortunate event, she moved away from the Beverly Hills area. In fact, it was one of a couple reasons that eventually led her to meet and fall in love with Ricky Vestellini. Of course, that was all water under the bridge now however it was what happened and now, reflecting back on it all, Maude found it very hard to forget what he did to her. Anyway, be so as it may, like so many times in the past, the sometimes-unmerciful hands of destiny were about to intervene again. Ken Stackford was on the phone, and she was at a total loss for words as to what to say by the unpredictability of the moment. In reality, it had been six years or so since she had spoken with him so you might say, she was speechless. Well, being the diplomatic person she was, not to mention a good sport, after stumbling around with a few very difficult minutes of trying to find the right thing to say, they eventually began to fill each other in on what was going on in their lives. At this point, Maude thought better of the situation and very prudently suggested, they get together for lunch sometime. Yes, believe it or not, Maude actually took the initiative to do that and at no surprise to her, Ken quickly accepted her invitation to meet for lunch. Actually, she could only assume that's what he had in mind anyway. Why else would he be calling? Perhaps, he was lonely these days. Who knows, she thought to herself. Anyway, they made plans to meet at a favorite restaurant of hers, one that she use to visit quite frequently, when she lived in Beverly Hills, some years ago now. The fact of the matter is she wouldn't have any idea what he had in mind until they discussed a few things over lunch. In the meantime, she would just have to be patient. As for the conversation they had that day, Maude made him aware of the fact she had children now, however much to her surprise, Ken indicated that's what he was looking for. Actually, she found that hard to believe however there was always the possibility he could have changed so there really wasn't any sense of speculating on that anymore until she met him for lunch. Needless to say, that was something that she would probably be able to deduce if she had a little time to spend with him and of course, having dinner with someone most certainly fell into that category. At this point in their conversation, she found out Ken had been struggling with alcohol addiction for the past five years although he quickly inferred that was a thing of the past now. In fact, if Maude understood him correctly, Ken said he hadn't had a drink in nearly a year. Well, that was all good and fine with her, and she didn't hesitate to compliment him on a job well done because that was actually a very good accomplishment however Maude was more concerned about his maturity. Needless to say, that was the reason why they went separate ways, years ago and that would more than likely be the reason why they would go separate ways again if she were to have another relationship with him. Anyway, she was hoping in the worst possible way, he had changed. The fact, Ken wasn't drinking anymore was a sign that may be the case so she was optimistic, he may be ready to settle down after all. Actually, any future time they spent together would depend on that and at this point, Maude really wasn't in the position to make that determination yet. In fact, it's the reason why she wanted to meet Ken for lunch. Obviously, the more she knew about what he had been doing and what his future goals were, the easier it would be for her to make a decision on whether or not to pursue him for marriage. Needless to say, that just happens to be what she was doing nearly six years ago however the last time Maude did that with him, it was an absolute disaster. Realistically speaking, the most important thing of all now was to determine if he was sincere about having a long-term relationship with her, which by the way would mean marriage this time. Anyway, putting all that aside, it was the first time she had anything to get all excited about in the way of another man since her marriage to Ricky ended in divorce. Granted, she hadn't been thinking about that for some time now however due to the fact she was human, if she were to give it some thought, the desire to do so was still there. Like you might expect, it was going to be just a question of whether or not, Ken had grown up to the point of being able to accept responsibility. The last time she saw him, he seemed to be only interested in one thing and that was having a good time. You know, fun and games. Life's a party and let's party some more. In fact, Maude was certain, it was the reason why, he was having relationships with more than one woman at a time and as I said before, that really wasn't at all what she had in mind. Perhaps, Ken had a different view of what happened to their relationship, some years ago, however Maude could not prove otherwise so she had already decided to give him the benefit of the doubt because she liked Ken Stackford. He was a good-looking man with a lot going for him and if he really put his mind to it, there wasn't too much he couldn't do. She was certain of that. Anyway, in a situation like this, in most instances, it would be wise to proceed with caution, and it goes without saying, that's what she planned on doing. In the meantime, there was a lot to take into consideration however right at the moment, all she wanted to do is savor the good memories she had with Ken. After that, the door was open to other possibilities. Perhaps, she would even marry him but first she wanted to see if he had changed from his promiscuous ways of yesterday.

CHAPTER 33

A steady flow of traffic was moving in and out of the East Side Restaurant as Maude took a moment to park her Ferrari in the parking lot next to the building. Through the years, she very often went to this restaurant, and she could honestly say, it was one of her most favorite places to eat. Between having a lot of steady clientele and serving some of the best Italian cuisine around, it made all the sense in the world to dine there whenever she had an opportunity to do so. In this particular case, she liked the atmosphere of the restaurant really well. It was casual. No suit and tie were required and reservations were optional. In fact, she felt at home there. Needless to say, she liked that aspect of the restaurant best however with the food being so good, there wasn't any way she could pass up an opportunity to go there. Perhaps, that wasn't always the case, however more often than not that's where she went. Admittedly, if you were to ask her how she felt about the food they served, I'm sure she would have said, it's well worth the visit. Anyway, regardless of what she may or may not have said about the restaurant, on this occasion, that's where Maude intended to have dinner. Perhaps, another time, she would dine out at different restaurant, but in the meantime she had a dinner engagement with Ken Stackford and that clearly took precedence over everything else.

Anyway, as you might think, just as soon as she found a place to park, she pulled the keys out of the ignition of her car and hurried inside the restaurant to reserve a table. Actually, Maude wasn't certain what time Ken would get there so rather than sitting around like a bump on a log, a drink was ordered in an effort to try and utilize some of her time with the hope he would be right along. Well, as it turns out, he arrived at the restaurant about ten minutes later which wasn't bad at all. Waiting a half hour or more for someone to show up gets a little tedious sometimes but ten minutes was a piece of cake. In this particular case, what made the situation so awkward was she hadn't seen him in nearly six years. In fact, Maude wasn't even sure if she would recognize him, however that fear was soon dismissed the moment she spotted him walking through the entrance to the restaurant. On this occasion, Ken was wearing a navy sport coat with a wine-colored turtle neck shirt and a pair of matching slacks. He looked great! Actually, he was a good-looking man to begin with, and the way he was dressed was eye catching to say the least. As a matter of fact, by all appearances, she could honestly say, Ken was one of the best-looking guys she ever dated. In truth, she thought Ken would be dressed a little more casual than he was but his sharp looking appearance certainly didn't hurt anything. Furthermore, and also somewhat surprisingly, it didn't look like he'd aged at all from the last time she saw him, and that was truly amazing. Usually, a person's age will come to surface as they get older, however in his case, he still looked as young as ever. Anyway, be so as it may, Ken walked over to the table she was sitting at and gave her a great big hug, saying, "It's really nice to see you again, Maude! I hope life is treating you well! It has been quite some time since I've had the pleasure of your company and I can honestly say, I miss the good times we had together in years past. In fact, when I look back on it all, I certainly have to admit, they were some of the best days of my life however at the time, I was so wrapped up in a couple of other things, I didn't realize that. Anyway, I sincerely apologize for that." By this time, they were both seated at the table and well emersed in their conversation. At this point, Maude replied, "I'm truly sorry things didn't work out for us back in the day we were the best of friends however when I learned you were sleeping with another woman, I was crushed. In fact, I was so crushed that I thought of committing suicide and on more than one occasion, I might add. Take a minute and put yourself in my place, Ken. Can you imagine how I felt? You were where the sun rose and set in my life! To say, I was upset is the understatement of a lifetime. In fact, if you really want to know, I was hurt so badly by what you did that I swore to god I wouldn't ever let another man into my life again. You meant the world to me, Ken and as you already know, it was the reason why, I thought it was best to call an end to our relationship. In fact, quite frankly, I was truly devastated by what you did to me. Believe it or not, it had nothing to do with me not liking you because that couldn't have been further from the truth. I just didn't want to share you with another woman, that's all." Obviously, Ken understood what Maude was trying to tell him and he really didn't blame her at all for the way she felt about his immature adventurism. At the time, Ken looked at the situation a lot differently however in hindsight, he had to admit, what he did was wrong. On the other hand, there wasn't any way to change the past. He clearly made a mistake however that was all water under the bridge now. Perhaps, with any luck at all, he'd be able to make it up to her. At least, it was worth a try anyway. Yes, that was Ken's thought as he quickly began searching for the right words to explain his side of the story. In truth, he had done that before however it was unclear to him whether or not he had done that effectively. Finally, at a partial loss for words, Ken stated, "First of all, before we get any further into this conversation, your next-door neighbor was the one who told me you were back in Beverly Hills. I'm sure you have been wondering about that and it's only natural to question that. Secondly, as unbelievable as it may sound, I'm really and truly sorry about the unfortunate incident you walked in on when we were dating each other, a few years ago. If you had any idea how bad I felt about the whole thing, perhaps, you might have looked at things differently. I made a mistake, Maude and now, I ask your forgiveness. In fact, quite frankly, if it means anything to you, as a result of that falling out, we had a few years ago, I took to drinking after we broke up and it took me the better part of five years to recover from being an alcoholic. Furthermore, and believe it or not, the woman you caught me in bed with meant absolutely nothing to me. She was just a one-night stand. A friend of mine set the date up. I'm sure you thought I was banging some slut or worse yet a whore, but that really wasn't the case at all. The woman in question was a very nice person, and also a very good friend of mine as well, however if it makes you feel any better, after that night, I never saw her again. In fact, if I remember correctly, in the days following that unfortunate incident, I tried to make it up to you however you wouldn't let me. At any rate, now years later, I would like you to know, I take full responsibility for what happened. I made a mistake! I should've just simply declined what my friend had lined up for me because I already had a girlfriend. That being you, Maude. Granted, in most people's eyes, what I did was not only uncalled for, but it was also an inexcusable act of childlessness as well. I do not dispute that. Not then or now! I just ask your forgiveness, that's all." At this point, he took a slow deep breath and continued on, "If it means anything to you, I've regretted that night every day of my life since. Now, before we go on with this conversation any further, there's one other thing you should know. It comes with great regret to have to say this, but I also think it's worth mentioning. The person who set the whole thing up that night had a crush on you, Maude. In fact, quite frankly, if I don't miss my guess, he wanted to break us up because he wanted you as his girlfriend as much as I did. Anyway, the way things turned out, he never had a chance to pursue you after we broke up because you moved out of the area." Then, he took another deep breath and tried to gather his thoughts again while she looked on in silence. Finally, he stated, "I have to admit, at the time, it probably looked like I was trying to romance any woman I could get into bed however that really wasn't the case at all. I really did like you. In fact, I still do for that matter. Anyway, I rest my case. I sincerely apologize for that unfortunate incident. Now, if you can find a place in your heart to forgive me, perhaps, you and I can go forward and build a long-lasting relationship together in the days ahead. In fact, I am sure we can do that if you still want too." Needless to say, she was flabbergasted! In all the years she knew him, never had she gotten that much information out of him. It was actually unbelievable! Even when they were dating each other a few years ago, he rarely said anything. Now, for some unexplained reason, she couldn't turn him off. Actually, Maude realized he was trying to explain his side of the story of what happened back in the day they were the best of friends so his way of being communicative was viewed as a good thing.

Furthermore, over the course of the past five or six years, Ken had learned the art of communication and that was obviously a good omen too. Anyway, there was total silence between the two of them for a moment or two as Maude thought about what Ken said. Then, just as she was about to answer him, he added, "There really isn't all that much more I can say about what happened between us in days past. As a matter of fact, like you may've already surmised, if possible, I would like to move forward from here. I think I have covered all the bases and now, I would like to hear from you." At this point, not only was Maude totally dumbfounded by what he said but she was also speechless as well. Ken actually admitted to making a mistake and you might say, Maude didn't think he was capable of doing that. Not in a million years did she ever expect to get that kind of response from him. Anyway, she was now carefully mulling over what he just finished telling her. "Well, what did you have in mind, Ken," she asked? "I assume, your desire to see me again isn't just one of your social calls and that you are actually serious about having a relationship with someone. Needless to say, the last time we were seeing each other you seemed to have just about everything on your mind except me. Of course, that could have been a bad perception on my part however at the time, that is definitely the way I saw it. Now, without rambling on any more than I have too about that, I would really like to hear what your intentions are now." Fortunately for her, he got the gist of what she was trying to tell him and a second or two later, he replied back to her saying, "Once again, believe it or not, I made a mistake and the falling out we had was all one big misunderstanding, Maude. I never meant to hurt you. In addition to that, if there was some way to make it up to you, I would do so in a minute and that's about all there is to it. Now, as for having a serious relationship with you, perhaps, even getting married, I would like too however you're going to have to forgive me for any past injustices before a relationship between us is going anywhere. Actually, everything will more than likely take care of itself if you're willing to do that. Take a chance on me, Maude. I will not let you down! I promise! Just let me back into your life and things will be good again. Obviously, I don't have a magic wand to make things perfectly right between us however I'm still confident we can patch things up and move forward together. In fact, quite frankly, if marriage is what you're seeking, there's a good possibility I can make that happen for you. It's not too late to do that! We are still young and there's plenty of time to enjoy life together. I give you my word, I'll be faithful to you and there won't be any other women. Trust me, Maude. It will be different this time." "Well," she replied, "you sound very sincere, Ken and I certainly would not fault you for those kind of intentions. Furthermore, I believe what you told me over the past few minutes however there's a couple of things involved here so even though the decision sounds like an easy one, there's a lot more to it than that. First of all, if I can find the right person, it is my intentions to get married again. Rest assured on that. Believe it or not, I miss having the presence of a man around if you see what I'm driving at. In this particular instance, there is another factor involved. I have children, Ken. In fact, to be more precise, I have two girls and a boy. Actually, my oldest one just started school, so I have some very challenging days ahead of me. Since their biological father isn't going to be around for them, I have to admit, it would be nice, if they had someone to look up to you like yourself, Ken. Anyway, as far as my marriage goes, I made a mistake. There certainly wasn't any question about that. Actually, I woke up one day and realized who I thought was the most perfect guy in the world, no longer cared for me. At first, I was extremely hesitant to look at things that way however a short time later, I discovered he was seeing another woman. Needless to say, that changed everything. That obviously meant, he didn't love me anymore so I thought it would be best to go separate ways. Actually, he was the one who filed for divorce, but I would have taken the initiative to do that myself had he not done so. I'm not a hundred percent sure what happened however I will say, the failure of our marriage wasn't my fault. Anyway, for the record, the whole, unfortunate thing came to light when I made the fateful decision to look in to what my husband was doing every evening because he sure as hell wasn't spending the time at home with me and the kids. Well, like you might think, Ricky said, he was just hanging out with the guys at one of the local bars however after finding him doused in perfume one evening, I had some very strong doubts about what he was doing, so I thought it would be a good idea to follow him home from work some evening. Anyway, make a long story short, that's what I did however as you may have guessed by now, that is when I made the startling discovery, my dearly beloved husband was screwing another woman. At that point, I was heartbroken beyond words but it was far better to have known what he was doing than to have pretended everything was fine between us. Needless to say, after that unfortunate revelation, I didn't see any sense of staying married to the man. Actually, I would've tried to work things out with him however the passion wasn't there anymore, so I decided against doing that. As a matter of fact, judging by his infatuation with that other woman, there probably wasn't any chance I would have been able to work things out with him anyway and that's really all there is to it. I'm a divorced woman, Ken and that has been the case for some time now. Sadly, the worst part about it all is he doesn't even know he has a son," Maude finished saying as she wiped the tears away from her eyes. At this point, a bit of silence filtered through the air as Ken reflected on what she just said. Not only had she unloaded all her dirty laundry on him but it didn't take a genius to realize she was being honest with him as well. Anyway, as you might suspect, Ken immediately felt sorry for her, however until he knew more about her overall situation, he wasn't sure what the best way to proceed would be. Obviously, a lot of variables in life exist, and when children are involved, it gets even more complicated than that. Anyway, after thinking about it for a minute, he went onto say, "I'm very sorry about what happened between you and your husband, Maude but everything happens for a reason. At least, that's what I've been told anyway. Did you ever stop to think what happened to you may actually turn out to be a blessing in the days ahead? I realize, that's looking at things in the most positive light possible however from what you told me, I would say, you made the right decision. Going separate ways with your husband was unquestionably the right thing to do. Divorce, regardless of how painful it might be, allows a person to have a second chance on life. One way or another, whether it or not it does, life goes on and for someone like yourself to be so young, it would not have been a good idea to have thrown your life away on a bad marriage. It goes without saying, there are all kinds of men out there that would love to have you for their wife so I wouldn't take it upon yourself to dwell on it. You did what you had to do! It's as simple as that. In reality, you cannot change the past anyway, so my advice to you would be to forget what happened and look to the future by redirecting your train of thought on something more up lifting. Furthermore, I'm really sorry you had such a bad experience with your marriage however that has happened many times over the years through the course of time. Neither do I blame you for all the animosity you have towards men. You certainly deserve a hell of lot better treatment than you received, present company included. Anyway, rather than beating a dead horse to death about something that isn't changeable now, let's take a minute to order something to eat. I would like to marry you, Maude however that's something you don't want to rush into. Take some time to think about it. That's a very big decision for anyone to make and I sure as hell wouldn't want you to be unhappy. You're too fine a person for that to happen. In fact, quite frankly, if I am not the right person for you, I can always try and find you someone. I know a lot of people in the area so that may be possible. Now, for the other reason we're here, from what I've heard, this restaurant serves very good food so let's enjoy ourselves and have a nice evening. As for seeing me again, well, that is up to you however you could start by giving me an opportunity to meet your children. Perhaps, tomorrow might be a good time to do that. I have the day off so I will be free to do that. Of course, I don't mean to rush you on this matter, but I would really like to meet them, Maude." At this point, she gave Ken one of her most pleasant smiles and replied, "I am sure they're anxious to meet you as well, Ken. I've already told them you're a good friend of mine so it should be a fairly easy thing to do. Now, as you suggested a moment ago, lets indulge ourselves on some of their fine cuisine before the entire evening is gone." At this juncture, he nodded his head to her in total agreement with what she said so after the waitress brought their meals to the table, they enjoyed a fine meal together. In fact, by the time the evening was all said and done, Maude had to admit, the evening went a lot better than she thought it would. She also realized, there was a very good chance they would be able to rekindle their friendship and it goes without saying, she didn't think that would ever happen.

CHAPTER 34

Ken usually worked Saturday's. Actually, it was voluntary on his part however it was the only way he could get caught up on some of the paperwork that had a tendency to pile up during the course of the week. He was the chief executive officer of a leading manufacturer of women's clothing and in many instances, the job was quite demanding. Anyway, like you might expect, if he didn't put the extra time in at the office, some things wouldn't get done so in order to maintain his high paying job, he put in a lot more hours than he would have preferred too. Furthermore, it was the only way Ken could meet the company's deadlines they mandated of him so if he wanted to get paid, this was the way he had to do things. Anyway, be so as it may, this Saturday Ken had decided to take the entire weekend off. Of course, when he got back to the office on Monday, he would be inundated with more paperwork than he cared to think about however the weekend was too important for him to do it any other way. In this particular case, he planned on spending the weekend with Maude and her family. Actually, it would be the best way to liven up his personal life a little, which had been suffering a bit of late so this is what he was going to do. Besides, the paperwork he normally did Saturday mornings could always be done Monday night and that was good enough for him. Right at the moment, he wanted to get back into Maude's life in the worst way so that really narrowed down his options. More importantly, the company did not care what he did just as long as the work got done. Anyway, with that in mind, Ken was going to make the most of this weekend away from the office and for more than one reason, it was probably a good thing he did. Actually, most things in life can wait for another day however his personal life was in need of repair so rather than putting it off any longer, he had decided to begin working on that next. In this particular case, that meant he was going to see an old friend.

Anyway, as it turns out, after a quick call to make sure Maude was at home, Ken headed over to her house. It was a short drive from where he was living, probably, no more than fifteen minutes so it was going to be an easy thing for him to do. As for Maude, she just happened to be watching a little television in her living-room when he arrived at her estate. At any rate, like you might think, upon noticing, Ken's car had pulled up in front of her house, she jumped off the sofa and went to answer the door. In fact, due to her quick action, long before he had a chance to ring the doorbell, she had ushered him into the house. Well, so far so good, Maude thought to herself. Admittedly, if a relationship with Ken was to be attained, this would probably be the best way to achieve that. Needless to say, she was actually quite elated, he wasn't wasting any time pursuing her because the longer it took him to follow up with his intentions to be a part of her life again, it more than likely meant, Ken wasn't interested in getting married and that's not at all what she had in mind. Anyway, since, he was immediately taking the initiative to come see her, that meant, he may be serious about marrying her after all. That was good news. Actually, what concerned her the most was whether or not, he had grown up enough to take on a little responsibility because in years past, that was something he wasn't unaccustomed to doing. Hopefully, that aspect of Ken's life was behind him now because if it was, Maude was going to pursue another relationship with him. In fact, to be more precise, she was going to try and get him to marry her. At least, for the time being, that's what the plan was anyway. Perhaps, that initiative would change at some point in the days ahead however right at the moment, she wanted to get him to redirect his attention to her family. Needless to say, that was her goal and objective. If she was able to do that, it stands to reason, she would more than likely be able to reel him in hook, line, and sinker. I realize that's probably a very tacky way to put it however that is what Maude intended to do. In this particular instance, thanks to her next-door neighbor, that had already happened. Now, it was time to work on him a little and the way everything was unfolding, that was something she did not have to put off any longer because he was already in the process of paying her a visit. From her perspective, everything was headed in the right direction. Anyway, as you may've already guessed, this was what Maude was thinking about when she went to answer the door that day. Anyway, now more excited than ever to rekindle their friendship, she did not waste a minute in inviting Ken into the house. In fact, long before either one of them realized it, the winds of a matrimonial destiny had them sitting down inside her living-room and well versed into a prolonged conversation. "Well," she stated, "It's nice to see you again, Ken. I was hoping you didn't make a stranger of yourself. I mean that sincerely. We still have a lot of things to talk about however I'm not on a schedule of any kind so time is obviously something I have a lot of." "I understand what you're saying," Ken replied. "Unfortunately, due to job obligations, I don't have as much time on my hands as you do however other than that aspect, our feelings are mutual. Anyway, it's a real pleasure to be here. I mean that sincerely. I apologize for not being here sooner but I wasn't able to get out of bed until ten o'clock this morning so you might say, I am running a little behind schedule. Usually, I work Saturday mornings but not this weekend. I'm taking this one off. The fact of the matter is I have been working a lot of overtime lately so I felt like sleeping late this morning. In this case, all that really amounted to was a little extra rest. At any rate, that's why I stayed in bed until ten o'clock. Believe it or not, for all of the overtime I work, I don't receive any additional compensation. No bonuses, no salary adjustments, no overtime pay, no incentives, no anything. I work my ass off for them every day and they don't even give a shit. Actually, to some degree, I would not expect anything from them however you would think they'd be a little more accommodating. Well, they aren't. Obviously, I'm just another number in their computer system that's all. Perhaps, that's an awful thing to say about your employer however it's the god's honest truth. If I were to walk out the door tomorrow, they would find someone to replace me, and it would not take them very long to do so either. I'm absolutely certain of that. Anyway, I truly apologize for getting carried away with the short comings of my job however as you can see, it bothers me. They pay me well, but I have to put in more time than I would prefer in order to make the kind of money I do. I still hope to be able to walk out the door someday however I do not see that happening anytime in the near future. Of course, if and when that does happen, it would mean, I found another job. Anyway, I believe I've said enough about that. Most people have problems and job obligations and so do I. In fact, I would be one of the first ones to admit it. Anyway, with that said, perhaps, it would be a good idea to move onto bigger and better things, like yourself, Maude. Furthermore, I hope we can have a good, meaningful relationship together with a long-range goal for getting married but that will be entirely up to you." At this point, Maude replied, "No it's not too late to do that Ken however right at the moment, I would like to show you around the house and have you meet my family. In fact, quite frankly, if I don't miss my guess, they're anxious to meet you, Ken." Then, before he had a chance to say another word, she had the maid bring her girls into the living-room so they would be able to see their mother's old friend. Actually, the only one that wasn't present was little Ricky, however he was in his bedroom sleeping so Maude told Ken, she would look in on him a little later. Needless to say, she did not have any intention of waking him up if it wasn't necessary and Ken totally agreed with her. Anyway, as fate would have it, they spent the rest of the morning and the better part of the afternoon getting reacquainted with one another again. By and by, it was time for lunch and like you might expect, her maid served them with an appetizing meal of spaghetti and meatballs. It was a simple dish however like always, the food she prepared was absolutely delicious. Furthermore, that gave them more time to talk about their current state of affairs, which was actually what Maude was hoping to do anyway. When they were dating, a few years ago, there wasn't enough communication going on between them. In fact, that's one of the reasons why their relationship didn't work out for them last time. Needless to say, that meant they had to learn how to communicate better and so far, it looked very promising. Now, if things continued to go well, it looked like getting married might be possible. Anyway, as expected, the two of them touched down upon just about everything they could think of for the next hour or so. It was at this point that Maude told him about the estate she owned in Oregon. As I said before, they had a lot of things to talk about and this particular subject was a very good example of that. Anyway, like you might think, one thing led to another and before either one of them realized it, they had made plans to spend the following weekend up there. In this particular instance, it was going to be a good opportunity to work on the intimate side of a relationship again and you might say, that was something they hadn't done for a while. Actually, she was fairly certain Ken would like the place, however she was more concerned about something else and that was, his maturity. Hopefully, he was ready to settle down however she still had her doubts about that. One way or another, spending some time alone together the following weekend would more than likely bring that to light. At the very least, she would be getting away for the weekend so in all likelihood, it would be a good thing to do. Besides, she hadn't seen the place in a while, so it was time to take a look at the place to see if everything was in order there. For a couple of very obvious reasons, she hadn't been in a hurry to go back there however with Ken back in her life now, a lot of things were changing rather quickly. Anyway, after lunch that day, they took Margaret and Vanessa out to see a Saturday afternoon matinee at a local movie theater while her maid tended to little Ricky. Like you might expect, the movie was an animated Walt Disney film and the kids loved it. As a matter of fact, both of the girls sat on the edge of their seat throughout the entire movie. Neither one of them said a word. They just sat there, totally engrossed in the movie however that did not come as any big surprise to Maude. More often than not, they were easily amused, and such was the case that day as well. Actually, at one point, due to the fact, they were so quiet, Maude gave thought to the notion, something might be wrong. Generally speaking, when they were at home, a fight of some sort usually broke out between them somewhere along the way during the course of the day however she did not have to break them up today. For some unexplained reason, they were behaving like a couple of angels. In fact, she could not have asked for a more perfect child on either one of their accounts. In hindsight, that was because of Ken's presence. Obviously, in not knowing what to expect from someone who might potentially turn out to be their father, they wanted to be on their best behavior.

Anyway, the day flew by quicker than either one of them expected it to and everyone had a good time. Since plans were made to spend the following weekend in Oregon, Maude couldn't have been any happier than she was that Ken had agreed to travel up there with her. First of all, it was a great opportunity to get intimately reacquainted with Ken. Secondly, Maude hadn't been anywhere since she came back to the United States so it was going to seem like a vacation to her. Chances are, Ken was going to feel the same way about that as she did, because his job was very demanding, and he hadn't taken any time off recently. Of course, until now, he really hadn't had any reason for wanting to do that however with Maude back in his life, everything was changing for him rather quickly as well. As for Maude, she wasn't sure, if she would be able to handle the emotional ties that were attached to the property in the state of Oregon. Needless to say, some of the fondest memories of her life were spent there. Even though it had been only for a short time, a lot of personal feelings were associated with the place. Neither was there any sense of denying that and she would have been the first one to admit it if she had been asked. Anyway, everything else appeared to be headed in the right direction at this point in time so she wasn't supporting any complaints whatsoever. In fact, for the first time in a very long time, she was looking at things in a positive light again. For a while after she had the falling out with Ricky, that wasn't the case at all. Anyway, now that things were beginning to look up again, hopefully, things would continue to go well for her in the days ahead. At least, that's how she was looking at it anyway. As I said before, the only thing she wasn't sure of was how her emotional state of mind would be once she saw Ricky's old estate. Granted, Maude owned it now however a lot of heart felt memories were left behind there. That meant, she might have to sell the estate at some point along the way. One way or another, she was determined to go back there. It was the only way

Maude would be able to find out, just exactly what her personal feelings were in regards to the place, now that she and Ricky had gone separate ways. Anyway, she would have her answer shortly because that's where they were going next weekend. Actually, under the circumstances, I am sure most people would probably sell the estate however time would tell, whether or not she did that. In the meantime, it was her intention to enjoy the property for as long as possible. In fact, she had a feeling Ken was going to like it really well so there wasn't any sense of jumping to conclusions at this point. Who knows, perhaps, he would even fall in love with the place and Maude would end up retaining the property after all. In truth, all Ricky's old estate was originally going to be used for anyway was a summer home so perhaps, that was still possible.

As for how the rest of their current weekend went, most of it was spent, filling each other in on how everything was going since they last saw each other. Of course, as you might expect, that took in a lot of territory however Maude wasn't in any hurry to reestablish their relationship anyway so that really wasn't a bad thing. That's not to say she wasn't looking forward to getting married again, however she wanted to make sure Ken was ready to settle down before making a commitment to do that. Needless to say, because she had kids it was very important that was the case. In fact, quite frankly, Maude wouldn't settle for anything less than that. Anyway, like you might think, she told him all about her previous husband and how they came to meet. Then, she even took the time to relate their highly unfortunate camping and fishing adventure to him, when bad luck bit them in the ass and they ended up being stranded on an island, somewhere out in the middle of the Pacific Ocean for a week. Believe it or not, Ken thought that story was an amusing tale however as I said before, it was actually a frigging nightmare for her and Ricky. In fact, she said if her memory served her correctly, neither one of them thought, they would ever get off the island. Actually, it was thanks to a fishing vessel that they eventually were rescued. Ken said it was a miracle they ever made it off the island and of course, he was right about that however that wasn't anything she didn't already know. In other matters, Maude told him how she came to buy her own estate up in the state of Oregon and also about the unbelievable stash of coins she found beneath the house as well. Furthermore, not only did Maude make him aware of that but she also informed him that when she moved to France, she sold that property. After that, there wasn't too much more to say about her summarized life story over the past six years however she did briefly touch down upon her time in Nice, France. Maude said it was a beautiful place but her heart still belonged to her home in Beverly Hills. As for Ken, he took the time to elaborate to Maude about a couple of relationships he had, and then he reluctantly went onto tell her about his dependence to alcohol which lasted for the better part of five years. Needless to say, they both aired out a lot of dirty laundry over the course of the afternoon and through the week ahead. In fact, they both agreed, it was a good idea to do that. Logically, by telling each other the details of their personal life, it stands to reason, that would more than likely pave the way for a good marriage in the days ahead if they decided to pursue that course of action and of course, that is what they had in mind. Now, it would be just a matter of finding out what fate and destiny had in store for them. At this point, it looked like they were headed in the right direction with only the best possible intentions for getting married and living happily ever after. Of course, things of that nature can change on a moment's notice however for the time being, the state of affairs between them certainly appeared to be fine. For her sake, hopefully, everything would turn out well for her this time. Needless to say, she had already made at least one very big mistake when she married her first husband. Of course, the odds of making the same mistake twice wasn't very likely but everything considered, Maude thought it was best to take a chance on Ken even if it meant throwing caution to the wind again. Certainly, marriage doesn't come without any risks or problems but if the bottom fell out of another marriage, she would be devastated right to the point of absolute hysteria and it can be noted, under those circumstances, hard telling what she would do. Maude had been through a lot in recent years and the rigors of that stress had taken a very unfavorable toll on her so there was a possibility something terrible might happen in the days ahead.

CHAPTER 35

As it turns out, Ken got out of work early and that gave Maude all the time she needed to charter a plane via a private carrier to the city of Portland. It was always nice not having to rush about doing anything so Maude was thankful she was able to do things that way. Actually, it was a quick flight, however like it so commonly does in that part of the state, they were greeted by a hard pouring rain. Of course, that didn't come as any big surprise because it just so happens that is what it was doing the first time she traveled to the state of Oregon. In fact, it was raining hard then and that is was raining harder than ever now. Anyway, it didn't take her very long to realize that was a common occurrence in Portland and being used to that sort of thing, the weather didn't dampen her spirits at all. Actually, in all due honesty, if Maude understood things correctly, the National Weather Service was calling for intermittent showers the entire weekend, so rain was to be expected. In this particular case, the rain was coming down very hard when they stepped off the plane however the chances of it lightning up at some point along the way was very good so it wasn't given too much thought. In fact, regardless of the undesirable situation, Maude had every intention of making the most of the weekend because there was too much was at stake for her to look at it any other way.

At any rate, they didn't have any problem renting a car so once their luggage was loaded into the car, they took off for Tierra Del Mar. Furthermore, at Maude's suggestion, they took the scenic drive. It was something she wanted Ken to see. Needless to say, the coast of Oregon was a magnificent sight to behold so she didn't want Ken to miss that aspect of the area. Anyway, for that reason, it was decided, they would take the route that allowed them to drive along the coast. In reality, it was supposed to be a weekend for rest and relaxation so there wasn't any hurry to get to Ricky's old estate in Tierra Del Mar. For that reason, they didn't hurry about getting there so it wasn't until around 8:00 o'clock before they pulled into the driveway of their desired destination. Furthermore, since, it had been a few years since she had seen the place, she wasn't sure what to expect so she got out of the rented car and began to look around the property to see if everything was in order. Much to her surprise, the overall condition of the property was still in good shape. In fact, other than having paid the taxes on the property, Maude hadn't done a thing to the estate and to the best of her knowledge no one had been living there either. At any rate, from what she could see, it was in the same condition it was when she left there, some years ago. Actually, she told Ken, it didn't seem possible so much time had gone by however that is pretty typical of life. Very often, a person will look one way, then the other, blink a couple of times and years of time has gone by. Anyway, at this point, that's when she began thinking about what six years can do to a person. Obviously, a world of things had happened to her. First of all, she had children now. Secondly, her first marriage was a man-made disaster in every sense of the word and Maude was living in the United States again. What else could go wrong? In addition to that, she was all the wiser for having gone through all that however that didn't rule out the possibility of making more mistakes along the way. Of course, she realized in being human, each and every day brings new challenges and there isn't anyway a person can change that. Furthermore, it would be safe to say, only time itself can heal physical and emotional wounds. As for how she was doing with that, in her opinion, she had handled everything really well. In fact, so well, it's the reason why she was dating another man now. Anyway, like you might expect, after assessing the overall condition of the house and surrounding property, she quickly concluded, the estate would be marketable in its present condition if she chose to sell it. Like I said before, she wasn't entirely sure about that yet although it was definitely one of the reasons why she was there. Needless to say, she wanted to see if she would be able to let go of the emotional ties that were attached to the place. Of course, her other reason for wanting to be there had everything to do with the fact, she wanted to find out if they were compatible for marriage however with all due honesty, she still had her doubts about that. The last time Maude tried to do this with Ken, he was not ready for a relationship at all and that included marriage. Anyway, with much of these, often tiresome thoughts racing through the innermost caverns of her mind, they eventually got around to walking up to the front door of the house and went inside. Thankfully, they stopped by a store on the way there and that gave them a few basic food necessities for the weekend. Earlier in the week, she had the power turned back on so they would have electricity to run whatever they needed over the course of the weekend so there shouldn't be any problems with that either. Anyway, as you might think, by this time, Ken was duly expressing his thoughts about the place by telling her the property was located in a very picturesque area however he could also see out of the corner of his eye, something was troubling her. At this point, Ken wasn't sure what that was however for the time being, he opted not to say anything. In fact, he was fairly certain, the bewildered look Maude had in her eyes was directly related to memories of her first husband. A person wouldn't be human if that were not the case. Anyway, shortly after showing him around the interior of the house, they eventually made their way into the kitchen and had something to eat before sitting down in the living-room to relax for a while. Needless to say, that gave them another opportunity to get to know one another a little better and like I said before, that was one of the reasons why she opted to make the trip to Tierra Del Mar that weekend. First of all, she wanted to know if he had any interest in the property. If that turned out to be the case, then, she would have another thing to take into consideration. The truth of the matter is Maude wasn't sure if she would be able to live there if it came right down to it so that might pose a problem for her in the days ahead. Anyway, like usual, time went by very quickly that evening however not before they had an opportunity to discuss several other matters of importance. Finally, along towards the hour of 11:00 o'clock, she suggested they head upstairs and go to bed. Like you might think, Ken immediately agreed, it was a good time to call it a day so with that in mind, they proceeded upstairs to the guest bedroom. At this point, she came to the conclusion, this is where they would sleep. Unfortunately, the master bedroom held memories of years past so for obvious reason, she didn't want to sleep there. Actually, Ken very quickly made the assumption that was the case and nothing more was said about that for the time being. He'd just go along with the situation as it stood and leave it up to her to bring up the matter of her first husband when she was ready to do so. In the meantime, Ken wanted to enjoy every moment of the occasion and after a little love making, he drifted off to sleep however she was not able to do that. Like you might think, she could not get Ricky out of her mind. In fact, shortly after he fell asleep, Maude quietly got out of bed and sauntered off down the hall to Ricky's old bedroom. It was where the two of them became the best of friends years ago and now, those memories began to flood her mind. At this point, Maude realized, she had made a mistake by not selling the place and she began crying at the very thought of the first night they spent together there. It wasn't that she made a mistake in giving Ricky a divorce however it had everything to do with the fact, this was where she fell in love with a man that in her opinion, befriended her. Actually, that may not even be the correct way of putting it however it wouldn't have changed the end result of what she now felt. Unfortunately, her mind was thoroughly submerged into the past and that very thought continued to overwhelm her as she sat down in one of the chairs inside of what was once Ricky's old bedroom. Needless to say, this particular evening brought one of the most memorable nights of her life to mind, which isn't necessarily a bad thing however for Maude that wasn't the case at all. It was due to the kind of person she was although much of what she was feeling had more to do with the fact, the man she fell in love with in Tierra Del Mar was no longer around. Generally speaking, she was a very sentimental person so it was difficult for Maude to let go of things that most people wouldn't have given a second thought too. In fact, at that very moment, Maude was trying harder than ever to get a grip on her emotions as the memory of her time spent with Ricky continued to flood her mind. Needless to say, the love she gave him was still anchored deep into her heart and now that she had gone back to the place where it all began, it was literally haunting the hell out of her. Anyway, much to her disappointment, Maude was not able to get the memory of Ricky Vestellini out of her mind. First of all, that meant, it was a mistake to go back to Tierra Del Mar however Maude wanted to be absolutely certain, she didn't have any remorseful feelings toward Ricky or to what he did to her. Sadly, as time continued to creep by that night, she began having second thoughts about Ricky. Perhaps, Maude had been a bit too hasty with her decision to divorce him when they might have been able to work things out with time. Furthermore, that pointed to only one thing and that was, she had made a mistake by walking away from someone she loved dearly at one time. Anyway, regardless of what may or may not have been, after a few minutes went by, she walked over to the terrace doors and gently pulled them open. In a matter of seconds, a very invigorating breath of fresh autumn air whisked through the room, leaving her with an almost whimsical feeling inside. Needless to say, at this point, not only was she feeling a bit melancholy, but she also quickly found herself reflecting on how her marriage to Ricky went. Then, ever so slowly, a little more time went by as she continued to stare off into the darkness of the night. In fact, it was now encompassing her every thought as she walked out onto the terrace to get some fresh air. Thankfully, it stopped raining over the course of the past hour so she had a good opportunity to see the moon as well as the stars, I might add. It was then, a little off in the distance, she could visibly see the lighthouse and without a warning of any kind, the memory of marrying Ricky up inside the turret of that building came to mind. Once again, she found herself totally overwhelmed with emotion as tears began to fill her eyes. If only Ricky could have been a little more faithful to her, things would've been different, she was quick to point out to herself. It was definitely the cause of their failed marriage. In fact, as much as she hated to admit it, that very thought was bothering her badly now as Maude began questioning her decision to grant him a divorce. Perhaps, for her children's sake, it would've been better for them to have tried to work things out over the course of time however Maude didn't think of that when the bottom fell out of everything. Anyway, she was now at odds with herself over that, in addition to not being sure of what would be the best thing to do with his old estate. If she didn't sell it, something told her, it would turn out to be a thorn in her side and that was obviously something she didn't want to deal with. At this point, there wasn't any doubt left in her mind. She would have to sell the property. It was as simple as that. In fact, quite frankly, there were too many adoring memories left behind where she now was for her to hang onto the property. She was certain of that now! Originally, it was her intentions to use the estate in Oregon as a summer home but she could see her innermost feelings didn't want her to do that. Actually, like you might think, right at the moment, there was one other thing that was eating away at the back of her mind and that was whether or not she was making the right decision about Ken. Granted, he was a nice man however he was not anywhere near as passionate as Ricky was. Worse yet, he cheated on her before so it wouldn't come as any big surprise if he did that to her again. They say, lightning doesn't strike in the same place twice however that does not necessarily mean it won't happen again. In reality, that was something she may have to deal with at some point in her life if she were to marry him. For that reason and not at all unexpected, more uncertainty began to flood her mind. She wanted to believe that wouldn't ever happen to her again however what if it did. Would she be able to handle marriage infidelity again? At this point, she shuddered at the very thought of what could happen. Furthermore, she had children to think about so it might be a good idea to look around for someone else. Granted, she hadn't done that yet, however when the man she used to think the world of suddenly comes back into her life, what else could she do? Obviously, Maude could've flat out refused to see him however she wanted to give him one more chance. Actually, with all due honesty, she liked Ken. It was just a question of something else, that's all. In fact, that's the reason why she was with him now. Needless to say, she was still undecided as to what the best thing to do would be. If he had grown up some, since the last time she saw him, everything would be fine. That, she was certain of! Anyway, at this point, another warm autumn breeze gently whisked through her hair, alerting her to the fact, it was time to go back inside the house. At two or three o'clock in the morning, it was obviously late in the night, however the troublesome frame of mind that kept her awake had also decided something for her. She was going to sell Ricky's old estate in Oregon and in regards to Ken, she would give him another chance. With that in mind, she turned around and went back inside, only to find Ken standing in the doorway that led into the room. "I didn't mean to startle you," he stated, "but I noticed you weren't in bed, so I began to wonder where you were. What's going on, girl? Do you realize, it's 2:30 in the morning? Obviously, something is bothering you unless you're just out for a breath of fresh air which I doubt very much is the case." At this point, Maude nodded to him in acknowledgment of what he said and replied, "I was thinking about my first marriage and some of the memories that were left behind here. In fact, I now realize, more than ever, I'm going to have to sell the estate regardless of whether or not this place is something you might be interested in. I'm really sorry to have to put it to you that way without any kind of explanation however as much as I hate to say it, Ricky's old estate is haunting the hell out of me. As you can clearly see, I wasn't able to sleep at all tonight, so I wanted to be alone to think about some things. Unfortunately, a very special part of my life is buried deep within the walls of this house so you should know, it's difficult for me to come back here and expect everything to be the same as it was before. Originally, the idea of maintaining the estate for a summer home sounded like a really great idea however I can now see that isn't going to be possible. Too many pleasant memories from days past are badgering my mind every time I re-live something I once did here. I hope you understand what I'm trying to tell you, Ken." At this point, he walked over to where she stood and wrapped his arms around her warm sensuous body in an effort to console her from the troublesome thoughts that were overwhelming her mind. Maude was apparently hurting very badly inside however he didn't immediately know what to say. In fact, quite frankly, he was at a loss for words. Not only could he see, the memory of her first husband was bothering her but he could also see something else was bothering her as well. Finally, Ken replied back to her saying, "Hey, whatever's going on inside that head of yours can wait. It's the middle of the night! Why don't you come back to bed, Maude? I can see you're tired. Thinking about problems regardless of whether or not they're solvable is a very stressful thing to take on at this hour of the night, and if it just happens to be something you can't change, you aren't doing yourself a favor by thinking about it. You do realize that don't you?" At this point, she very slowly nodded her head to him in agreement because he was right about that. There wasn't any sense of hashing this out inside her head at this time of the night. It wouldn't change anything. Needless to say, Maude would have to come to terms with things another time. Right at the moment, she couldn't absorb any more anything. There was silence in the room for a moment as she tried to digest what he told her. Finally, he said, "Hey, I have an idea. Let me give you one of my tranquilizers. My doctor prescribes them to me for my insomnia. In fact, if I don't miss my guess, it will more than likely help you get a good night's sleep. Now, will you consider taking one?" "Well," Maude replied, "seeing that you put it that way, I suppose it won't do any harm to try one." At this juncture, he walked over to the nightstand next to the bed and retrieved the container of sleep medication out of one of its drawers. "Here," he said, "Take one of these and we'll discuss what's bothering you in the morning." "Okay," she replied. "I guess it's worth a try." With that said, she proceeded to do as he suggested and about twenty minutes later, she was sleeping soundly. In the meantime, a very puzzled and bewildered Ken Stackford began thinking about things as well. He was certain Maude wasn't telling him everything however if he was patient, perhaps, everything would come out in the wash in the days ahead. For the time being, Ken was content to just wait and see what happens. With that said, a few minutes later, he fell back to sleep. It would be daylight soon and there were a lot of other things that had to be discussed however the circumstances of their newly rekindled friendship had to be dealt with another time. Right at the moment, in the waning hours of the night, some rest was in order. Tomorrow was another day and with any luck at all, maybe it would turn out to be a good one. In the meantime, they both slept as soundly as anyone could while the thought of what the next day might bring gave light to the possibility better days were coming. Not only for him but for her as well.

CHAPTER 36

By the time Maude awoke from her night's sleep the following morning, there wasn't any question in her mind, as to what she was going to do with Ricky's old estate. As a matter of fact, it was going up for sale, just as soon as she could get it listed with the real estate agency in Tierra Del Mar. Needless to say, after giving it a lot of careful thought last evening, Maude realized she wouldn't be able to keep the property. There were too many haunting memories left behind there to really consider doing anything else. In fact, quite frankly, the matter was apparently a thorn in her side and it had to be removed from not only her sight but from her mind as well. That meant, regardless of the consequences, the estate in Oregon had to go. Maude was absolutely certain of that now. Anyway, with that thought plaguing the hell out of the back of her mind, a few minutes later, she headed into the bathroom to freshen up a bit. Actually, all that really meant was Maude was going to take a shower, get dressed and after a bite to eat, she would venture off into town to take care of the business of selling the property. It was her usual early morning routine and right at the moment, with circumstances as they were, she wanted to get busy with her state of affairs. Anyway, once her personal hygiene was taken care of, on her way downstairs to the kitchen, she stopped by the room Ken was sleeping for a minute to ascertain whether or not he had gotten out of bed yet. After a quick observation, nothing of the sort had happened which meant either sleep came naturally to him, or he took some of the same sleep medication she did last night. One way or another, regardless of the reason why Ken was still asleep, Maude began making plans for the entire weekend, long before he got up that day. Of course, as a matter of priority, the property in Oregon was going to be put up for sale first, and then, with any kind of luck at all, Maude would have the rest of the day to spend with Ken. At least, that was the plan anyway. Anyway, her very meticulous mind soon went to work on coming up with an idea for something they could do later in the day. Perhaps, they would take a short drive down the coast and have a picnic at one of the rest areas along side of the road. That sounded like a fun thing to do, and it would be a great way to enjoy the fine day it was outside as well. In fact, if she got busy, they would more than likely have the entire afternoon to do that. At this point, she was already considering it a plan, however she would ask Ken, if that was something he might be interested in doing when he got up. As for the rain they were experiencing the day before, it was nowhere to be seen. Obviously, it was just a few passing rain showers because the National Weather Service was calling for a nice weekend. Actually, that's all she could really hope for and with any kind of luck at all, perhaps, that is how everything would turn out. Anyway, she continued to mull these things over inside her head until she heard the distinct sound of a toilet being flushed upstairs. That meant Ken was getting out of bed. That's good, she thought to herself. Now, she would be able to get things moving along. In her opinion, it would not be a good idea to take off out the door without letting Ken know where she was going so that would no longer be an issue. She would finish having breakfast, then, just as soon as Ken came downstairs, she would go to the real estate agency in Tierra Del Mar to take care of some business that needed tending too. Before venturing off on that errand though, it was her intentions to discuss their options for things to do while they were in Tierra Del Mar over the weekend. Anyway, regardless of what was eventually decided upon while he was upstairs taking a shower, she made some coffee and polished off two or three donuts. Once her hunger had been satisfied, rather than wait for Ken to amble on downstairs, she changed her mind and ran upstairs to inform Ken what her plans were. Like you might expect, the moment Maude told him she was going into town to put her property up for sale, Ken couldn't have agreed with her more that was unquestionably the right thing to do. Needless to say, he said if something like that was going to bother her that much, then it was obviously in her own best interest to sell the place. Anyway, it didn't take her very long to make him aware of what she was going to do. From there, she made a quick statement, something to the effect, "I made a fresh pot of coffee, Ken. All you have to do is pour it and indulge yourself in some of the donuts we picked up at the store yesterday. As you may've already guessed, I just finished having breakfast myself so I'm off to the real estate office now." "Okay, Maude," he replied. "I'll be anxiously awaiting your return. By the way, have you given any thought to what you want to do this weekend?" "I am glad you mentioned that, Ken," she answered. With the real estate business on my mind, I nearly forgot. I was going to ask you if you might be interested in going on a picnic this afternoon however if you have something else in mind, we can forgo that and proceed with some other kind of activity. Actually, whatever you want to do is fine with me." Generally speaking, Ken was an easy person to get along with and it took him all of two seconds to reply back to her that a picnic would be a good thing to do so that was agreed upon. Anyway, with that said, a moment later, she gave him a kiss on the cheek and headed off out the door to take care of business. As for Ken, while Maude was in town, tending to real estate matters, he took a quick shower, got dressed, and headed downstairs to have a bite to eat. In this particular instance, he opted to have bacon and eggs along with some orange juice instead of the coffee and donuts, she had. Actually, that was usually the way Ken started his day on the weekends anyway. Monday through Friday, he would deviate from the usual bacon, eggs, and orange juice for breakfast by opting for a dish of oatmeal or perhaps, one of the other cooked cereals however in most instances, he had bacon and eggs. It was something he liked really well so that's what he usually had. As for a hot cup of coffee, under normal circumstances, he tanked up on that at work. Actually, it was sort of a routine for him but like most of the things he had to deal with in the due course of his employment, a set routine was very beneficial to him and not a hindrance at all. In truth, he was a creature of habit anyway so for him to routine something was just an everyday run of the mill thing for him. It's how he felt most comfortable so that's the way he did things. Whether it was a work issue or a non-work issue, it didn't really matter. He would approach things in that manner. Needless to say, that was just one aspect of his personality but in his opinion, it was the best way to get something done.

Anyway, during breakfast that morning, he began running a few things through his head. First of all, job obligations to the company he worked for was badgering his mind because when he returned to work on Monday, he would have some catching up to do on his most current work project at his place of employment. In fact, he would more than likely have to work late a couple of evenings next week to compensate for that however he wanted to be with Maude this weekend so it was the only viable option available to him. The reality of it all was Ken didn't want to take a chance on having his relationship with Maude fail this time so he planned on spending as much time as he possibly could with her. Obviously, with regards to all matters great and small, it was important they trust each other, in addition to respecting one another's boundaries as well. Ken was at fault for violating the latter when they were dating the last time they were having relations together while Maude had failed to trust his intentions for having more than one woman around. Needless to say, for those reasons, they didn't have the best of relations when this happened some years ago now however Ken was confident that wouldn't be an issue this time. Of course, things like that take in a lot of territory however they both agreed, it would take a good commitment on each one of their parts to maintain a good healthy relationship together. Anyway, like you might think, because their relationship failed the last time they were going together, he was mulling this thought over really well during breakfast that morning. In fact, it was actually something Maude had done a lot of as well however right at the moment, she was taking care of business in town.

As for Ken, no sooner had he finished eating breakfast, when it occurred to him, it might be a good idea to take stock of what they would be able to take with them if they were to go on a picnic that afternoon, which of course was what they planned on doing. With that said, he took a look around the kitchen to see what they had for food and concluded, it wouldn't be necessary to stop in a convenience store to purchase some more food because thanks to a little good planning on Maude's part, they were already stocked up on most of the things they would be needing over the weekend. Anyway, as you might think, Ken was busy trying to have everything ready to go by the time Maude got back from the real estate agency so they would be able to take off for the afternoon. As to where they were going on a picnic, Ken didn't know, however if he didn't miss his guess, she more than likely had a location all picked out. Needless to say, Ken knew her well enough to know that was one of the things she would've taken the initiative to plan out ahead of time. In fact, quite frankly, to be well organized and to plan things out in advance is a good way to be. Obviously, if he were more like that, he wouldn't have to put in so much time at work. Of course, Ken was quick to realize this however like with most things in life, saying one thing and doing another are two different things. Perhaps, with time, he would be able to pick up on some of her organizational skills. In the meantime, there wasn't any sense of thinking about it because he wasn't at work. He would deal with that new way of thinking when he got back to the office on Monday. Right at the moment, he was waiting for Maude to return from her business matters in town. Furthermore, due to the fact, she had been out for a while, it stood to reason, she would be back shortly. In fact, chances are, Maude would be right along, and sure enough, about a half an hour later, his premonition turned out to be correct. She had returned from her trip into town. Anyway, upon arriving home, the first thing she did was take a look around the house to see what Ken had been up to while she was out. Actually, as you might think, Maude didn't have far to go because the moment she stepped into the kitchen, she found Ken putting food inside a cooler. In this particular case, in knowing the circumstances of what she wanted to do that afternoon, what he was doing did not come as any surprise. As a matter of fact, she was pleased he had taken the initiative to get things ready for their picnic. Anyway, with it being late morning and with things apparently in order, she smiled at him and said, "Well, I can see you've been busy getting things together for our picnic. I hope you've come up with a good idea in the way of food, Ken. To be perfectly honest with you, I'm not sure what we had kicking around in the refrigerator that would be good for a picnic, so I will have to trust your judgment on that." "Well," Ken replied, "in not being sure what you wanted to take for food on the picnic, you might say, I was a bit limited on options for putting together a good meal. I hope you like barbecued chicken because we've got plenty of it inside the refrigerator. In addition to that, I threw together a tossed salad. It will go well with the barbecued chicken. If that doesn't too appealing, I'm open to suggestions however if you want something other than that, we'll have to stop into a store on the way down the coast." At this point, Maude replied back to him saying, "The barbecued chicken and salad will be fine, Ken. I'm not all that fussy when it comes down to what I eat for food. More importantly, we'll have the afternoon to do whatever you want to do and if I don't miss my guess, you are going to like the place I've picked out for a picnic." "Actually, it doesn't matter where we go or what we do just as long as I'm with you, Maude," he stated. "I would also like to say, one more time, I'm sorry about some of the mistakes I made in the past, however that's all behind us now. Trust me! Better days are coming!" At this point in their conversation, she replied, "Well, believe it or not, after we broke up a few years ago, I missed you a lot, Ken. Granted, I was extremely upset when I found you in bed with another woman, however the truth of the matter is I thought the world of you." "That's really nice of you to say that, Maude however I take full responsibility for the bad falling out we had the first time we were going together," Ken replied back to her. "You know, it would mean a lot to me to have you as my lawfully wedded wife, Maude. Actually, I would like to try and make things up to you for any past injustices I may have unintentionally inflicted upon you. Furthermore, to set the record straight, I damn near drank myself to death after we broke up last time. Believe it or not, I loved you very much. Anyway, I want you to know, it's not too late for us to build a life together. It's just going to take a little time, that's all." Needless to say, what Ken said made a lot of sense and as you might think, that left her speechless for a moment or two before she was able to reply back to him. Perhaps, Ken was a changed man after all, she thought to herself. At this point, she let out a sigh and replied back to him saying, "No, it's not too late to be the best of friends again, Ken. In fact, quite frankly, I would like that. As for getting married, I think that may be possible. In fact, if it means as much to you as it does to me, then, I want you to be a part of my life for as long as we're alive. They say forever is a long time however if that's what forever really means, then, let's spend the rest of our life together. Think about it, Ken. I'm not in a hurry however I would like to marry you. When the time is right, let me know. Right at the moment, I think it would be a good idea to get busy or neither one of us will be doing a thing this afternoon and that's not all what I had in mind. Actually, just in case you weren't aware of it, a person couldn't ask for a better fall day. The sun is out shining brighter than ever and there isn't a cloud in the sky. In fact, quite frankly, I wish every day of the year could be like this." At this point, without saying another word, Maude got a couple of soft drinks out of the refrigerator and threw them into the cooler and just like that, they were ready to go. Anyway, with that said, Ken grabbed the cooler that was packed with the food they were taking with them on their picnic and brought it out to the rented car they were using, whereby, seconds later, they were on their way to their destination. Actually, the place they were traveling too wasn't really that far away however it was where Ricky took her whenever he got the urge to get romantic. It was a place she would never forget, and chances are it was a place Ken would never forget either. Anyway, after a brief stop along the way to pick up a few additional things for the picnic, they continued on their way. As for the route they were taking, it just happened to be one of the more scenic drives in the area and about twenty-five to thirty minutes later, they were there. As a matter of fact, it took him all of two seconds to realize why she chose to go there. The area was breathtakingly beautiful. Not only was it a very scenic spot overlooking the ocean but it was well secluded on both sides of the road by a lot of deciduous trees too, so it undoubtedly had the makings of a great place to have a picnic. With that said, amid the truly awe-inspiring splendor of a beautiful autumn day, Ken and Maude spent the rest of the afternoon there, relishing in the thought, better days were coming. If not immediately, certainly in the days ahead.

CHAPTER 37

By the time early evening arrived, Maude thought it was best they head back to Ricky's old estate and without any disagreement from Ken, that's what they did. Actually, the afternoon went by quickly however that wasn't an uncommon occurrence because in most instances, time goes by quickly. As expected, things went well and even though they did not have time to enjoy anymore of their outing, they agreed to do it again sometime. In the meantime, with only a little more time to spend in Oregon that weekend, they thought it would be a good idea to move onto some other things. Anyway, with the warmest part of the day behind them, they didn't have any other recourse than to return home. In fact, it was the only practical thing to do. As you might think, they discussed several things over the course of the afternoon, and no sooner did they get back to Ricky's old estate, when Maude suggested they go into the living-room and talk about a matter she had finally come to terms with. Actually, to be more precise, Maude had changed her mind about something. Not in the I don't want to do this sense, but in the let's do this as soon as possible sense. Well, as far as Ken was concerned that was fine with him so he took a seat in the living-room and waited for the direction of the topic to make itself known. Obviously, she had a desire to talk about something that wasn't discussed earlier in the day however he wasn't certain what she had in mind. Generally speaking, it's a woman's prerogative to keep a man guessing anyway so Ken wasn't surprised by her request to speak with him about something of obvious importance. Anyway, with things apparently headed in the direction she wanted it too, Maude excused herself for a moment and went into the kitchen to make a couple of drinks. Ken had a whiskey and tonic while she opted for vodka and orange juice. At the very least, it might benefit her in the long run because of the nature of what she wanted to discuss with him. First of all, she wanted to know what he thought about her estate in Oregon and once again, Ken told her that he liked the place a lot however his advice was don't let it influence her decision to sell it. In truth, it was fairly obvious, what she wanted to do with the property however due to the circumstances of the situation, Ken did not blame her for wanting to do that. Actually, at some point along the way, he had a feeling they were going to get married and if that happened, nine times out of ten, he wouldn't have the time to travel up to Oregon anyway. Needless to say, he made sure Maude was aware of that fact although in all due honesty, it wouldn't have made any difference because she wanted to sell the estate before it ruined her life. At this point, Maude was satisfied with his overall perspective on what she should do with the property, so she pressed on further with what she wanted to discuss. In this particular instance, she actually took the indirect route for her goal and objective, however that meant Ken had to listen to the story about the unfortunate adventure she had with her first husband when they got stranded on the island out in the Pacific Ocean due to a miscalculation on Ricky's part. Actually, until now, she hadn't gone into any of the details of the adventure, she had only briefly mentioned it on a couple of occasions, but with the rest of the evening to themselves, she thought it was a good time to relate the entire story to him. Anyway, like so many times in the past, he was quick to sympathize with her although you might say, that was fairly typical of his personality. In fact, Ken didn't waste any time telling her how lucky she was to have been rescued. Of course, this was nothing Maude didn't already know but it still felt really good to get the story off her chest one more time. Furthermore, and not unexpectedly, she kept on talking about how they managed to survive the horrifying ordeal of being stranded on an island out in the middle of the Pacific Ocean for an hour or more before Ken suggested, she take him out to see the lighthouse. Actually, Maude had a tendency to overdo things a bit, in addition to being a little forgetful at times, however Ken overlooked that particular idiosyncrasy as one of her shortcomings.

Needless to say, no one is perfect and she sure as hell wasn't however flaws in her nature were something she would never own up too. You just agreed with her and listened to what she had to say. In fact, on many occasions, she said what she wanted to hear and wow unto you if you tried to tell her otherwise. She was definitely a bit stubborn and that added to her very obvious shortcomings however on the plus side of it all, she was a very beautiful woman.

Anyway, if you remember correctly, Maude had already promised to show him the inside of the lighthouse at some point over the weekend and it goes without saying, there wasn't a better time to do that than right now so with that in mind, a short time later, that is what they did. It can also be said, at this point in the evening, both participants were a bit intoxicated however that did not slow them down in their endeavor to see the inside of the lighthouse. Of course, by now, the daylight hours of the day were nowhere to be seen. It was dark outside however that didn't deter them from doing what they wanted to do, nor did it stop them from what they would actually end up doing before the weekend was over. Anyway, not unexpectedly, the moment they were inside the turret of the lighthouse, she began crying. Unfortunately, the emotional pain of having been married there a few years earlier literally came rushing to the forefront of her mind. At first, Ken was a little baffled by her sudden burst of emotion however long before he could say anything to her about that, he understood it had to do with past memories that were experienced there. For a moment or two, he remained quiet. As a matter of fact, Ken let the natural course of events take control of the situation, which in this particular instance, really amounted to no more than taking her into his arms and consoling her for a short period of time. Obviously, it had everything to do with her previous marriage. Of course, he didn't know exactly why she was crying although Ken was smart enough to realize her sudden burst of emotion would've been caused by something she did here when she was married to Ricky Vestellini. Anyway, as you might suspect, she continued to sob uncontrollably for a lot longer than he thought however she eventually came around to her senses and was able to explain to Ken why she was crying. At this point, she had calmed down a bit and that allowed her to tell him this was where she married her first husband. In truth, Maude may have mentioned this to him before but he didn't immediately recall her doing so. Well, be so as it may and certainly the circumstances of the moment, Maude told him the whole story of how they ended up getting married in the turret of the lighthouse, now, some years ago. Furthermore, since marriage is usually a once in a lifetime thing, Ken could see why the memory of what took place here must have meant a lot to her. Anyway, Maude continued on with her story until there was literally nothing left to tell. Finally, after exchanging a few more words and feelings about a very memorable experience that would remain etched in the back of her mind forever, they went back to the house. Actually, it was getting late in the evening anyway however she had one more thing she wanted to discuss with him before they headed off to bed that evening and that subject was marriage. Actually, it was the reason why Maude thought a couple of drinks might help ease the situation a little because men usually get all worked up over a matter like this and sometimes, they even run in the other direction when something of this nature is brought up. Anyway, on the way back into the house, it was extremely apparent, she didn't want to think about it anymore. In fact, quite frankly, it was time to take a chance on life again. Maude was certain of that so rather than beating around the bush anymore, she came right out and asked Ken the inevitable question, would you like to get married inside the turret of the lighthouse? Actually, believe it or not, that was the subject matter she wanted to touch on earlier in the evening anyway however until now, she hadn't been able to get up enough courage to ask him not to delay his desire to do that. Well, as you might think, Ken was a bit surprised by Maude's explicit candor and also by the fact, she wanted to get married inside the turret of the lighthouse however he quickly implied that was all right with him. He didn't have any issues with that. As a matter of fact, that's what he wanted to do anyway. It was just a question of whether or not she would consent to do that. As far as Ken was concerned, she was just exactly what he was looking for so with all due honesty, he wanted to get married. Normally, under circumstances such as this, that doesn't usually happen however in this particular case that scenario was about to unfold and there wasn't anything on god's green earth would be able to change that.

Anyway, with the question of getting married out in the open now, Maude and Ken went back into the living-room of her estate and sat down on the sofa to talk about this pressing matter a little more. In truth, it's usually the man that pops the question, hopefully at the right time, but in this particular instance, Maude took the initiative to do that even if it meant being rejected for whatever reason Ken saw fit as an excuse for not getting married. He had already told her that is what he wanted to do however doing one thing and living up to another are two entirely different things. Maude was fairly certain that's what Ken's intentions were. Furthermore, just in case you weren't aware of it, it is fair to say, Maude wanted a special person to share her life with again. It would be just a question of whether or not she chose the right person, that's all. Needless to say, her last marriage was a disaster. Of course, there wasn't any guarantee her next marriage would turn out any better than her first, but she had decided to throw caution to the wind. In truth, from what she could see, Ken appeared to have grown up so she was inclined to believe, he was worth taking a chance on. Actually, for the sake of her children, she thought it would be a good idea to find someone. She obviously didn't need any financial assistance. Anyway, now back inside the living-room of her estate, she fixed both of them, one last nightcap for the occasion and then, she pursued the subject of marriage. As you might think, the inevitable was about to happen but Ken wasn't showing any kind of resistance so that was obviously a good sign. In fact, he was actually just sipping on the drink she while she assessed the situation. At this point, it's also safe to say, it did not take her very long to know where she was going with their conversation. What she found somewhat puzzling was the fact he was able to consume alcohol. It was her understanding, once a person is an alcoholic, they can't have alcohol anymore or they'll go right back to drinking, but there wasn't any indication that was the case with Ken. In fact, he didn't appear to be concerned about that at all so you might say, she wasn't concerned about that either. Actually, she really and truly believed what he told her when he said it wouldn't be a problem, so the matter was dropped. By now, she was beginning to get a little restless as well as a little anxious because it was time to see if they could be the best of friends again. Anyway, with that in mind, she went on to explain, her reason for wanting a man in her life again. Needless to say, in being human, she truly missed the intimate side of life and secondly, unless she was mistaken, it would be a good idea to have a man around the house anyway. That way, her children would have someone to look up too in the years ahead or at least, that would be the case from the masculine side of a human life. Granted, if everything went well and nothing happened to her, they would always be able to turn to her for support when they needed guidance, however it was still her belief they would also benefit from having a male figure around the house. Anyway, with these thoughts bouncing around inside her head, she began to share her inner most feelings with Ken over the course of the next hour or so, while he listened very carefully to what she had to say. By now, he could clearly see where their conversation was going and like a true gentleman, Ken finally got around to officially proposing to her. Actually, it was her understanding, that's what he was looking to do anyway so she didn't see any reason why she couldn't help things along by dropping a few, good, subtle hints and as it turns out, it worked. The truth of the matter was she had made up her mind, if Ken didn't ask her that fateful question, sometime this weekend, she was going to look elsewhere for a man. Elated that Ken was willing to get married after all, she jumped off the sofa and proceeded to give him a great big hug. Then, Maude looked into his eyes and planted a deeply passionate kiss on his lips. At first, Ken was a little stunned by her sudden advances however that more than likely had to do with the usual repercussions associated with drinking alcohol over a period of an hour. Actually, from his perspective, he felt great and with everything headed in the right direction, he planted a retaliatory kiss upon Maude's lips just as soon as he recovered from the passion of her own kiss. What else was there left do but make love to her right there in the comfort of the living-room, so that's what he did. Finally, after the sexual gratification of the moment filled both of their hearts, well beyond anything that could be described in words, they sat down and began making plans to get married. In fact, it was something they both wanted to get out of the way as soon as possible because until they did so, neither one of them would feel satisfied or be able to enjoy life the way they would like too. In the meantime, regardless of any past indifference's, they both appeared to be ready to take the next step and of course, that was marriage. Anyway, a few minutes later, the matter was agreed upon, right down to where they would get married and as you may've already surmised, their vows were going to be taken in the turret of the lighthouse again. Furthermore, it was also decided, rather than waiting around to do this, the following day is when their marriage vows would be taken so shortly before they went to bed that evening, he called Reverend Nelson. Actually, at her suggestion, he did this because she wanted the same pastor she had before. Well, in the course of twenty minutes, the matter was all taken care of. They would take their marriage vows at 1:00 o'clock the following day. Obviously, it was on a short notice, however he inferred it wasn't anything he hadn't done before so he agreed to do it Sunday afternoon. As for Ken, due to work obligations, just as soon as they were married, they had to fly back to Beverly Hills. At least, that's what the original plan was anyway. There was a little flexibility in his schedule, so it was possible, they could leave Tierra Del Mar, later in the day on Sunday. In the meantime, now, more anxious than ever to get on with their relationship as a married couple, they headed upstairs to try and get some sleep because the following day was already literally knocking upon the door of their destiny. Of course, that kind of observation can only be seen from the perspective of the divine presence of God, which in this case, that assumption may be viewed as authentic, real, and right down to the fact, that's where their lives were headed. As for the precise nature of what lay ahead of them in the months to come, that was anyone's guess, but it was in her own best interest to keep an eye on Ken and I am sure she was aware of that when she made the decision to marry him. Needless to say, because of his past track record with women, it would be a good idea to do that. Obviously, if that hadn't been the case, Maude would have been able to look at things a lot differently, and in the end, she wouldn't have suffered the injustices life so unfairly sent her way.

Anyway, when Sunday morning arrived and after a fairly good night's rest, she suggested they go out for breakfast and since, he didn't voice any objection about doing so, the later part of the morning was spent at a restaurant in Tierra Del Mar. The fact of the matter is they had plenty of time to get back home before 1:00 o'clock so they went in search of a place to eat. Anyway, as it turns out, about fifteen to twenty minutes later, they were seated inside a small family diner on the outskirts of town. Furthermore, in this case, she had dinned there before so there wasn't any question about the quality of the food. In fact, quite frankly, for a casual place to eat, the cuisine was nothing short of spectacular. In addition to that, the restaurant was in a good location so that afforded them the time to do this. Anyway, one thing led to another and in a very short period of time, they were feasting on a very enjoyable meal. About an hour later and as fate would have it, they left to go back to Ricky's old estate. On the way home, she casually pointed over to the old Kimball mansion, which of course she used to own. Actually, her reason for doing that had to do with the fact, that's where she met Ricky. Until now, it had totally slipped her mind to show Ken the house however there wasn't any better time than the present to do that so a stop along the way was done so he could see where she use to live. Needless to say, even though she was there for a very short period of time, some very unforgettable memories were left behind there. Anyway, as you may think, she was elaborating on how that all came to be as they pulled up into the yard of Ricky's old estate. "As you may have guessed, at that point in my life, we were neighbors," she stated. "Then, one day, right out of the blue, this nice-looking Italian man was standing directly in front of me at the door to my house. Well, in being human, I have to say, I couldn't resist the temptation to get to know him so I asked him into the house, we had coffee, we talked a bit, and the rest is history. Actually, there's a lot more to the story than that, but for the time being that's all you need to know. Not that I am trying to hide anything, but it will give us something to talk about another time. Right at the moment, we need to redirect our attention to another important matter and that's taking our marriage vows. Reverend Nelson will be here shortly, and I want to be ready when he gets here." Well, as you might think, Ken was quick to agree with her on this, so they proceeded to go inside the house to attend too any last-minute business that needed to be taken care of. Actually, for Maude, all that really amounted to was a fresh change of clothes and a quick shower. She wasn't certain if Ken had anything to do, but she was to learn a few minutes later, he changed into a more formal attire. In fact, to be more precise, Ken put on a suit and tie however she quickly reminded him, it wasn't necessary to do that, so he wasted no time putting something on that was a bit more casual, which in this case was a polo shirt and slacks. Maude was dressed in jeans and a blouse. Needless to say, it wasn't a formal wedding so she didn't see any sense of getting all dressed up. Granted, it was a special occasion, however it really wasn't necessary to do that. At any rate, once that was decided upon, they went into the living-room to wait for Reverend Nelson to get there. Thankfully, he was right along, so they didn't have very long to sit around and contemplate the situation and it turns out, about fifteen to twenty minutes later, he was knocking at the front door. At any rate, now readier than ever to take their marriage vows, they went to the door to let him in. Then, after a few amicable words were said, amid the confusion of what they were about to do, they headed out to the lighthouse. Actually, it came as no surprise to Maude that Reverend Nelson remembered marrying her here before and of course, she immediately owned up to having married her first husband in the same manner. Anyway, as you might suspect, with the formal introductions out of the way, and now out at the lighthouse, it left the task of climbing up the stairs of the structure until they were safely inside the turret of the lighthouse. By now, it was twenty minutes past the hour of 1:00 and like always, time was going by quicker than anyone wanted it too with the exception of Reverend Nelson. Of course, he was bound by duty to do the inevitable and since he was being paid well to do this, he didn't have any complaints. Anyway, as fate would have it, in the short time he was there, the participants in the wedding ceremony were officially married. In fact, the whole thing was over within a matter of twenty minutes. In this particular case, the pastor wasn't too long winded, so things moved right along until there wasn't anything left to be said. At this point, Mr. Nelson told them he had to be on his way, and with nothing left to be tended too, they went back down the flight of stairs to the bottom floor of the lighthouse. Then, as you might think, he took a minute to wish them the best of luck in the endeavor they were about to embark upon and shortly thereafter, he left. Anyway, with the thought of what had to be done over the course of the next twenty-four hours and to get things moving along in the right direction with some degree accuracy, like returning to California for instance, they headed into the house to pack their suitcases. The fact of the matter is Ken had job obligations that required his attention so it was necessary for him to be at work the first thing Monday morning. Needless to say, that meant, they were going to fly back to Beverly Hills that afternoon. Anyway, with that goal and objective in mind, an hour or two later, they were on their way to the airport in Portland, Oregon. Like before, Maude made arrangements ahead of time so a plane was waiting for them when they got there. Actually, it was the only reasonable way they had to fly back to California without waiting in line to get on a commercial flight. Anyway, as it turns out, everything went on schedule, and a couple of hours later, they were back in California. To be more precise, Beverly Hills. In fact, they were back at her estate in literally no time at all however the way she planned everything out, you might say, the weekend went very well indeed. Now, if everything continued to go well, everything would be fine. Hopefully, that would be the case however as much as she hated to admit it, something in the back of her mind told her things might not work out the way she wanted it too. In truth, she had been screwed over before and for that reason alone, she still harbored reservations about the marriage she entered into. Obviously, she wished in the worst possible way that wasn't so however because she was human, the reality of it all was anything could happen. Furthermore, she realized that even though Ken appeared to have grown up enough to bear the weight of a wife and kids upon his shoulders, uncertainty was still gnawing away at the back of her mind. Actually, as you might think, she had been reluctant to forgive him for any past injustices however everyone has a right to change, and it was Maude's sincere belief Ken had. Needless to say, she would know that all in good time. Believe it or not, in many ways, what happened to her through the years wasn't entirely her men's friend's fault. A lot of it had to do with the kind of person she was, however in her apparent shortsightedness, she wasn't able to see that, nor would she have ever admitted that. Furthermore, and with regards to what Maude had to deal with from one day to the next, even if she had been able to see things in a better light, it probably wouldn't have made any difference because the men that were a part of her life used her, and in the end, that's what inevitably motivated her into doing what she did.

Part VIII

CHAPTER 38

A couple of months went by and everything seemed to be going well. There weren't any arguments to speak of and their marriage was coming along just fine. In fact, you might say, she was actually quite pleased with the way things were going. Needless to say, Maude was the kind of person that liked to have a man around the house so Ken fit in really well with her plans for an ideal family. At any rate, the day after their marriage vows were taken, he didn't waste any time moving in with her as destiny soon found Ken relocating all of his belongings to her estate in the fine city of Beverly Hills. Actually, between that and trying to get caught up on some paperwork at the office, Ken was a very busy man for a few days however he didn't seem to mind that. For some reason, he liked to spend time there even though he claimed they didn't treat him well. At any rate, going from bachelorhood to family man evolved into a smooth transition for him and in a matter of a week, life had returned to normal. Like always, routines were followed most of the time and everything seemed to fall into place really well. No one had any complaints and for the most part, life was good. Perhaps, like any marriage, little things came up from time to time that had to be addressed but other than that, everyone was making out just fine.

Anyway, it turns out, autumn was unseasonably warm that year. Most of the days had an abundance of sunshine and Maude's oldest daughter began school in September of that year and much to her surprise, Vanessa Ann adapted really well to her new environment. Needless to say, Maude was extremely pleased about that however there were times when she missed having her daughter around the house during the day. Actually, Vanessa's younger sister, Margaret was lost for a while after Vanessa started school. In fact, she very often went from one room to the other looking for her older sister. Then, Maude would take a few minutes to reassure her Vanessa had not gone very far, and that she would be home later in the day, however regardless of how many times she did that, Margaret would still go around the house looking for her. Of course, both of Maude's girls were very close to one another, not only in age, but in everything else as well. At any rate, it took Margaret some time to adjust to her older sister's absence at school however she eventually did, and life soon returned to normal at Maude's house.

Anyway, at least for a while, her new marriage appeared to be going well. With Vanessa in school and Margaret entertaining herself for a good portion of the day by watching television or engaging in one of those things young children do, Maude would often take to her study to do a little writing. After lunch, about the time Vanessa got home from school, Maude would redirect her attention to both girls. In fact, they usually found a game to play while their younger brother slept soundly in his crib upstairs. Then, late in the afternoon, their stepfather would come home from work. At this point, they would sit down to supper and have a good meal. In the evening, a lot of television was watched after family time at the supper table, at least Maude did anyway. It wasn't unusual for Ken to look at the paper and go to bed early. Job obligations at work seemed to expend most of his energy. Occasionally, a matter of importance arose and when it did, a very lengthy discussion followed until the matter was resolved. Anyway, for the most part, everything was going well, and with the holiday season creeping up on them, the kids were getting excited about the thought of Santa Claus paying them a visit. In the meantime, all of their daily routines were predictable, and life continued on as usual for Maude and her family. Actually, it was about this time that Maude brought up the subject of having another child with Ken. Well, much to her disappointment, Ken didn't want to pursue that route for a while. Initially, Ken told her if that is what you want to do, we'll do that however somewhere along the way, he changed his mind. At first, she was a little miffed by his desire not to pursue the route of having another child however as disappointed as she was about that, she tried to remain optimistic Ken would change his mind about that in the months ahead. For the time being, that wasn't going to happen and that left a bit of uncertainly rolling around in the back of her mind because it was a good indication her second marriage might not work out for her either and of course, that weighed heavily upon her heart.

Anyway, shortly before the holiday season that year, the bottom fell out of everything. At this point, it goes without saying, the course of Maude's life was about to take a horrible turn for the worst as their marriage hit another snag during the middle of November that year. In fact, it was a day she would always remember. Not in the good sense of remembering something but in the bad sense, like when something haunts the hell out of you the rest of your life. Anyway, right out of the blue one day, Ken called from the office and said he had to work late. Well, at first she didn't give it a second thought because she knew Ken had a very demanding job however a short time later, a red flag popped up in the back of her mind alerting her to the possibility she may be having more marital problems than she originally thought. Of course, that was the last thing she needed to have happen however the reality of it all was that's the same thing Ricky told her when the bottom of her first marriage. Suddenly, a world of fear gripped her heart because that's what happened when she was married to Ricky. Granted, there were times when Ken had to work on a job-related project for ComTech, which inevitably led him into putting in extra time at the office on the weekend however that's as far as it went. In fact, to be more precise, Saturday mornings were usually a sure bet, with regards to what his profession required of him but if it also became necessary for him to work late on one or more evenings of the week, it would be a problem. In fact, you might say, it made her wonder what he was doing with all of his time away from home. At any rate, with regards to what Ken was doing at work, she had every intention of giving him the benefit of the doubt until she had reason to believe otherwise. Actually, what worried Maude most was the possibility he might be pursuing the route of marriage infidelity like Ricky did. In reality, he could be working on a project that needed his attention and if that turned out to be the case, he didn't have anything to worry about. On the other hand, if Ken was actually doing what she thought he may have been doing, she had a problem.

Anyway, because Ken's request to work late came on the heels of a last-minute statement made in a very obscure manner, it seemed to indicate something was amiss. At any rate, he told Maude that he wouldn't be able to make it home until around eleven o'clock that evening. Well, of course, that immediately prompted her to ask Ken why he had to work late on one of the week days. His answer, just simply was, it was necessary for him to do that and since, she was not the kind of person to press the matter into some kind of irreversible confrontation, nothing more was said about it. Actually, she found out later from the horse's mouth itself, the company he worked for was in the process of installing a new computer system. Not surprisingly, he claimed his boss wanted him to give them a hand with the implantation of it. The truth of the matter is, he was the best there was at what he did so his request to work late for a few nights made all the sense in the world to her. At this point, Maude had decided to accept what Ken said as the god's honest truth. Surely, he wouldn't be numb enough to have an affair with another woman. They had only been married for a couple of months. At any rate, the more she thought about it, the more she came to the conclusion, he may actually be doing what he claimed he was doing. Obviously, it would be a very good idea to stay in good standing with the company you work for so she didn't fault Ken for wanting to give them a hand with things. In truth, she was afraid he would do the same thing to her that Ricky did so the fear of an extramarital affair weighed heavily upon her mind. Was it a justifiable concern? Yes, it was, because of what Ken and Ricky did to her in years past so she was very there was reason for concern. In fact, in this case, Maude was certainly well within her boundaries for taking issue with Ken for what he was doing away from home.

At any rate, another week or two went by and Ken continued to work late each and every night until she couldn't take it anymore. She had to know what he was doing, or her mind wasn't going to let her rest until she did so. At this point, to appease her mind, she made the decision to look into the matter. Maude wanted to know whether or not Ken was actually giving ComTech a hand with the installation of a new computer system. The truth of the matter is that thought kept returning to the forefront of her mind through this difficult time in her life. Surely, you wouldn't think it would take forever to install a new computer system however that seemed to be the case with Ken so for obvious reasons, she had decided to fix up a nice meal and drop in unannounced at work to give it to him. Of course, that endeavor would be done in a very discreet manner, one in which, by the time he realized what was going on, it would be too late for him to do anything except to say, how kind of you to bring me in a meal, dear. In fact, she had already made up her mind, if Ken was working on the installation of a new computer system like he said he was, she would make things up to him by making arrangements with a travel agency to take a vacation to some exotic island somewhere. On the other hand, if Ken was doing something he shouldn't be doing, he had a lot of explaining to do.

Anyway, during the course of an afternoon, on a weekday towards the end of November, Maude put together a seafood casserole and headed out the door for Ken's place of employment. Obviously, her maid could look after the kids for a while. In fact, it was the only way she would be able to see how well he was coming along on the installation of his company's new computer system. At any rate, since his employer was located only a short distance away from her estate in

Beverly Hills, it wasn't going to take her very long to get to his office but it would be a matter of staying cool, calm, and collected while she looked into the matter though because she was sorely afraid she was in the process of being screwed over again. Needless to say, that had happened to her before and if it happened again, Maude wasn't sure what she would do. Anyway, once again, she was about to find out just how unfair life can be sometimes. As for how she made out on the way to Ken's office, well, I believe that can best be summed up best by saying, Maude ran three traffic lights and a stop sign before pulling into ComTech's parking lot. Usually, she was a much better driver than that however right at the moment, not only was Maude's patience wearing thin, but the thought of what Ken might be doing behind her back was irking the hell out of her. As a matter of fact, due to an overall lack of sleep over the past couple of weeks, Maude was actually quite fatigued.

At any rate, putting all that aside, Maude was now more determined than ever to find out if her beloved husband was screwing another woman. Until now, with regards to what Ken may have been doing, she had given him the benefit of the doubt however may god have mercy on his soul if he was doing what she thought he may be doing. Anyway, as you might think, right at the moment, Maude was lost in thought as she tried to decide what she was going to do next. After a moment or two went by, Maude concluded, regardless of the consequences, she was going to put her plan into action so she got of her car and headed for the building Ken's office was in. Now, it was time to enter the building however as she suspected, the security guard wouldn't let her go in to the building. Needless to say, the man wanted to know the nature of her business before he let her go any further, which of course meant, she would have to have to explain the reason why she was there. Anyway, she quickly explained to the man her husband worked for ComTech and that he was working late. Obviously, being the dedicated housewife she was, Maude said she wanted to bring a freshly made casserole up to her husband and that seemed to satisfy his curiosity, so he asked her to wait a minute while he rang Ken's office to inform him his wife was here. Needless to say, at this point, if the element of surprise was to stay on her side she had to act swiftly so she told the officer her visit was supposed to be a surprise. Well, it wasn't any skin off his teeth what Maude did or didn't do just as long as she didn't pose a security threat to anyone inside the office building however for security reasons, the man wanted to see some identification that proved she was who she said she was. At this point, she pulled out one of her husband's identification cards and showed it to him and upon seeing it, he allowed her to enter the building.

Anyway, it didn't take her very long to figure out where his office was located. It was on the third floor of a ten-story building. Actually, there was a list of names on the wall leading out of the main entrance to the building that provided the information Maude was looking for, so she had no trouble finding Ken's office. At any rate, it only took her a couple of minutes to find his name on the wall and upon learning where she needed to go, she headed for the elevator. There, she pressed a button that took her up to the third floor of the building, where upon she exited the elevator, and began walking down the hall. First, she had to go left, then, she had to take a right, and a moment later, she came to a stop about fifteen feet away from his office. At this point, she heard a good amount of chatter going on inside a room that appeared to be a small lounge located directly across the hall from where Ken's office was, so Maude quietly made her way over to the door and peaked inside. Sadly, what she saw next was enough to make a grown woman cry. Her beloved husband was aggressively fondling the breasts of an attractive woman on the far side of the room. "Of all the luck," she muttered beneath her breath. "That son of a bitch has done it to me again!" She was furious and rightfully so. Furthermore, it was also quite apparent, Ken was still a lady's man. At this point, she didn't know whether to cry or throw up all over the floor. It was another one of the most difficult situations she ever had to deal with. Actually, believe it or not, Maude thought he was a changed man however that wasn't the case at all. Anyway, much to her regret, Ken had a drink in one hand and was pursuing the woman with his other. Needless to say, in her eyes, what he was doing was extremely disgusting and totally uncalled for and as you might think, she could barely stand to look inside the room. In fact, the urge to vomit was there as the reality of the situation sank in. Obviously, Maude's second marriage wasn't going to turn out any better than her first one had and the prospect of that happening made her even more sick to her stomach. At this point, Maude took another look into the room, only this time Ken's right hand quickly darted up her skirt in total defiance of the woman's modesty as she began to moan rather loudly. Once again, she felt like vomiting. In fact, by this time, the woman was groaning in ecstasy as Ken kissed her passionately on the lips. "God damn that good-for-nothing bastard," she cursed beneath her breath. "He's definitely worn out his welcome with me." At any rate, as she proceeded to monitor the situation from just outside the room, things appeared to be getting a little out of hand inside the employee's lounge as she tried to decide what to do. Actually, Maude was all but certain Ken was serious about settling down and raising a family however it was now quite apparent, she had been mistaken about that. Anyway, she continued to watch her husband's foolhardy behavior for a little longer. Then, after another moment or two went by, the woman in question unzipped the fly on his pants and began blowing him off. Needless to say, by this time, Ken was groaning in ecstasy too as the woman proceeded to make her husband feel like he had died and gone to heaven. Of all the disrespectfully ignorant things Ken could have done. Damn him, she thought to herself. Needless to say, it was extremely heartbreaking to see Ken with this woman, and even more heartbreaking to know her second marriage had just gone down the drain as well. Anyway, she was now absolutely certain she should've never married him. As a matter of fact, the bout of overwhelming nausea that had been plaguing her since making the discovery Ken was having an extra-marital affair continued to plague the hell out of her as Maude thought about what her next course of action would be. At this point, she had a strong yearning to walk over to where Ken sat in the lounge and unselfishly unload the casserole in his face but she was quick to decide against doing that. She would leave the building in a civilized manner and deal with things at a later time however her marriage to Ken was over.

Anyway, after she got over the initial shock of what was happening, rather than watch the woman finish blowing her husband off, she took off down the hall in a miserable fit of rage with the seafood casserole tucked beneath her arm. First, she got to the elevator. Then, after gallantly fighting back a few tears, she proceeded to press the button that took her down to the main floor of the building. From there, Maude stuffed the seafood casserole in a waste basket and exited the building as quickly as possible. Once she reached the parking lot, she found her car rather easily and without wasting anymore time or thought, she quickly threw her Ferrari in gear and sped off down the road. Needless to say, her only immediate plan was to go home and cry for a while. At any rate, when Maude got home, she left instructions with her maid to make sure the kids got to bed on time and that under no circumstances was she to be disturbed. At this point, Maude went directly to her bedroom and locked the door. Needless to say, she wanted to be alone for a while. Obviously, her maid sensed something was wrong however as to what that was, she didn't know. Furthermore, she didn't want to pry into the matter so for the time being, whatever was bothering her would have to wait until another day. In reality, Lisa knew Maude would tell her about what happened somewhere down the road, so she took the non-combative approach to the matter. As for Ken, Maude said he wouldn't be coming home for a while however she didn't elaborate on the reason for that other than saying, he was working late at the office again. When he actually got home later in the evening, her maid was supposed to say, she wasn't feeling well, and under no circumstances was she to be disturbed. Then, with a highly strained smile, a moment or two later, Maude reassured Lisa everything was all right, and that was the end of their conversation. In fact, it was her understanding she would see Maude in the morning. At any rate, the moment Maude made it upstairs that evening, she actually made a quick stop to the bathroom, where she threw up in the toilet. How she had made it that far without doing so she didn't know, however once that unpleasantry was behind her, as stated before, she went to her bedroom and locked the door. Well, so much for another marriage, Maude thought to herself as she tried to remain calm in the midst of a catastrophe. Unfortunately, as positive and up-beat as she tried to be, that way of thinking didn't last very long because within a few minutes of having landed on the top of her bed, she began to curse the ground Ken walked upon. In fact, as far as she was concerned, Ken didn't exist anymore! He was the lowest of the lows! Scum of all scum! Trash of all trash! You get the picture. It was very unfortunate he had taken the initiative to get a piece of ass elsewhere however that's what happened and now she had to deal with the matter. In fact, there wasn't any sense of denying it because she had seen it with her own eyes, so as far as she was concerned, he could go to hell. In fact, it was her forgone conclusion, Ken would pay for his careless infidelity. She was certain of that however at this time, she was uncertain what the best form of punishment would be.

At any rate, that was all she could take for one day. After hashing things in her head for an hour or more, she called it a day. Tomorrow, she would give the highly unfortunate matter a little more thought, and then with any luck at all, she would be able to make a decision on what to do with Ken. Right at the moment, Maude could honestly say, everything was pointing to an irreconcilable differences divorce. Perhaps, she would be able come up with a better solution to the problem happen however as things stood now, she didn't see that happening. Of course, that would definitely exclude any chance of patching things up and living happily ever after together however she didn't have any desire to do that anyway. No, something a lot more meaningful had to be done about his fidelity, however at this point, just exactly what measures had to be taken to get even with him for his careless promiscuity remained to be seen. Anyway, as you might think, that is what she was thinking about when she fell asleep that night. Obviously, she wasn't going to rule anything out, including the despicable act of cold-blooded murder. Until now, the thought hadn't actually occurred to her but with circumstances as they were, she intended to give the idea a lot of very serious consideration. In fact, quite frankly, Maude was willing to take any measure necessary to resolve the problem and that included murder.

CHAPTER 39

No one knew exactly what time Ken got home that evening however when they sat down to breakfast the following morning, Maude wasn't in a very talkative mood. In fact, it didn't take him very long to realize something was bothering her so he took the initiative to find out why she was being so quiet. Not unexpectedly and much to his disappointment, every time he brought up the subject of why she was being so distant to him, Maude gave him the silent treatment. At first he thought, it might have something to do with his desire not to have another child however Ken eventually concluded, it was far more likely she had a lot on her mind. Anyway, be so as it may, shortly after one way conversation took place between her kids and their mother, he frustratingly headed off to work. Actually, he had more important matters to attend to at the moment so rather than worrying about that, he headed off to work. Realistically speaking, there wasn't any reason why he couldn't address the matter another time so he left things as they were for the time being.

Perhaps, if he had enough time, later that evening, he would try and resolve things. In reality, he was endeavoring into a new business adventure at work and that was occupying most of his time these days. Of course, in this particular instance, I'm referring to one of his fellow employees. I believe her name was Jennifer Johnston. She was a very pretty divorcee, who was having a hard time getting her life in order, and as you might think, Ken felt sorry for her. Admittedly, she was looking for someone to have a relationship with, and perhaps, for no other reason than to find the right man to tango with, if you'll please excuse the expression, she just happened to set her sights on Ken Stackford. As for her exact intentions, there was a little uncertainty to the situation, but it stands to reason, she was looking for another husband. Furthermore, she knew, Ken was married however she also realized, if she was persistent enough, there was a possibility she might win out over his wife, Maude Derringer. In fact, it can be further stated, Jennifer Johnston was more than likely looking for some additional revenue to supplement her already depleted income, so he had plenty of reason to be concerned. Unfortunately, Ken didn't that see this, so he was very quickly targeted for his financial resources. From his perspective, all he wanted to do was to appease his sexual appetite, which had been suffering of late so for the time being, Ken thought he would try to have the best of both worlds. Obviously, he didn't have any desire to end to his marriage with Maude because if that were to happen, he stood to lose a lot of money. It was a difficult situation but he was a game player and a chance taker, so he intended to pursue the object of his affection.

Anyway, as you might think, the tension between Maude and Ken continued to get worse over the course of the next day or two until it was extremely apparent, their marriage was surfing on dangerous waters. Perhaps, that isn't the best way to put it but they were definitely headed for a divorce on the grounds of marriage infidelity again. Of course, Ken didn't know that however I believe, that's what Maude had in mind. Actually, after having made the highly unfortunate find, Ken was having sexual relations with another woman, Maude wasn't sure what she was going to do. It's true, after sleeping on it for a couple of nights, many ideas took to root in her mind, none of which was more ominous that an act of cold, blooded murder. Obviously, that is a horrendous thing to contemplate doing, however believe it or not, Maude eventually came to the conclusion, not only did Ken have to go but her estate in Oregon had to go as well. She would try to kill two birds with one stone. Of course, that meant taking a chance on something that would more than likely get her a life sentence in prison if she got caught doing that however Maude wanted to get even with him for what he did to her, and that would probably be the easiest way to settle things between them. Obviously, if she could come up with a well thought out, strategic plan of action, there was a good possibility, there wouldn't be any more pain and suffering on her part. Needless to say, from that point on, the rest would be history. Anyway, as it turns out, Ken had absolutely no luck at all in getting what he wanted to know out of Maude so he eventually gave up pursuing the matter. What was bothering her was going to remain a mystery. Furthermore, since Ken did not see any sense of trying to get an answer from her, his endeavor was soon abandoned. In fact, quite frankly, as far as he was concerned, it would've been much easier to have gotten blood out of turnip, than it would have been to understand that woman or at least, that's how he looked at it anyway. Whether or not, that was a true and accurate statement, remained to be seen. I've heard it said, it's a woman's prerogative to keep a man guessing and perhaps, that's the way she wanted it with Ken too. Who knows! Anyway, regardless of what Maude was thinking or what she had in mind, a day or two later, shortly after Ken went to work, she headed out the door to purchase a handgun. It also goes without saying, by now, Maude was hell bent on putting him in the ground and the sooner that happened, the happier she would be. There wasn't any question about that. It would be just a question of whether or not, she got away with it, that's all. Anyway, as you might think, not only did she devise a plan to murder her husband, but she also devised a plan to get rid of her estate in Oregon as well. Granted, it was early in the month of December, however it was also unusually mild fall and winter, so she didn't see any reason why she couldn't pull the whole thing off. Believe it or not, the only thing she wasn't sure of was whether or not God would find a place in his heart to forgive her for committing a cold blooded, premeditated act of murder. As for when this was going to happen, perhaps, with any luck at all, next weekend. That was only a few days away. She could be patient. In the meantime, she would have to put up with things as they were for a little while longer. Now, with regards to her exact plan of action, well, it seemed only logical to murder her husband at Ricky's old estate up in the state of Oregon, and then, she would burn the building to the ground with his body inside. Of course, if things were done right, the law enforcement authorities would be led to believe an act of god, like a lightning strike from a severe electrical storm was responsible for what happened. Obviously, she didn't know a thing about electrical wiring, or she would've pursued the route of faulty wiring in an old house but no such luck was on her side so that idea was eventually abandoned. Her goal and objective was to make the whole thing look like an accident. If she was able to succeed in doing that, no one was going to know what happened. She was confident of that. On the other hand, if for some reason, it didn't work out that way, then, in all probability, the law enforcement agency in Tierra Del Mar would suspect she was behind the unfortunate tragedy that was going to take place there shortly. In reality, the worst thing that could happen was she would go to prison for a few years, however in the end, she concluded, it was a chance worth taking. Needless to say, she wanted to get even with Ken for his marriage infidelity, and with any kind of luck at all, she would succeed in doing so. It was as simple as that. As for her estate in Oregon, she would file an insurance claim on it, just as soon as it burnt to the ground. Since, it was insured against fire, theft, and everything else for that matter, chances were, she would not have any problem making an insurance claim on the property. At least, that's what she was counting on anyway. If for some reason it was determined the fire was an act of arson that would obviously complicate things a bit however she was willing to take the chance.

Anyway, as I said a moment ago, she went out and bought herself a small handgun at the general store on the outskirts of town and when the proprietor of the business asked her what she wanted the gun for, she told him it was for self-protection. Whether or not, he believed what she said was highly questionable however the most important thing of all was regardless of what the man actually thought, he did not refuse the sale of the gun to her. In this particular instance, her reason for wanting to purchase a handgun was probably one of the most common excuses in use these days when a person is trying to attain a firearm and as you might think, the gentleman who waited on her didn't ask any further questions. He just simply accepted her alias driver's license and one other form of fake identification and she was good to go. It was as simple as that. How she came about such an easy fabrication of identity is actually a long story however good fortune came her way in literally no time at all so the matter was all taken care of. Now, with any luck at all, no one would ever be able to trace the gun back to her, in the unlikely event, the police made a connection and tried to implicate her for the murder of her husband. Of course, that was based on the premise, that would never happen and if the whole thing went as planned, she didn't have anything to worry about. As a matter of fact, for the time being, Maude had already decided not to give it anymore thought. It looked like, she was going to be able to get away with murder and it goes without saying, that's all that really mattered.

Anyway, on this particular day, early in the week, sometime later in the evening after Ken got home from work, Maude suggested, they spend the weekend at her estate in Oregon. As you might think, he was surprised by her impromptu request to do that because they hadn't spoken to each other in a couple of days. At first, Ken was somewhat reluctant about going, however after giving it some thought, he came to the conclusion, it might be a good opportunity to patch things up on the home front, which in this particular case, amounted to marital problems. He still didn't know what was troubling Maude and in reality, Ken didn't have a good excuse not to go anyway. Anyway, as anticipated, he did come up with some kind of justification that allegedly explained why he was still working late at the office but unknowingly to him, she already knew the reason why he was spending a lot of additional time at ComTech. Believe it or not, he even had enough nerve to say, the project he was working on was taking a lot longer to complete than he originally thought however he further stated, there was a very good chance, things would be finished up by the time the holiday season was over. Of course, all the while he was saying this, she was saying to herself, likely story. In truth, after having looked into what he was doing at work, there really wasn't too much she didn't already know. At first, she thought about hiring a private investigator to keep tabs on her delinquent husband however she eventually concluded, it would be best to do nothing at all. She would murder the son of a bitch. At the very least, it should logically remedy the situation. If it didn't, she would be greatly surprised. Anyway, as you might expect, Ken told her a lot of hard work went into the project he was working on for ComTech, so she just brushed his statement aside in favor of getting even with him the first chance she got. As for how the rest of their discussion went, well, not a hell of a lot more was said between them however in the end, Ken agreed to fly up to Oregon with her this weekend, even though there was a lot of uncertainty in the back of his mind that led to some strong reservations about doing so. In the meantime, she was sorely afraid the hate and resentment in her eyes would betray the innocence of what Maude knew about Ken and the affair he was having with another woman. Needless to say, if that were to happen, it would cause even more problems for her, and of course, she would prefer that didn't happen. Anyway, if everything went as planned, he would step into the trap she laid out for him, and perhaps with a little luck, his existence, and everything else attached to him would be buried forever within the annals of time.

CHAPTER 40

By the time Friday afternoon arrived, Maude was having second thoughts about what she was going to do over the course of the weekend however when you take into consideration, what she intended to do was actually premeditated murder in the first degree, then, I guess it would be fair to say, the fact she was rethinking the whole thing over, didn't come as any big surprise. It's true, she wanted to extract her pound of flesh from Ken for his ungracious, foolhardy adventures with another woman, yet at the same time, the inner most caverns of her mind were bothering her more than she would care to think about. Perhaps, human nature was at work because her highly astute conscience had already taken a turn for the worse as she pondered the thought of what she was going to do. Normally, she would only fret over the little things, like her overall appearance however today Maude was concerned about her plans for the weekend so while the very thought of what she was going to do was ravishing her mind, Ken made arrangements with his employer to get out of work early on Friday. In fact, at this point, you might even say, nothing was holding them back from flying up to Oregon later that afternoon. Actually, Ken had a lot of flexibility in the hours he worked at Comtech so the prospect of getting out early wasn't really any big deal at all to him. Anyway, as expected, she was waiting patiently for the hour of his destiny's calling to become a reality and if she had anything to do with it, which of course, she most certainly did, at some point over the weekend, she was hoping to achieve her goal and objective. First, she had to find a way to get her beloved husband up to Tierra Del Mar and to the best of her knowledge that very pressing matter had already been taken care of. Now, it would be just a matter of time until Ken's appointment with destiny bit him right in the ass. From her perspective, that wouldn't be a very long-time span, however because of the nature of her intentions, the day would probably go by slowly.

As for how Maude felt about selling the estate in Oregon, like I said before, the sooner it was sold, the better off she would be, because the love she once had for Ricky Vestellini was still haunting the hell out of her. Furthermore, since, she hadn't been able to sell the property over the course of the past couple of months, you might say, she was anxious to take matters into her own hands with that too. Granted, she could always lower the selling price of the property however if things went as planned over the weekend, she wouldn't have to worry about that particular matter anymore. In reality, it was a thorn in her side anyway so if something were to happen to it, there wasn't any way she would be brokenhearted. In fact, considering the circumstances, Maude was going to be elated, if and when, that strike of good fortune actually came about. At this point and certainly without any reservations, Maude eventually came to the conclusion, she wasn't going to back down from her plans to get rid of Ken or the estate in Oregon. In truth, the very thought of what she was going to do was tormenting the hell out of her mind however she intended to stand her ground on that. Both, Ken, and the property in Oregon had to go. In fact, quite frankly, there wasn't any question about it. Obviously, if everything fell into place the way she wanted it too in the course of a few hours, she would more than likely be able to kill two birds with one stone. It was actually all Maude could hope for and like a cobra full of venom, she was ready to strike.

Now, let's discuss the psyche of the mind for a moment. A person's personality or soul, if you prefer to call it that, it a very complicated thing. Of course, there's the ego, in addition to the conscious and sub-conscious parts of the mind. Needless to say, a human brain is complex to say the least although everyone is born with a certain level of intelligence and then, depending on the kind of person they are, their level of intelligence is increased by one of two things. Knowledge will be attained through life experiences or by reading another person's thesis on life. Books can be an excellent source of information as well. Anyway, the reason I bring this matter up has a lot to do with

Maude's highly questionable mind stability. It's true, she was a very deep, intellectual person, and wise beyond her years, however every once in a while even the very best of us snap. You know, what I'm referring to don't you, well, that would be a person's sanity. Actually, we all have a breaking point, where simple things become difficult, and life's adventures take a turn for the worse. There's paranoia, depression, schizophrenia, anxiety, as well as many other so-called afflictions of the mind. In really bad cases, I suppose instability of the mind could lead a person to think they were going crazy. That happens sometimes. In this particular case, I'm not entirely sure what description would best describe Maude's apparent psychosis, but it was quite apparent, regardless of the fact she didn't have a clue in the world she was mentally ill, the nature of what she was about to do really says it all. The truth of that matter is most of us have a breaking point and the same can be said about Maude too. Needless to say, circumstances as they were, she was thinking irrationally although she had no idea that was the case. Anyway, there's always the first time for everything, including committing a criminal offense, which undoubtably takes in a lot of territory. Granted, committing an act of arson, or committing an act of murder definitely fell into that category but as regrettable as it was, that was the road she was headed down. Obviously, she had no idea she was mentally ill, and perhaps that was to her advantage but regardless of whether or not that was the case, Maude was more determined than ever to get rid of Ken, and her estate up in the state of Oregon. I suppose you could make the argument she had a bit of a temper, but even if that was true, the evil side of her mind was now at work. Anyway, everything was going as planned and to the best of her knowledge, Ken didn't suspect a thing. In fact, Maude thought he was going to look at her request to spend the weekend in Tierra Del Mar as an opportunity to patch things up between them and of course, she was right about that. Realistically speaking and at no surprise to her, their marriage had been suffering a lot in recent days so common sense told her, Ken would want to fly up to Oregon for the weekend. Needless to say, that was where their marriage officially began and if she had anything to do with it, that's where their marriage would officially end. Anyway, as you might think, he was aware that something was wrong because she barely spoke to him of late. It also stands to reason, that's why he wasn't sleeping with her every night like most husbands would do. No, she kept insisting, he sleep in one of the other bedrooms and without having too much choice on the matter, that's what he was doing. Actually, Ken was hoping, she would eventually get over whatever was bothering her however that hadn't happened yet. In the meantime, the only thing Ken would acknowledge is he was working late every night so the company he worked for would be able to install a new computer system. Admittedly, Ken wasn't going to be in the position to use that excuse much longer, so there was obviously a lot of uncertainty going on in his life, not only with his own marriage but also with the woman, he was having an affair with. Anyway, regardless of whether or not, Maude had any idea of what he was doing behind her back, Ken thought it would be a good idea to give her a little extra attention for a change. In fact, as unbelievable as it may sound, what he was doing at work had nothing to do with a desire to end his marriage with Maude because that really wasn't the case at all however it had everything to do with an opportunity to help one of his colleagues at work though. Actually, it was his understanding, the woman he was having an affair with, just went through a very ugly divorce and was currently looking for a casual encounter with someone. Well, that's where Ken came in. Anyway, as luck would have it, the woman in question was a very open-minded person, not to mention, a very passionate lady, so when she came onto him one evening, Ken totally lost his resistance. To make matters worse, Jennifer Johnston was a very persuasive woman, so it did not take him very long to succumb to her demands. Anyway, if he understood her correctly, and Ken was fairly certain that he did, the impression he got was Jennifer's previous husband was an absolute asshole. Needless to say, that happens sometimes and like you might think, that's where she made up her mind to dump her husband. Of course, without having actually met the man, he wasn't able to confirm that however due to recent developments, he concluded, that was probably the case. Anyway, as for dealing with Maude, sooner or later, he would have to make a decision on whether or not he would stay married to her or move onto greener pastures with Jennifer. If he did the latter, Ken stood to lose a lot of money. In fact, there was a very good chance, it's the reason why she was pursuing him. She knew Ken's wife was a very bankable writer so there was a good possibility that might be the case. In truth, Maude was a filthy rich woman these days, so he had all the motivation in the world to patch things up with her. Anyway, like you might think, at this point, Ken was giving a lot of serious thought to what he was going to do next. Granted, it wasn't an understatement to say, he liked Jennifer really well however she obviously didn't have the money Maude had either. In conclusion, Ken thought it would be a good idea try and salvage his marriage even though he had some strong reservations about doing so. In reality, as much as he would prefer to stay in a relationship with Jennifer, his better sense of judgment told him that the right thing to do was make amends with Maude and continue on with his life. Anyway, with that highly troublesome thought in the back of his mind, the decision was eventually made to fly up to Oregon with his beloved wife on Friday, which if you haven't guessed by now, had arrived. Logically, this would be a step in the right direction for making amends with Maude, in addition to the fact, it would be taking a much better financial route as well. Obviously, he would have a good idea as to how everything was going to go by the time Sunday afternoon arrived. Actually, there was an outside chance, he might even have an answer before that. As for Maude, she was a woman on a mission and just sort of saying, she had every intention of getting rid of Ken even if it meant going to prison for the rest of her life. Most people would have settled for some type of divorce settlement however in her mind, that wasn't an option. In fact, quite frankly, regardless of how stable her mind actually was, she wasn't going to sleep well until Ken was in the ground. Obviously, if what she was about to do was never meant to be, then so be it. She accepted that as a part of being human even though she knew damn well, it could also mean the end of her life as well. If she got caught, she might get the death sentence, yet, Maude was determined to do what she had set out to do. That was certainly something to be concerned about however as you might have already guessed, she was steadfast in her decision to murder Ken, and nothing in the world was going to change her mind about that. She was truly convinced now was the time to take care of the matter. Of course, that is said from the perspective of a person that more than likely wasn't running on eight cylinders however like everything else in life, many times, it boils down to how that's interpreted by someone else. Beauty is undoubtably in the eye of the beholder, however if a well-planned out infraction of any kind isn't provable, then, it would be safe to say, the person in question should be given the benefit of the doubt. In this particular case, with regards to what she intended to do, one could use the same basis to make an argument on her behalf for Maude's stability of mind. At any rate, everyone has choices in life and Maude had unquestionably made hers, so from her perspective, it was time to rectify a very undesirable situation.

Anyway, as it turns out, everything went off as scheduled and they arrived in Oregon that evening at her Oregon estate, shortly before dark. Like before, she chartered a plane to get them up to the city of Portland, where upon arrival, they rented a car and drove to Tierra Del Mar. The amount of day light that time of year had the sun setting at an early hour however that didn't even come close to dampening her spirits. Part of the reason for that had to do with the fact, it was the holiday season and back home, in Beverly Hills, she was busy with commitments to her kids. In fact, it was a very special time of the year for them as they waited for Santa Claus to pay them a visit. As for Ken, he was hoping to begin working on rebuilding his marriage to Maude over the weekend. Needless to say, things hadn't been going very well between them and as much as Ken hated to admit it, by this time, he concluded, the fault of that happening must have been his own. Anyway, with these thoughts racing wildly through his highly stressed mind, just as soon as they arrived at her estate in Oregon, all of the essential things needed for their weekend getaway was unpacked, and then it was onto the living-room to unwind a bit before calling it a day. There was a lot to talk about. In fact, as much as they would've liked to deny that very obvious statement, it was not possible to do that. There were matters that needed discussing again, none of which they really cared to discuss however in light of the marital problems they were having, it was essential for them to do that, or they would obviously be going separate ways. Actually, for Maude, every minute that went by was one step closer to what she came here to do and that was murder Ken. I suppose, if a person was to look at the situation from a position of neutrality, there was plenty of time over the weekend, not only patch up their marriage but to do something together as well. In reality and as you might think, that was the least of her concerns as she tried to keep her distance from Ken whenever possible. Granted, Maude had been treating him coolly over the past couple of weeks however if she had any intentions of murdering him and she most certainly did, she was going to have to warm the situation up a bit. Needless to say, victory is usually attained from the element of surprise, so it was obviously necessary for Maude act like she wanted to be Ken's best friend again. Perhaps, that wasn't going to be the easiest thing to do however it would be the best way to proceed with the weekend. Anyway, they were both at odds with themselves for the very awkward situation it was, in particularly, Ken. Actually, she had a hell of a lot more certainty set in her mind than he did. Like I said, Maude knew what she wanted to do, and I don't think there was anything in the world that was going to change her mind about that. As you might think, his first thought was to try and address the problem as soon as possible however he eventually came to the conclusion, it would be best to let her bring the subject up and just go along with whatever she wanted to do over the course of the weekend. Needless to say, he didn't want to make things any worse than they already were. As for Maude, the fires of hell were literally blazing away in her eyes so for the time being, he was going to pretend everything was fine. Needless to say, that wasn't a good omen for Ken and as far as Maude was concerned, it was too late to make amends. Regrettably, too much damage had been done for her to travel down that road again. No, Maude was bound and determined to get even with him for his marriage infidelity. In fact, as far as she was concerned, there wasn't anything that was going to save him now. Once again, it would just be a matter of finding the right moment to do what she came here to do. It was as simple as that. Unfortunately, at this point in her conversation with Ken, the actual concept of murder began to resonate loudly through her mind until the sound of the word was deafening. Would she be able to carry out her plan to murder him after all? Once again, Maude began having second thoughts about she wanted to do, in addition to having doubts about her sanity. Obviously, a sane person wouldn't commit murder so that got her to thinking all the more. Perhaps, it wasn't the best thing to do, she thought to herself. Then, another terrible thought gripped her mind. What if the act of murder she was about to commit haunted the hell out of her for the rest of her life? Would she be able to live with herself with something like that on her conscience? Needless to say, right at the moment, Maude was at a loss for words and at odds with her own thoughts because the weight of what she planned on doing was eating away at the back of her mind again. Then, just as quickly as her mind wandered off in the direction of usual disaster, her alter ego took control of her body, reassuring her everything would be fine. Give it some time, she muttered to herself. Of course, upon doing so, Ken immediately picked up on the last thing she said and quickly inquired of her what she was referring too in her mumbling state of mind. He could see she was having a hard time with something. At this point, Maude told him, she was thinking about selling her estate in Oregon and as you might think, that made all the sense in the world to Ken so nothing more was said about it. Anyway, like it so commonly does, the evening went by very quickly, and through it all, Maude tried harder than ever to stay cool, calm, and collected without showing any sign of discontentment with their marriage even though Ken knew darn well something was wrong and that had been the case for a couple of weeks now. In reality, she did not want to alert Ken to the fact he was on her hit list, and this hit list wasn't the kind that falls into the category of reaching number one or being number one. You might even say, this kind of hit list, usually gets a person time in prison. Anyway, it was now very obvious to anyone who was not blind of sight, it would be a question of whether or not, her conscience held up over the weekend and in the days ahead. Actually, right at the moment, the odds of that happening were in her favor because the National Weather Service was calling for severe electrical storms over the weekend. Needless to say, that is what she was hoping for. The truth of the matter is, if everything went as planned, Ken would perish in a horrific blaze of fire. Believe it or not, an unfortunate strike of lightning was going to make a direct hit on her estate in Oregon while he was sleeping and the law enforcement agency in Tierra Del Mar would be led to believe his death was an accident. Surely, it would be a simple matter to take care of. In fact, by this time, an ingenious plan of action had been well formulated inside her mind. Obviously, the first thing Maude had to do was murder Ken. That's where her erroneously registered handgun was going to come in. She would set the estate on fire, and then she would take off down the road with the intentions of getting the hell out of the area as soon as possible. Anyway, with any kind of luck at all, no one would ever know the better of it. She was fairly certain of that. Actually, if she was able to do things this way, she wouldn't have to depend upon the theory of faulty wiring, which in her opinion was a little risky. Anyway, for that reason, Maude had decided to go with plan B because if the weather did what it was supposed to do over the course of the weekend, she would have it made. In truth, that's what she was counting on and perhaps, if things didn't go too badly, that's how everything would turn out. In the meantime, she was trying to stay attentive to what they were discussing so Ken would think she was considering an act of forgiveness that would eventually be bestowed upon him at some point along the way. I believe, it's also safe to say, that wasn't going to happen however it was to her advantage for him to think that for everything to fall into place the way she wanted it too. Anyway, as it turns out, a little while later, after having watched television for the better part of the evening, it was decided they would call it a day. Actually, Ken was the one who suggested they do that and as you might think, she went along with his desire to go to bed. Unfortunately, it was a very awkward feeling for her though because she hadn't slept with Ken for a couple of weeks. In this particular case, it was also quite apparent, she was very adamant about making Ken believe their marriage was on the road to recovery and as you might think, that was a hard thing for her to do. Anyway, Maude reluctantly headed off to bed with him, hoping in the worst possible way he would be happy that she was giving him a piece of her ass. In reality, he was probably getting that from Jennifer over the course of the past couple of weeks anyway however she had already deemed this a necessary action in order to gain his trust again. Actually, it was a very undesirable situation, but it was the only way she would ever be able to succeed in what she wanted to do. In fact, if Maude had her information right, at some point during the weekend, she would more than likely be able to take matters into her own hands, which in this case meant, Ken didn't have very long to live. At any rate, a barrier as wide as the Mississippi River stood between them, and for that reason, she was hoping to put this miserable chapter of her life behind her this weekend. Actually, she had until Sunday to get what she came here to do taken care of and like a true optimist she was certain her endeavor to put Ken in the ground would turn out to be successful. Anyway, after going through the motions of absorbing some of his unwanted love making, much to her delight, Ken fell asleep seemingly satisfied with what he had accomplished in bed that night. As for Maude, it turns out, she didn't immediately fall asleep but that was due to the fact she was engrossed in deep thought. In fact, to be more precise, she was praying for the worst possible electrical storm to ever hit the area. In the meantime, she closed her eyes and tried to get some rest. She would know when the time was right to take the appropriate action and it goes without saying, the moment of truth had not yet arrived.

CHAPTER 41

Somewhere in the early morning hours of dawn, Maude awoke to the sound of thunder echoing off in the distance. A flash of light followed, then silence filtered through the air for a moment or two. At this point, excitement as well as adrenaline began to flow through her veins. It was the severe electrical storm she was hoping for. Now, she would be able to go ahead with her plan to get rid of Ken. In fact, right at the moment, that is what she wanted to do more than anything in the world. Then, a smile appeared on her face. Ken won't know what hit him, she thought to herself. Soon, another clasp of thunder echoed about the perimeters of her bedroom. Another flash of lightning followed. By this time, she was literally ecstatic because it appeared all her prayers had been answered. Anyway, as you might expect, a hard pouring rain was soon beating down upon the roof of the house and in the course of a few minutes, the area was amidst a severe electrical storm. At any rate, now more delighted than a pig in shit, her overall desire to make

Ken pay for what he did to her came to the surface of her complex personality. In fact, as stated before, as far as she was concerned, divorce wasn't an option, however murder was and it goes without saying, that's the course of action she had decided upon. Anyway, after giving her anticipated action a little more thought, the need to get even with Ken eventually won out in her mind. At this point, she took a long slow deep breath and gently rolled over in bed to see if Ken was awake. He was sleeping. Thank god for tranquilizers, she thought to herself. Obviously, if she had any chance of succeeding in her endeavor this evening, it would be necessary to have the element of surprise on her side. Anyway, now satisfied this was the opportunity she was looking for, she quietly slipped out of bed and walked over to the bureau where she had taken the time to hide the handgun she purchased for getting rid of Ken. By now, it was extremely apparent, there would never be a better opportunity to do what she wanted to do than now. At any rate, she was quick to glance at the clock on the nightstand next to her bed. It was five minutes after the hour of three o'clock. The perfect moment had finally arrived. Anyway, there, in the quiet stillness of the night, Maude began fumbling around the inside of the top draw of the bureau in an attempt to find the handgun she had conveniently put there after arriving in Tierra Del Mar. Unfortunately, as she did, the quiet stillness of the night began to reverberate loudly through her head until she felt like screaming. Another moment went by. Needless to say, Maude was feeling a bit uneasy again as guilt came rushing to the forefront of her mind. If the unthinkable happened, she would go to prison. Certainly, not a very pleasant thought however that is what she was thinking about at that point in time. In fact, quite frankly, an inner voice inside Maude's head kept telling her to abandon her plan to murder Ken. Caution, she told herself. Murdering Ken Stackford or anyone else for that matter is against the law. Then, she began to recoil in fear at what the consequences of an action like that would be. Another moment or two moment by, yet she was still struggling with her intentions to murder Ken. Needless to say, indecisiveness was tugging at her heart. By now, she was having second thoughts. At this point, she took another deep breath as perspiration began to roll down the side of her face. Then, as the practicality of the situation filtered through her highly distraught mind, she glanced at the clock on the nightstand one more time. It was now 3:15 in the morning. Time was going by quickly. If she didn't act soon, she wouldn't be able to get rid of Ken. The truth of the matter was it would be light soon, and he would be waking up so she couldn't afford to waste another minute thinking about what she was going to do. Then, once again, she began questioning her motive for murdering Ken. At this point, she wasn't sure if she could do it. Worse yet, what if she didn't get away with it? What if the law figured out what she did and locked her up in prison? In fact, just that thought alone was enough to make her re-think her actions. Furthermore, was it the right thing to do? From the legal side of it all, no, it wasn't and morally speaking, murder was a sin in the eyes of god. What if god actually struck her dead for giving the son of a bitch what he deserved. Then, she shuddered at the thought of that. That was definitely not what she had in mind however she didn't have any control over that. Anyway, while trying to keep all of this in perspective, Maude very slowly began to load up the magazine of the handgun with bullets. Obviously, if she was going to go through with this act of murder, it was time to inflict her punishment on Ken. At this point, she took another deep breath of air and turned around to face the bed he was sleeping in. More thunder and lightning crashed outside the house as the stillness of the night was broken by the sound of the severe electrical storm that was passing through the area however Ken continued to sleep soundly. Actually, it was a miracle, he was sleeping through the entire thing but she quickly noted, that was to her advantage so with the handgun placed securely in her right hand, she walked over to the side of the bed where Ken was sound asleep. It was time to put the son of a bitch in the ground, she thought to herself. Then, in a brief flash of memory recall, Maude started thinking about the first time he broke her heart and once again, she wanted to cry out in agony. Yet, she remained strong in her conviction to murder him as she tried to brush off the emotional pain of that past injustice. Needless to say, regardless of how badly Maude wanted to change the past, there wasn't any way she could do that, so it was senseless to dwell on it. Then, she thought about what happened a couple of weeks earlier, when she found him screwing around with another woman. It was extremely heart breaking to say the least! Actually, Maude thought for sure he had grown up enough to accept the responsibility that went along with being married however much to her disappointment, he hadn't. In fact, Ken had done it to her again. Another moment went by and the rain continued to beat down upon the roof of the house. At this point, Maude took one last look at her beloved husband. Damn that cursed son of a bitch, she thought to herself. In fact, quite frankly, now, more than ever, she detested the ground Ken Stackford walked upon. Then, she cursed his name beneath her breath one last time, knowing darn well he had used her again. Needless to say, it was undoubtably time to give Ken his just reward for his infidelity. Then, with the profound courage of a woman on a mission, she spoke his name out loud. Much to Maude's surprise, he didn't awaken. Perhaps, she didn't say his name loud enough, she thought to herself because he should've heard what she said. Another second or two went by, then, she said his name again. Still, there wasn't any response. The fact of the matter is she wanted to let Ken know what she thought of him and the only way she could do that was to have his attention. He continued to sleep soundly. Finally, on her third attempt to wake him up, Ken opened his eyes and blankly stared at her through the darkness of the dimly lit room. "Do you know what time it is," he exclaimed! Then, long before Ken had a chance to say another word, at a distance of three or four feet away from the bed, she began pumping his body full of bullets. "You god damn ungrateful son of a bitch," she yelled! "May you rot and burn in hell for what you did to me! You're a great big asshole, Ken! In good faith, I put my trust in you again, and you let me down. In fact, quite frankly, you broke my heart. Well, just in case there's any question about it, this is the end of the road, Romeo," she finished saying as she emptied the entire contents of the revolver into his body. There, it's done, she thought to herself. Now, there wouldn't be any reason to agonize over that asshole any longer. At this point, Maude bent down over his limp body to check for a pulse and as you might think, there wasn't any. He was deader than dead. Now, it would just be a matter of covering up her footsteps and then, she would be on her way. It was unquestionably an unfortunate matter however everything was going as planned so just as soon as Maude tied up a couple of loose ends, she would make a quick and methodical retreat. At any rate, it was obviously in her own best interest not to leave any clues behind as to who may have done this. Needless to say, the whole thing was supposed to look like an accident and if she had anything to do with it, that is how the police would view it. Anyway, with that in mind, she quickly tucked the handgun back into her purse and got dressed. Then, Maude took a moment to gather up all the shell casings from the bullets she used and then, she went out to the boathouse to get one of the gasoline cans that were stored there. Thankfully, they were still full so you might say, she had fuel to fan the fire that was about to erupt inside Ricky's old house. It also goes without saying, that's what Maude needed to finish the undesirable job she was now in the process of doing. At any rate, with the can of gasoline in hand, she hurried back to the house because it would be light soon. Obviously, time was of the essence so Maude went back upstairs to the bedroom Ken slept in and doused his body with gasoline. Then, she walked over to where his cigarette lighter sat upon the top of his nightstand and picked it up, before walking back over to the bed. At this point, with the now partially empty can of gasoline tucked beneath her arms, she set fire to the bed and to the floor surrounding it. Suddenly, the room burst into flames and a moment later, a very appreciative Maude Derringer raced down the stairs and out the front door. Now, with any luck at all, by the time someone realizes the house is on fire, it will be too late to do anything. Anyway, before leaving the property, she brought the gasoline can back out to the boathouse and then, after making sure the door to the building was locked, with her purse in one hand and a set of keys in the other, Maude headed for her rented car. It was undoubtably time to make her getaway because the building would go up in flames shortly. At any rate, with that in mind, she got in the car, started the engine and she sped off down the road. Needless to say, she was headed for the city of Portland. In fact, if

everything went as planned, Maude would catch a flight out of Portland International Airport and fly back to Los Angeles. For obvious reasons, she didn't make reservations ahead of time so she wasn't certain how long it would take to get in and out of the airport. Anyway, by the time she made it to the airport that day, the sun was beginning to rise however with it being the month of December, that was to be expected. Actually, the most important thing of all was she had gotten away from Ricky's old estate without anyone being the wiser for it. At any rate, upon making her arrival at the airport, Maude took care of the rental car and immediately booked a flight on the next commercial jetliner headed to Los Angeles. As you might think, the plane Maude chartered to Portland the day before was only a one-way flight so it was necessary to do what she did. Of course, the original plan was to drive back to Beverly Hills on Sunday afternoon with Ken however that wasn't going to happen now. In fact, if and when an inquiry was made into her husband's disappearance, Maude would say, Ken chose to stay behind in Tierra Del Mar to catch up on some badly needed rest. Needless to say, it sounded like a good alibi to her. Furthermore, since Maude's maid as well as a few of her close friends knew she was having marital problems, she was fairly certain no one would give a second thought to the reason why she flew back to California alone. Anyway, her departing flight back to California left right on schedule at eight o'clock that morning and a couple of hours later, she was back in the city of Los Angeles. At any rate, from the airport terminal, she took a taxi and by nine o'clock, she was at her home in Beverly Hills. Thankfully, everything went as planned and Maude could not have been any happier that it had. Anyway, upon arriving at her estate, she quickly informed her maid Ken had decided to stay in Tierra Del Mar until the following day to try and finish up some very important paperwork for ComTech. Then, she went onto to say, with it being the holiday season, she didn't see anything wrong with coming home and spending the time with her children while Ken tried to work things out on paper for ComTech. In reality, that's what she planned on doing anyway however more importantly, what she said seemed to appease the mind of her maid so for the time being anyway, nothing more was said about the matter. In the meantime, Maude was at a loss for how to proceed amidst some very rough waters in the days ahead however like always, whenever the going got tough, she always managed to find a way to move forward, and such was the case this time as well.

CHAPTER 42

L ater that afternoon, Maude received a call from the Tierra Del Mar police department. It wasn't an unexpected call by any means. In fact, you might say, it was call she had anticipated at some point along the way. It was just a question of when, that's all. Anyway, she quickly braced for the worst, while the person in charge of the investigation spoke to her about the property she owned in Tierra Del Mar. First of all, as a matter of formality, he told her that he had some news to share with her and then, he furthermore stated, as much as he would prefer not to be the bearer of bad news, he said it was his duty to do so. At that point, an overwhelming whirl of fear began to well-up inside of her for obvious reasons. Needless to say, Maude was concerned about what the cause of the fire was determined to be. Of course, that was something she was already aware of due to her involvement in the unfortunate event that happened that weekend, nevertheless, she had to sound surprised because she didn't want the officer who was conducting the investigation to think she had something to do with it. At this point, panic began to set in because if they were to suspect foul play like arson or worse yet, someone murdered her husband, Maude was in deep shit. At any rate, she literally held her breath in suspense as the officer told her about what they thought may have happened to her house in Tierra Del Mar. In fact, the man said it really wasn't all that uncommon for a strike of lightning to make a direct hit on a house and burn down but the truth of the matter is, the actual cause of the fire had not yet been determined. He said the matter was under investigation though however all indications seem to point to a strike of lightning. As for the rest of the property, no damage had been done. The boathouse, the lighthouse and Ricky's old yacht were still there. Actually, when she set everything in motion earlier in the day, she was not sure how everything would turn out in the end, so part of what the man told her was news of things she knew nothing about. Anyway, if things continued to head in the right direction during the course of the investigation, she wouldn't have anything to worry about, and as far as she was concerned, that's all that really mattered. At this point, she took a deep breath, not knowing what the officer was going to say next. In fact, there was actually a bit of a pause in their conversation as the man she was speaking with tried to assess the situation. Needless to say, he had to decide how he was going to bring to light the rest of what he had to tell her. Anyway, with some taxing reluctance, the man went onto say there was one other thing she had to be made aware of. Much to her supposed disappointment, the remains of a body was found in the charred aftermath of the fire. At this point, Maude said her husband was supposed to have been staying in Tierra Del Mar over the weekend, which in turn prompted an obvious ghast of surprise from her, oh my god, you mean to tell me my husband perished in that fire. Then, she quickly tried to act the part of a very upset woman, who, when they find out their beloved is dead is extremely distraught. At any rate, that prompted the officer to say, as of yet, no one had filed a missing person's report so he was a bit puzzled by who the identity of the man that perished in the fire might be but now that Maude had shed a little light onto the situation, the officer said he would look into the matter further for her. The truth of the matter was the incident was under investigation, however he did stipulate, it appeared, the origin of the fire wasn't arson and that it was probably a strike of lightning that had burned the house to the ground. Of course, if any new information came along that may change the direction of the investigation. At this point, he did pass along his deepest sympathy to her if that was indeed her husband who perished in the fire. Once again, he did say, the identity of the man had not yet been determined, however based on what she told him, it was very likely it was her husband. At any rate, once she regained her composure, Maude went onto inform the officer her husband wasn't supposed to be home until later in the day on Sunday so she didn't have any reason to suspect anything was wrong. Not only was that part of her alibi but it's also the reason why she didn't file a missing person's report. Needless to say, the officer quickly swallowed the entire story that was given to him, hook, line, and sinker. Actually, in reality, for all either one of them knew Ken could have left her estate in Oregon before the old house was struck by lightning and may have been on his way back home to Beverly Hills at that very moment. Anyway, at this point in their conversation, he apologized for being so vague about things however the reality of it all was, not much more could be said about the matter until a thorough investigation was done. In fact, she would have to be patient while the law enforcement agency in Tierra Del Mar looked into the matter. If and when they had more information to share with her, he would let her know. At any rate, without anything else needing to be said, their conversation soon came to an end but as anticipated, the telephone call she had been expecting left things up in the air a little as to what her future might hold. Anyway, immediately following the conversation with the police office in Tierra Del Mar, she got into her liquor cabinet and made herself a drink. To be more precise, she made herself a gin and tonic. Then, after taking a few deep breaths of less than fresh air into her lungs, she went back into the living-room to explain to her maid what the officer from Tierra Del Mar was calling about. Needless to say, she thought it would be best to keep her abreast of what was going on, not only with the whereabouts of Ken, but with her property in Oregon as well.

Anyway, the next couple of days were spent sitting around the house on pins and needles waiting for an answer from the Tierra Del Mar police department that would say what caused the fire and what happened to her husband. Unlike most days where time usually went rocketing by, such was not the case for Maude. At any rate, she eventually accepted that fact and tried to keep busy until she heard from the law enforcement agency in Oregon. In the meantime, the suspense of what they might determine continued to badger the hell out of her mind. Finally, six or seven days later, she received another call from the police department in Tierra Del Mar, only this time, the officer in charge of the investigation said there wasn't any evidence to support either arson or homicide. The fire was thought to have been caused by a strike of lightning and her husband met his end through asphyxiation. Furthermore, DNA samples determined the badly charred remains of the body found in the upstairs bedroom of her house were Ken's. It was conclusive. What she didn't totally understand was no mention at all was made of anyone finding traces of gasoline on his clothes, but she had already decided if that conclusion was reached, she was going to say Ken had been working on his boat the previous evening, and probably just fell asleep with his clothes on. At any rate, that was not determined and in the end, she didn't have to fabricate anymore lies to cover up for what she did. Anyway, as you might think, the man in charge of the investigation gave Maude her condolences and in the due course of another moment or two, their conversation came to an end. At this point, she realized everything was going to be alright after all. In fact, it was now obvious, she was free and clear of any wrongdoing. Thank god everything worked out for the best, Maude thought to herself. Then, not unlike a person who wasn't playing with a full deck of cards, she began to gloat at her accomplishment. Needless to say, she had literally gotten away with murder, and no one was the wiser for it. As a matter of fact, in Maude's opinion, Ken Stackford got just exactly what he deserved and she felt no remorse whatsoever for what she did.

Anyway, after this new revelation of information, none of which Maude wasn't aware of, she had a couple of loose ends to take care of before the matter would finally be laid to rest. The first thing she had to do was inform the company Ken worked for that he would not be returning to work. Actually, as you might think, when Ken didn't show up for work on Monday, ComTech, inquired about his whereabouts however it wasn't until now, that Maude was able to give them a definite answer as to what happened to her husband. At any rate, once that was taken care of, the next thing she did was buy a plot of land in a neighboring community cemetery and then, she had his ashes buried in an unmarked grave. Anyway, once that matter was out of the way, she made a call to her insurance agent to let him know her property in Oregon had burned flat to the ground. Then, like anyone else would do, she filed an insurance claim for the loss of her estate, and soon everything was all taken care of.

In the meantime, with the despicable Ken Stackford matter taken care of, she concluded, there wasn't any sense of dwelling on the past any longer so it stands to reason, now, she would be able to turn her attention to some other things. In fact, in literally no time at all, happy days had descended upon her again, and soon destiny found her putting together some new ideas for another work of literature. As always, time passed by very quickly and long before she realized it, the holiday season was over, and another year had come and gone. Then, spring was quick to arrive and with it came a new hope for better days ahead. Obviously, the past fall and winter had not been very good to her however with her optimistic attitude, she began looking ahead to what appeared to be the beginning of a much more promising year. Granted, she just went through her second failed marriage in a matter of a year or so, but she didn't look down upon that as a failing on her part. In fact, as far as she was concerned, both failed marriages were the fault of Ken and Ricky, but she got three beautiful children out of it all and that was something she didn't regret.

Then, with everything seemingly going better than ever that year, one day, along towards the end of May, she received a letter from her first husband. In his correspondence to Maude, he expressed his desire to see her again. Needless to say, she was flabbergasted to say the least. Of all the half-assed, insane things that could have happened to her and now this. Sweet Jesus, Holy mother of Christ, she thought to herself. As unbelievable as it was, Ricky had taken the initiative to see her again. First of all, it didn't come as any surprise to learn his relationship didn't go the way he wanted it too and secondly, because she told him she never wanted to see him again, she couldn't believe he would be so ignorant as to want to get back together with her again. In fact, as much as she hated to say it, both of her husband's had a very strong desire to be with women, in particularly, attractive women so when she learned Ricky's latest relationship didn't work out for him, that's more or less what she thought would happen. At any rate, she wrote right back to him saying, she would think about what he said. In truth, it didn't actually hurt to see him again just as long as she didn't commit herself to another relationship with the man. Anyway, it was a very difficult decision for her to make, regardless of whether or not she was actually running on eight cylinders. Obviously, that was debatable, however everything seemed to indicate that was the case because at this point, her diabolical mind concluded, she was going to murder Ricky as well. Of course, that decision more than likely had a lot to do with the fact, she had gotten away with murdering Ken so why not do it again. The truth of the matter is, there wasn't another more deserving man of that honor than Ricky anyway so Maude quickly concluded, she would murder him as well. In fact, that's what she wished she would have done when she found out Ricky was having an affair with another woman during the time they were married in France. Surely, that's not an excuse for doing something above the law however that's how she felt about it. Needless to say, he was the other person she gave credit to for ruining her life. At any rate, be so as it may, she was now more determined than ever to get even with him as well. Obviously, that meant she would have to commit another act of cold-blooded murder however that could be arranged easily enough. She would have to do things a little differently this time though because she didn't have the house in Oregon anymore. Actually, at this time, she still owned the property, the lighthouse, and his old yacht, but the house was gone so there was still a couple of possibilities there. In the meantime, she returned Ricky's call, saying if he wanted to come over and see where things went that was fine with her just as long as he realized, she wasn't getting married again. At any rate, it was apparently what he wanted to hear because within seconds of having said this, Ricky said he would make arrangements to fly to California sometime the following day. Needless to say, that meant if everything went as planned, he would be in Beverly Hills in a couple of days. Anyway, after exchanging a couple of stories, and talking about their current state of affairs, Maude stated there were some things she had to attend too and shortly thereafter, their conversation came to an end. In truth, she didn't want to talk to him any longer than she had too because

Ricky wore out his welcome with her when they were living together as a family in France. Furthermore, if you haven't guessed it by now, she wasn't the kind of person to forgive someone over a wrongdoing either. It just simply wasn't her nature to do that. At any rate, after thinking things over for a bit, she also went onto speculate, perhaps, Ricky had an ulterior motive for wanting to see her again. Surely, he wasn't numb enough to think she would marry him again. That wouldn't happen in a hundred and ten million years, she thought to herself. No, she was much too good of a person to consider doing something as foolhardy as that. Admittedly, Ricky was a very charming man but there wasn't any way she was going to let him back into her life. She was certain of that. No, on the contrary. Ricky was a marked man. In fact, even if he got down on his knees and begged her to take him back, she had no intentions of doing so. Her mind was made up. Ricky was going to go down the same way Ken had and there wasn't anything in the world that was going to change her mind about that. Needless to say, Mr. Vestellini had created too much emotional pain for her to look at it any other way, however that matter was thought to have been behind her for a while now. No, after that terrible falling out they had in France, Maude wasn't about to reconcile with him over anything although as stated before, it did come as a surprise he wanted to see her again. Needless to say, she wasn't sure of his reason for wanting to do that, but she was fairly certain it had nothing to do with wanting to get back together so she eventually came to the conclusion, it was his steadfast desire to see his children again that would bring his unwanted presence back to her door. In fact, as per their divorce agreement, Mr. Vestellini had been granted visiting rights to see his children if he wanted too but until now, Ricky hadn't made any attempt to do that. At any rate, regardless of what his reason was for wanting to come to see her and the kids, the truth of the matter was, in a couple of days, she would have to deal with his unwanted presence at her home in Beverly Hills. In the meantime, more undesired uncertainty began to torment her mind again as the course of her destiny was about to take shape one more time.

CHAPTER 43

As fate would have it, a couple of days later, Ricky was knocking on the front door of her Beverly Hills estate. Unlike most days, on this occasion, Maude went to the door to see who was calling. Usually, that's one of the things her maid took care of however she was expecting Ricky to show up at her house at any time so she took the initiative to do that herself today. Anyway, as she thought, Ricky Vestellini was indeed standing outside the door of her estate. The moment of truth had finally arrived. Whether she liked it or not, they would meet again. It was not going to be an easy thing for her to deal with however she would find a way to do it. At any rate, with the future course of her destiny having landed at her door, there weren't too many options left to her. In fact, little did Ricky know he was about to step into the final chapter of his life, or I'm sure he would have made plans to go elsewhere. As for her reaction when she saw Ricky standing at the front door of her estate, well, you might say, it wasn't the usual, it's nice to see you again. How have you been? That sort of thing. No, on the contrary. On this occasion, without any affection whatsoever and with circumstances as they were, she was as cool as a cucumber upon seeing her ex-husband again. At any rate, after a brief exchange of words, Maude asked him into the house. As expected, there was a bit of tension in the air between them and the situation was awkward to say the least. Anyway, in trying to be as polite and cordial as possible, she immediately offered to make him a drink and much to her surprise, he accepted her offer. Actually, if she had been in his shoes, she would've been concerned about being poisoned to death. Obviously, that was not the case however it was the first thing she thought of when she got him his drink. Anyway, with both of them being at a total loss for words, she showed him into the living-room, where he took a seat and they proceeded to get caught up on what was going on in their lives. It was a whiskey and tonic for Ricky and a fruit flavored rum punch for her. Usually, Maude had gin and tonic but this time she opted to have something different. At any rate, the first thing they talked about was how his flight to the United States went. Obviously, that wasn't a touchy subject to talk about so their conversation began there. Anyway, at no surprise to her, she found out, he didn't encounter any problems flying from France to Los Angeles, so the first part of their conversation went very well indeed. Ricky did say, he was suffering a little jet lag though but that was to be expected on a flight of that distance. Anyway, as it turns out, in what amounted to a very short period of time, one thing quickly led to another and soon they were talking about how things were going. All in all, their conversation moved along rather nicely, and it continued to do so until Maude mustered up enough courage to tell him he had a son. Needless to say, no mention of little Ricky was ever made to her first husband, however the moment she made him aware of this, he expressed a real genuine interest in seeing him. Of course, Maude being just as rotten as she possibly could in a very subtle manner, showed him around the house first. After fifteen to twenty minutes went by, she led him into a large playroom that her children used when they got out of school during the week. On this occasion, it was Saturday so both girls were home. In fact, they were actually out in the yard playing a game of tag when she pointed Ricky's daughters out to him through a large picture window inside the playroom. As to what the girls were doing, you might say, it was sort of a routine they followed from one week to the next and since it was Saturday, tag just happened to be one of the things they usually did on weekends. Obviously, like any father who hasn't seen his children in a while, Ricky quickly commented on how much they'd grown since the last time he saw them. At any rate, they proceeded to discuss the girls for a few minutes. Things like how they were doing in school were talked about. Finally, at her insistence, he went out into the yard to meet them. It was another very awkward moment. Neither one of the girls actually knew him because they were at too young of an age when their parents divorced. Anyway, after a couple of minutes went by, the brief interaction between Ricky and his two daughters were over so she had him follow her back into the house, where they proceeded to go upstairs and down a hall until he and Maude were standing in the doorway of a young child's bedroom. It was little Ricky's room. At this point, he looked in where the young boy was sleeping and admired his son for a moment, and then in not wanting to disturb him, Ricky followed her downstairs to the living-room where he learned they would be eating shortly. Actually, there were all kinds of other things that had to be discussed as well and sitting down at the dinner table would give an opportunity to do that. At least that's what the original plan was anyway however after some more catching up on what was going on in their lives, Maude unexpectedly suggested they go out for supper. Needless to say, it was something she seldom did, and it certainly wasn't the original plan, but when she learned the pot roast that was supposed to have been served for supper was burnt to a crisp, another plan was soon decided upon. They would dine out for supper that evening. In fact, since it was still early in the day, she was able to take the kids with her as well. Obviously, that wasn't always possible however this time Vanessa and Margaret were going with them. The maid would be able to look after little Ricky while they were out, so things were all taken care of. The truth of the matter is, he thought that was a great idea so it was decided, they would have supper at one of her favorite places to eat, which in this particular case was the Five Star Restaurant. As to how the restaurant actually got its name, that's anyone's guess however their food was rumored to be good so that is where they were going. Furthermore, it was only a short distance away from her house and with it being a casual no reservations required restaurant, it fit the occasion well. At any rate, they all had a good meal at the Five Star Restaurant and along towards the hour of seven o'clock, Maude gave Ricky the signal, it was getting close to the girl's bedtime so about fifteen to twenty minutes later, they left the restaurant in favor of going back to her house. Of course, it wasn't yet decided where Ricky would stay for the night so there was a bit of uncertainty in the air. Actually, at this point, the only thing she was certain of was she was going to murder Ricky just like she did Ken. In fact, it would be just a question of whether or not she got away with it again, that's all. As for how and where she got rid of Ricky, it would be in Oregon, but the details of how she was going to do it had not yet been decided. The truth of the matter is over the course of the past few hours Maude had run the idea through her head so many times that it felt like she had already murdered the man a couple of times over. At any rate, while that thought continued to eat away at the back of her mind, they drove back to her estate.

Anyway, by the time they returned home, the two girls were beginning to get tired, so she had the maid take them upstairs to get them ready for bed. Needless to say, at this point, the rest of the evening was Ricky and Maude's to do whatever they wanted however it was very doubtful it would be anything too memorable because she had too much hate and resentment inside of her for anything good to come out of the evening. Anyway, like when he arrived at her house earlier in the day, at her request, they headed into the living-room to have another drink. In fact, Maude thought it was best to get him a little intoxicated before she set her plan into motion so where the evening would lead too was unclear however in spite of her unquenchable thirst to get even with Ricky for what he did to her in France, perhaps, something good would come out of things after all. At any rate, after having made a couple drinks, she asked Ricky if he would like to fly up to Tierra Del Mar for the weekend with the intentions of spending some time on his old yacht. You know, like going deep sea fishing. Needless to say, it was something he enjoyed doing so Maude thought it would be the perfect way to get him there. Well, it turns out, that was the case. Ricky liked the idea so what she suggested was easily agreed upon. At this point, she took a moment to tell him about what happened to his old estate in Tierra Del Mar. As you may recall, after a very thorough investigation was done by the Tierra Del Mar police department, it was determined, the house was struck by a bolt of lightning and burned flat to the ground as a result of it. In addition to that, she elaborated further on how her second husband lost his life in that horrible fire. Then, she went onto explain in more depth, she had only been married for a couple of months when the tragedy struck. Of course, she stretched the truth a little by telling him she was heartbroken over the loss of her husband however with all do honesty, she couldn't have cared less what happened to him. Anyway, Ricky immediately expressed his sorrow to her over what happened, saying she didn't deserve to go through a traumatic event like the one she went through even though it most certainly happens sometimes. Then, not unexpectedly, he took a moment to thank her for giving him the opportunity to see her and the kids, however Maude quickly brushed the comment aside because she didn't have any interest in seeing him again. The truth of the matter is, she was very disenchanted with him over his marriage infidelity however at some point along the way, he had to make amends with her if what he wanted to do was going anywhere. Of course, there was no better time than the present to do that and perhaps, that's what he had in mind when he made the decision to see her again. Obviously, there wasn't any way to be certain of that, nor was there a way to change the past however for the first time since they divorced, Ricky apologized for that injustice. In fact, he further stated, it was something he regretted every day of his life but in most instances, once hurtful words are said to someone, it's difficult to undo the damage that was done and such was the case here as well. At any rate, after the apology was made, Maude didn't waste any time telling him she was making out just fine without him. Of course, that wasn't at all what he wanted to hear because that meant they would not be getting back together again. In truth, his exact plans had left her guessing as to what his intentions really were, but it was now obvious, he wanted to get married again even though she had no desire to do so. At this point, he wasn't sure how to proceed so he took a minute to think about what she said. In fact, he was quick to realize, either he had to get down on his knees and beg for forgiveness or destiny would more than likely end up sending him back to the French Riviera alone. Obviously, there were other options Ricky could pursue however his mind was set on Maude. Anyway, tension was mounting as she waited for an answer from Ricky with regards to her suggestion, they go fishing this weekend. Actually, he didn't see anything wrong with doing that however that wasn't what he was hoping to gain by having come all the way over to the United States to see her. At any rate, after a brief moment of silence, Ricky said he would go fishing with her. In reality, that was something he enjoyed doing anyway so what the hell, he didn't see any harm in doing that with her. Anyway, after a few very long tense seconds of indecision on his part, Ricky agreed to take his old yacht out, one last time. Of course, Maude was the one who owned the boat now, but just as soon as Ricky was no longer around, she was going to sell it. In the meantime, everything was headed in the direction Maude wanted it too. They would go to Tierra Del Mar; she would rent a room at one of the fine hotels in the area and sometime the following day, she would get even with Ricky for what he had done to her. Needless to say, when that happened, she would feel redeemed in the eyes of God and in the end, she would be free from the emotional pain he caused her, and everything would be fine.

Now, with regards to the rest of their conversation that evening, she had no intentions of marrying him so that matter was quickly brushed aside in favor of talking about the children they had together, and what the future may hold for them in the days ahead. Then, after a little while, their conversation took an even more conservative direction as they touched down upon some of the things that were going on in the news at the time. In addition to that, they also talked about a lot of other things as well but in the end, nothing was accomplished in the area of getting married again. That just simply wasn't going to happen. In fact, even the prospect of being good friends didn't appeal to her so there wasn't really anything else he could do. He did have visiting rights to see the children whenever he wanted too and that was something she had to honor.

At any rate, when it came time to go to bed, she gave him one of the guest rooms to sleep in. There wasn't any way she would sleep with him again so that was an easy decision for her to make. Actually, on Ricky's part, a little rest was in order. Needless to say, he was still suffering from a little jetlag, so he was content to call it a day anyway. As for Maude, she couldn't believe he would be numb enough to want to get back together with her again. To see his children, yes! That she could comprehend but to get married again was ludicrous to say the least. Actually, she was still a bit puzzled by his desire to do that however along towards the hour of nine o'clock, it didn't matter anymore. They had both gone to bed although in her case, as sad as it may be, she had only one thing on her mind and that was the number of days till Saturday because it was the precise number of days Ricky had left to live.

CHAPTER 44

They say most things in life happen for a reason and perhaps, that's true but regardless of that supposition, what Maude was about to do definitely fell into that category. Furthermore, as I stated before, because of the unlawful endeavor she was about to undertake and the previous one she got away with, it was a question of whether or not she was in her right mind. Theoretically, a person could debate that until hell froze over however whatever conclusion is actually derived at, things of that nature are usually very hard to prove. Anyway, be so as it may, after sleeping on it for a couple of nights, she concluded, they would drive up to Tierra Del Mar on Friday. At first, she thought they would fly up to Oregon on Saturday, but for more than one reason, she decided against doing that. They would get up early and head up there on Friday. Of course, as far Ricky was concerned, he didn't care how they got up to Tierra Del Mar so that was more than fine with him. Anyway, as it turns out, when Friday morning arrived, the weather was beautiful. In fact, it was a picture-perfect day in every sense of the word. The sun was shining brightly and without a cloud in the sky, they had a beautiful day to head up the coast to Oregon. As a matter of fact, for anyone who didn't have to work for a living, it was a beautiful day to enjoy. Obviously, for her it was a weekend she intended to use for taking care of business. In this particular case, to be more precise, Maude was going to remedy the Ricky Vestellini problem. That meant as far as she was concerned he was as good as dead. She would commit another act of cold-blooded murder and a very challenging 21st century world as well as herself would be all the better for it. Actually, she was convinced it was the right thing to do. Anyway, as you might think, everything was going as planned and she couldn't have been happier than a pig in shit about it. In fact, quite frankly, she was actually relishing the thought of murdering Ricky during the drive up to Tierra Del Mar that day. For anyone else, it would not have been the proper thing to do however for her, it appeared to be the only logical thing to do. Sadly, she was obsessed with getting rid of Ricky now that he had inadvertently popped back into her life. Yes, time had gone by very quickly. There certainly wasn't any question about that. Then, as Maude pondered the thought of what she intended to do inside her head, once again, second thoughts about the situation began to flood her mind. Could she be making a mistake? The thought had occurred to her but like words that go in one ear and come out the other without making a substantial impression on the person hearing them, the idea was soon forgotten. Anyway, seconds later and totally oblivious to the reality of what was going on outside the perimeters of her mind, Maude began to marvel at what she planned on doing this weekend. Obviously, she was hell bent on getting back at Ricky for what he did to her, however was it necessary to go as far as killing the son of a bitch? Unfortunately, at this point, everything was pointing to the fact, he was going to be the benefactor of her rage. Perhaps, that's stating the nature of the mission she set out to accomplish a bit fastidiously however in truth, that's what she was in the process of doing. Furthermore, and also in reality, it had only been a span of six years or so since she actually moved into Tierra Del Mar, and now, nearly returned to the area again, it was a struggle to push that thought out of her mind because this was where her journey with Mr. Vestellini began. Yes, the bitter side of her innermost feelings were coming to surface during the drive up to Oregon. Granted, the time that was once spent together there had the beginnings of the most pleasant adventure you could ever imagine but it turned into a nightmare in France. At least, from her prospective it was anyway. She was certain Ricky looked at it differently, but the damage was done, and she wanted to get even with him for his careless promiscuity even though it happened some time ago now. At any rate, such were the thoughts running through her head as they traveled through northern California and on into Oregon. In fact, that would continue to be the case until they reached their final destination with that being Tierra Del Mar. In reality, since that's where it all began for them, it was only fitting, that is where it all should end for them too.

Anyway, upon arriving in Tierra Del Mar that evening, they found a place to stay. Since, it wasn't a large community, it was also a rather easy thing to do. Actually, she was the one who chose the hotel they would be staying at and she was the one who checked them in as well. Like you might think, Maude stretched the truth a bit by indicating at the front desk, she would be the only occupant in the room. Of course, it goes without saying, while she took care of the business matters, Ricky ran across the street to a local bakery to get some munchies for their breakfast the following morning. Anyway, in a matter of ten or fifteen minutes, not only did she have them all checked into their hotel room, but Ricky was also successful in his endeavor to get some freshly made coffee and donuts, so everything was going as planned. Furthermore, she wanted Ricky to think, they would be staying in Tierra Del Mar for the weekend when in fact, Maude intended to make a quick departure from the area sometime the following day. That in itself, wasn't actually all that hard to do however when tomorrow arrived, she was uncertain about some things. In the meantime, after a quick shower to freshen up a bit, Maude suggested they get something to eat at a nearby restaurant so with that in mind, that course of action was taken. As a matter of fact, that endeavor went very well also. She ordered oysters on the half shell while Ricky opted to indulge on lobster. A little red wine helped round out the evening meal and then, it was back to the hotel they were staying at. So far, so good. Nothing out of the ordinary had happened and it appeared Maude was on track for an appointment with destiny. At least, all indications seemed to point to the fact, Ricky was about to meet his maker. Of course, that was based on the likely premise, she would bring an end to Ricky's life sometime the following day. At any rate, while these thoughts continued to occupy unwanted space inside the innermost caverns of her mind, the remainder of the evening was spent reminiscing about old times with Ricky. Actually, to be a bit more precise, everything they ever did together as a couple was thrown out upon the table, much the same way a person would air out their dirty laundry. Anyway, it was a really difficult evening for her to get through because she despised the ground he walked upon.

Anyway, be so as it may, along towards the hour of eleven o'clock, they decided to call it a day. The thought was, it had been a long and tiresome day, due to the fact much of the day had been spent on the road so a little extra rest wouldn't hurt either one of them. Thankfully, the way everything fell into place, Maude was able to get a room with separate beds, so she wasn't going to have to sleep with Ricky. Furthermore, for all she cared, Ricky could roll over and drop dead, however seeing that wasn't about to happen on its own, she was the first one to opt into going to bed. Actually, Ricky tried to talk her into getting a room with a single, king size bed however his effort to do so fell upon deaf ears. Needless to say, there wasn't any way she would give him her consent to do that so the matter was dropped. That should've been enough to tell Ricky he didn't have a prayers chance in hell of winning her over however he couldn't see the length of his nose, so everything went in the other direction of what he would've preferred. At least, the better part of the evening was conducted on the most pleasantest of terms although that probably would not have been possible without a little alcohol. Anyway, the persona she exuded throughout most of the day was one of lighthearted indifference so when the lights inside the room were shut off that night, Ricky thought he may have gained a little ground in his attempt to remarry her. Sadly, that wasn't even close to the truth however do to the undeniable fact, Maude's diabolical scheme had not been unfruitful, he went to bed with an optimistic outlook. On the other hand, her mind, was set on making it a historic weekend in every sense of the word or better put, it was going to be a weekend to remember. Perhaps, not in the conventional way but it was definitely going to be an unforgettable weekend and with any kind of luck at all, it would be one, Maude would be able to celebrate for many years to come. For most people, that would've meant having a fun adventure together and once upon a time, that would've been the case but that wasn't going to happen now. No, at this point in her life, it was just a question of whether or not she would be able to succeed in her endeavor to murder Ricky. After that, hopefully paradise would descend upon her and all the things that ruined her life would be laid to rest once and for all.

CHAPTER 45

After breakfast the following day, they drove out to Ricky's old estate. Actually, Maude hadn't seen the property since she was there with Ken last December so she didn't have any idea what kind of condition the property was actually in. The house itself had burnt flat to the ground during a severe electrical storm last year however the rest of the property still remained however that had yet to be verified by Maude and there was no time like the present. Anyway, it was only a short drive to the property from where they spent the night in Tierra Del Mar so even though it was a little later than normal for her, it was still early in the day. In fact, by the time they arrived there, it was only a little after nine o'clock in the morning. Needless to say, there was still plenty of time to accomplish what she intended to do so right at the moment, you might say time wasn't of the essence. Everything was going as planned though and that was a good omen. At any rate, upon making their arrival there, she quickly assessed the situation, and concluded, she must have did one hell of a good job in getting rid of Ricky's old estate because there wasn't anything left to the building now with the exception of the old yacht Ricky used to make frequent use of when he lived in Tierra Del Mar. Of course, Maude owned it now and under those circumstances, she was going to take full advantage of that aspect of what he left to her in their divorce settlement. As I said before, the estate had burned to the ground. In fact, the foundation was all that remained of the old house. Actually, the lighthouse was still there in addition to a boathouse that was used for the storage of a few outdoor things. Anyway, not unexpectedly, the better part of twenty minutes to a half hour was spent assessing the damage of the fire. Needless to say, a lot of good, heartfelt memories surfaced over that course of time, however in the end, they both agreed to put that very unfortunate matter behind them. Furthermore, even though a good part of their lives were buried beneath the rubble of that building, it was decided they would go forward with their plans to take his old yacht out for a cruise, and in the process of doing so, he would do a little deep-sea fishing as well. Yes, as unbelievable as it was and with circumstances as they were, Ricky was going to spend a little time fishing on his old boat or perhaps, I should say, that's what he thought he was going to be doing anyway. Unfortunately, little known to him, his profound desire to see Maude was about to bring an end to his life, and there wasn't anything in this world standing in her way from making that happen as Ricky Vestellini was about to become her next murder victim.

Anyway, as anticipated, they walked over to the boathouse where his yacht still remained anchored to the pier. It was the pleasantest of days. There wasn't a cloud in the sky and with not much more than a light breeze, you might say, it was ideal weather conditions for heading out to sea, so everything bode well for her. In fact, they reminisced about days gone by again. A lot of very memorable adventures had taken place in Tierra Del Mar, so it was only natural to savor the thought of some of the things they did together. It can be further stated, every now and then, past attachments become hard to let go of at some point in life, and it just so happens, at this time, she was dealing with similar circumstances. In this particular case, she had always been that kind of person and after taking a beating in two marriages, it was worse than ever for her these days. At this point, everything was still going as planned and as you might think, Maude was as happy as a person could be about that. Anyway, trying harder than ever not to show any sign of weakness for what she was about to do, she boarded the boat with Ricky. Normally, she would have been a little more receptive to his presence however with everything headed in the direction she wanted it to go, she thought it was best to stay emotionally detached from the situation. Needless to say, that meant, she didn't want her conscience bothering her if there was any way possible to prevent that from happening, so while Ricky looked the boat over to ensure it was in good working order, she sat there gloating like a lioness ready to strike its prey. At any rate, fifteen to twenty minutes later, he raised the anchor and they set out to sea while she proceeded to glorify in the soon to be events of his death.

Anyway, with that said, after having departed from the shores of Oregon, and in knowing the course of action she planned on taking, she suggested to Ricky, it might be a good idea not to go too far out to sea so ten or fifteen minutes later, he turned off the engines and dropped anchor. At this point, like a true gentleman, and also so he wouldn't incur her wrath over a trifling matter such as this, Ricky quickly assured her, they would not be going out any further to sea. Needless to say, from her perspective, that was to her advantage because once his poor excuse of a life was done away with, Maude had to head back to shore, so she wanted to be able to get out of the area as soon as possible. Anyway, with nothing more to do than what was already done, a moment or two later, he proceeded to get his fishing gear out of a small compartment on the right side of the deck and began to fish. Everything was going as planned, she thought to herself. Now, with any luck at all, she would be able to wrap up the final chapter of his life. At any rate, by now Maude had regressed into the inner workings of her psyche again, however that wasn't anything unusual for her because she was a very deep person. Then, suddenly, for no practical reason at all, a cold, calculated smile appeared upon Maude's face as she contemplated what she was about to do. At this point, fear and hatred began to filter through her mind as the last few minutes of Ricky's life flashed quickly before her eyes. Needless to say, she just simply couldn't get what he did to her out of her mind. In fact, every time she looked his way, she saw an asshole attached to a fishing pole casting out into the depths of the ocean. Surely, anyone who thought it was best to sleep in another woman's bed while being married to her obviously deserved to die. Yet, no matter how many times she tried to push the matter out of her mind, the thought of Ricky Vestellini banging away at the backside of Mona Aubert continued to torment the hell out of her. It wasn't as if she deserved to be treated badly. No, on the contrary. Not once did she ever do anything bad to him. So, why in the name of Christ did that have to happen to her? She didn't ask to be screwed over by a couple of assholes. Perhaps, she didn't use the best possible judgment in what she did over the course of time, but that didn't justify the actions her husband's took when she was married to them. At this point, Maude vowed to herself one more time, Ricky had to go! There wasn't any question about it. Actually, she would have been all right had he not come back into her life, but that wasn't how everything unfolded, and now with nothing but a desire to kill the son of a bitch, she regressed even further into herself. Ricky was going to get what he deserved and that was an early death. Now, if only her conscience held up, she would be all right. A little more time went by. Still, she reflected on the tragic course of events that had made an absolute wreck of her life. Unfortunately, no matter how many times she ran these thought through her head, she continued to reach the same undeniable conclusion, Ricky deserved to die. In fact, in her opinion he didn't deserve to be treated any better than to receive a burial at sea and you might say, that can be said in the broadest of terms. Obviously, it would be up to her to see that happened and as you might think, she didn't have any intentions of passing up the opportunity. At any rate, while these very troubling thoughts continued to plague the hell out of her mind, time went by quickly. Neither is that an uncommon occurrence, however in this case, with every minute that went by she thought about what had to be done. At this point, a pleasantly warm ocean breeze gently whipped across her face, bringing her around to her senses to where she actually was. Naturally, that brought her out of the deep, preoccupied thoughts her mind was struggling with while at the same time, there wasn't any way she could let go of the past either. Then, she told Ricky, just as soon as she had a bite to eat, she would do a little fishing with him, however in reality, that wasn't going to happen. She had no intentions of doing that. Anyway, he just simply nodded his head in acknowledgment to what she said and continued to fish in the waters around the boat. Thankfully, with some good planning on her part, Maude remembered to pack a lunch for their adventure earlier in the day so there was plenty of food to eat. At this point, she offered Ricky one of the sandwiches she made for them before leaving the shores of Tierra Del Mar, and much to her surprise, he accepted what she had in the way of food. In this particular instance, it wasn't anything to elegant. As a matter of fact, it was a peanut-butter and jelly sandwich. Little did he know that sandwich would be the last meal he ever ate. Anyway, while Maude proceeded to devour her sandwich down as quickly as possible due to an unexpected pang of hunger, Ricky ate his sandwich with one hand and kept fishing with the other. By now, she was watching him from a short distance away and like a die-hard combatant, ready to go to war, she continued to glower at him through the eyes of someone who was lost in the midst of hell. Needless to say, she didn't pity him at all and as far as she was concerned, he had only a few more minutes to live. Then, Maude's conscience began bothering her again. Obviously, Maude was only human, and like most people with an important decision to make, she began questioning her motive for wanting to murder Ricky. Was what she wanted to do a reasonable solution for the injustice she suffered at the hands of his ignorance? Then, to complicate things further, she started thinking about the good times they shared together in days past and the children she had with him. In fact, at one time, Maude loved him more than anyone in the world. Regrettably, she was at odds with herself again. Damn, the human psyche, and the many aspects of a person's intelligence. If only everyone thought alike it would more than likely be a perfect world however real life isn't like that at all. Perhaps, in theory or in a Utopian world that would be the case, however on planet earth, nothing of the sort exists. At this point, she was finding it extremely difficult to concentrate on anything except the course of action she intended to take. Furthermore, regardless of what she might have done in neglecting his personal needs, it wasn't any reason for him going somewhere else to get a piece of ass. All he had to do was bring his need to her attention and that would've fixed the problem right then and there however Ricky didn't do that. He took the deceitful approach and a divorce was the end result of his selfishness. Anyway, slightly dismayed, and at odds with herself, Maude continued to weigh out the pros and cons of committing another act of cold-blooded murder. Needless to say, while these horrendous thoughts took refuge in her mind, time continued to go by. First, ten minutes. Then, another ten minutes and still no decision was made on the matter. Actually, in truth, Maude had made up her mind at least three or four times that Ricky was as good as dead, however each time she gave the situation more thought, she began to question the morality of what she wanted to do. Then, even at somewhat of a surprise to her, she came to the conclusion, Ricky wasn't going to get an ounce of mercy from her. No, on the contrary. She would extract her pound of flesh from him. He was going down. In fact, quite frankly, Ricky was going down in every sense of the word because his grave was going to be at the bottom of the ocean he loved so much. In her opinion, Ricky would get what he deserved and that was death. Yes, that horrific five letter word that has a tendency to change a person's life forever. Granted, everyone has got to go sometime however she would get things moving along a little sooner than he would prefer. Obviously, an early death on his behalf would solve the problem. Yes, it was definitely time to get even with the son of a bitch and with that said, Maude finished the last morsel of her sandwich. Then, she took a deep breath, and was soon reaching down into her purse where she proceeded to pull out the handgun she brought with her, while anger, and the fires of hell continued to blaze away in her eyes. In fact, her emotional state of mind had been stretched to its limit. There wasn't any way she could turn back now. At this point, he was as good as dead. Anyway, tension kept building up inside her distraught mind, yet at the same time, she was determined to go through with her plan to murder Ricky. Since she succeeded in doing it before, she would succeed in doing it again. Then, droplets of perspiration began to roll down the side of her face as she assessed the situation. By now, she was convinced what she came here to do was the right thing to do after all so while he was engrossed in fishing, she took a few steps in his direction. Then, a few more. He had yet to realize, she was creeping up on him from behind. At this point, she took a deep breath. Obviously, if she shot him in the back, it would be a cowardly thing to do so she quickly reassessed the situation and decided that wasn't how she would kill him even though what she was about to do couldn't have happened to a bigger asshole. A couple more seconds went by. She had decided to create a diversion of some kind and then she would shoot him. It would as easy as that. Then, she paused just long enough to take in another deep breath of fresh air, and second or two later, with all the rage and fury of a woman hell bent on getting even with someone for the injustice they caused her, Maude yelled at him saying, "Ricky, you're a cursed piece of shit!" "I'm a what," he exclaimed! "I said you're a cursed piece of shit and I despise the ground you walk upon," she replied. "How dare you come back here to torment me some more after I explicitly told you I didn't want to see you again! In fact, either you have shit for brains or your head's stuck so far up your ass you can't see the light of day!" "How could you say something like that to me," Ricky exclaimed! "Actually, I can see by the gun in your hand, I must have done something else you didn't care for. Is there any way I can make amends to you?" "No, there isn't," she screamed, "but you can rot and burn in hell for what you did to me in France. I gave you my complete trust, and you turned around and threw it away on some worthless whore! How dare you be so damn insensitive to me and our marriage! You deserve no less than hell for what you did and believe it or not, that's where you're headed! Both you and Ken were nothing but assholes who displayed the same promiscuous temperament. As a matter of fact, it's just a question of which one of you had the biggest dick, that's all. Well, just so you know, from what I remember, Ken had that dubious honor. How does that make you feel you little prick?" At this point, Ricky started to say something but Maude immediately kept going on with her soliloquy, keeping the intense bombardment of words flowing freely at Ricky by saying, "It's clear to me all either one of you ever cared about was where you could stick that damn thing. You never cared for me, Ricky! All you wanted was a piece of my ass! I'm certain of that!" "That's not true," he stated. "I loved you dearly and I still do. I mean that with all my heart and soul. I just made a mistake, that's all." "Bullshit," she stated, "and to hell with you for your careless promiscuity." At this point, a disdainful smile appeared on her face, then she made one last statement, "Well, if you haven't guessed it by now, Ricky, it's time to kiss your sorry ass good-bye. This is the end of the road for you. Good-bye, asshole!" Then, long before he had a chance to say another word, she filled his body full of bullets until his body fell onto the deck of the yacht in a pool of blood. At this point, feeling satisfied with what she had done, she began to gloat over her accomplishment even in light of having committed an act of cold-blooded murder. Normally, something like that doesn't give someone a thrill but in her case, it did. Anyway, now it was time to clean up the mess she had made so with that in mind, the moment she came to her senses, she put the handgun back into her purse, and proceeded to where the anchor mechanism of the boat was located and quickly raised the anchor up from the depths of the ocean. Once that was achieved, she got busy with the rest of her plan. Needless to say, Maude had every intention of dumping his body over the side of the boat however it was important it was done the right way because she didn't want his body washing up on shore somewhere so she tied the end of the rope that supported the anchor to his body. Then, after making sure the rope was secure, and with his body hanging over the side of the boat, she used a knife from Ricky's fishing tackle box to sever the rope. At this point, his body as well as the anchor went spiraling down into the depths of the ocean below. The job was done. Maude had succeeded in her endeavor to murder Ricky. Now, it would be just a matter of getting back to the mainland and returning to her home in California so after going to the wheelhouse, she started the engines, and seconds later, destiny found her on the way back to Tierra Del Mar.

In the meantime, like she was so commonly in the habit of doing, Maude set her mind to thinking again, not only about what she had done but also about what the possible consequences of her actions might be. In reality, no one even knew Ricky was back in the United States, so it stands to reason there wouldn't be any reason to search for Ricky's body out in the depths of the Pacific Ocean or anywhere else for that matter. In fact, other than her immediate family, Maude was the only one who knew Ricky was in Oregon, so like a true detective, she began working on an explanation that would explain his current whereabouts. Obviously, he wouldn't be returning to Beverly Hills with her. That was fairly obvious. Furthermore, since she took the extra caution to ensure no one saw them drive up to her estate in Tierra Del Mar, chances are everything would be all right. At least, that's what she was counting on anyway. Actually, this particular stretch of coastline was visibly isolated so the odds of anyone having seen them together was very unlikely. In truth, to the best of her knowledge, the only incriminating evidence anyone could hold against her would be a photograph that depicted them together in Tierra Del Mar but there wasn't any, so she felt confident no one would ever be able to implicate her in anything related to Ricky's death if by some chance his body were to wash up on shore somewhere. Needless to say, Maude didn't think that was very likely, however on the off-hand chance it did, she would defend herself every way possible. At this point, and also from her perspective, it would be just a matter of tying up a couple of loose ends and everything should be all right. The truth of the matter was Ricky didn't have any living relatives, and since he was a loner, she was fairly certain no one would ever look into his disappearance. In the meantime, Maude had made up her mind to brush the matter aside in favor of forgetting Ricky Vestellini ever existed.

At any rate, the way everything unfolded that day, a couple of hours later, Maude was on her way back to California. Furthermore, and as a precautionary measure, before leaving Tierra Del Mar, she had the foresight to intentionally damage the yacht in a couple of places to make it look like the boat was targeted by vandalism. The truth of the matter is she planned on selling it along with the property, however to this point, she hadn't been able to do that. Perhaps, she was asking too much for the property. Granted, the old estate was gone but the lighthouse as well as Ricky's old boat was still there. In fact, she could always try and sell the yacht separately and in the days ahead that was something she would give strong consideration too because she wanted no part of his old estate in Tierra Del Mar anymore. Actually, there were a lot of things to take in to consideration however she was still confident that everything would turn out for the best in the end. As far as her immediate family went, she would say, Ricky changed his mind about getting back together with her and went back to France. Surely, no one, including her maid would ever guess what happened. Obviously, it wasn't the whole truth and nothing but the whole truth but it definitely explained the reason why he didn't come back to California with her and that's all that really mattered. Anyway, as stated before, Maude was on her way home, and with traffic being light, she was able to make it back to Beverly Hills by days end. As a matter of fact, she pulled into the driveway of her estate at about eleven o'clock that evening. All was quiet when she got there and she let herself in through the side door so no one would be awakened or startled by her unexpected return.

The truth of the matter was, she wasn't expected to be home until later in the day on Sunday anyway so to be home late Saturday night might cause her maid to be suspicious. Needless to say, right at the moment that was her biggest concern however everyone had gone to bed so she would deal with her maid and everything else sometime the following day. Then, she thought to herself, yes, it was all in a day's work, and it was going to be a good night after all. If only she could have foreseen, Ricky and Ken were not the right persons for her, perhaps, a more enjoyable life would have emerged from everything she did. Then, not unexpectedly, she started to count her blessings for all of the good things that happened to her through the years. First and foremost, she had three beautiful kids that she loved very much. That in itself was something to live for. Secondly, she had attained a successful career in writing and that she was very proud of too. No, perhaps, life wasn't that bad after all, she mused to herself. Obviously, she could have done better with a couple of failed marriages but that was all water under the bridge now. Then, once again, like so many times in the past, she realized it was time to move on with her life, and with that said, a few minutes later, in defiance of everything Maude had been up against and just before she went upstairs to call it day, the whole unfortunate mess that unfolded its hideous face in her direction seemed to dissipate into thin air. From this point on, life would be good, Maude told herself. Then, being fairly certain everything was under control and that she had nothing to worry about, sometime after midnight, she drifted off to sleep within the peaceful serenity of her home in Beverly Hills.

EPILOGUE

In the days following the untimely death of Ken and Ricky, Maude took a break from all of her activities with the exception of one thing, and that was to make sure kids were well cared for. Needless to say, it was her motherly instinct and it usually kept things interesting from one day to the next. In fact, what she didn't take care of her maid did, so it was a good arrangement. As for her conscience, there was a short period of time after the tragic deaths of Ken and Ricky that she was concerned about being a suspect in their murders however nothing ever came of it. Admittedly, that's what she thought would happen and thankfully, that's how everything turned out. Obviously, from an innocent bystander's perspective, they would've said she was as crazy as a loon in heat and perhaps, that was the case however she got away with what she did and in the end, as far as Maude Derringer was concerned, that's all that really mattered. Usually, even the craziest of people would've felt a twinge of regret about what they did however that wasn't the case at all with

Maude. In fact, she was quite satisfied with what she had accomplished. At any rate, like always, time went by very quickly and after a little rest, she continued on with her work in the field of literature. As for everything else at her estate in Beverly Hills, things very gradually returned to normal and in a fairly short period of time, Maude found happiness in life again through her children and through her writing. Believe it or not, even with all of the wealth she attained through a very prolific career in writing, Maude led a fairly simple life however she embraced that kind of lifestyle with open arms. In fact, she was typically a quiet person, and she didn't mind not being in the spotlight whenever the opportunity arose, and without having Ricky and Ken in her life anymore, life had taken a turn for the best and she was undoubtably as happy as a person could be about that. Anyway, from that point on, life was the way it should be for her as the pleasantries of a better life blessed her a hundred times over and whenever it was possible, Maude enjoyed every moment of her time in the years ahead as an abundance of happiness soon followed her wherever she went.

It can also be said, she never married again but that didn't disappointment her any. After a couple of failed marriages, there wasn't any way she would ever commit herself to another bad relationship. In fact, Maude very often cursed the ground men walked upon for all the good they ever did her, however on the plus side of it all, her children grew up and went onto have families of their own. Then, so typical of life, time went by very quickly and days became weeks, weeks became months, months turned into years, and long before she realized it, a lifetime of memories and living life the way she wanted to, had gone by. Perhaps, the most interesting thing of all was she didn't have any regrets in life. Both acts of justice she served on the men who ruined her life were well deserved. She was certain of that. It was just a question of whether or not she was in her right mind when all that happened, however as unbelievable as it may be, nothing more ever came of her mental state of mind during her lifetime. In fact, as time went by, she refused to talk about either one of her husbands, saying both marriages were unquestionably a great big mistake and obviously never meant to be. I will say, it was questionable as to whether or not Maude was right about that, however in her eyes, there was ample justification for what she did. At any rate, through the years and eventually in the end, after everything was all said and done, believe it or not, Maude never admitted to any wrongdoing to anyone, not her children or to anyone else for that matter. Needless to say, the circumstances that took the life of both of her husband's always remained a mystery, and other than Ricky and Ken, no one was ever the worse off for it. In fact, as stated before, she really and truly believed what she did was justified even though it should be noted, she committed a grievous sin in the eyes of God. At any rate, through the years following her disastrous marriages, she remained a lifelong resident of the community of Beverly Hill until the day she died at the ripe old age of ninety-three. At this point, it can also be said, for the most part, she lived a good life, and upon her passing, and also at her request, she was given a private funeral and was laid to rest in a cemetery on the outskirts of Beverly Hills, leaving behind assets worth many millions of dollars to her three children, and a legacy that will never be forgotten in the world of modern-day literature.